ROUTLEDGE LIBRARY EDITIONS: COLONIALISM AND IMPERIALISM

Volume 6

BRITISH HONDURAS

BRITISH HONDURAS

Past and Present

STEPHEN L. CAIGER

Routledge
Taylor & Francis Group
LONDON AND NEW YORK

First published in 1951 by George Allen & Unwin Ltd

This edition first published in 2023
by Routledge
4 Park Square, Milton Park, Abingdon, Oxon OX14 4RN

and by Routledge
605 Third Avenue, New York, NY 10158

Routledge is an imprint of the Taylor & Francis Group, an informa business

© 1951

All rights reserved. No part of this book may be reprinted or reproduced or utilised in any form or by any electronic, mechanical, or other means, now known or hereafter invented, including photocopying and recording, or in any information storage or retrieval system, without permission in writing from the publishers.

Trademark notice: Product or corporate names may be trademarks or registered trademarks, and are used only for identification and explanation without intent to infringe.

British Library Cataloguing in Publication Data
A catalogue record for this book is available from the British Library

ISBN: 978-1-032-41054-8 (Set)
ISBN: 978-1-032-41881-0 (Volume 6) (hbk)
ISBN: 978-1-032-41882-7 (Volume 6) (pbk)
ISBN: 978-1-003-36019-3 (Volume 6) (ebk)

DOI: 10.4324/9781003360193

Publisher's Note
The publisher has gone to great lengths to ensure the quality of this reprint but points out that some imperfections in the original copies may be apparent.

Disclaimer
The publisher has made every effort to trace copyright holders and would welcome correspondence from those they have been unable to trace.

BRITISH HONDURAS
PAST AND PRESENT

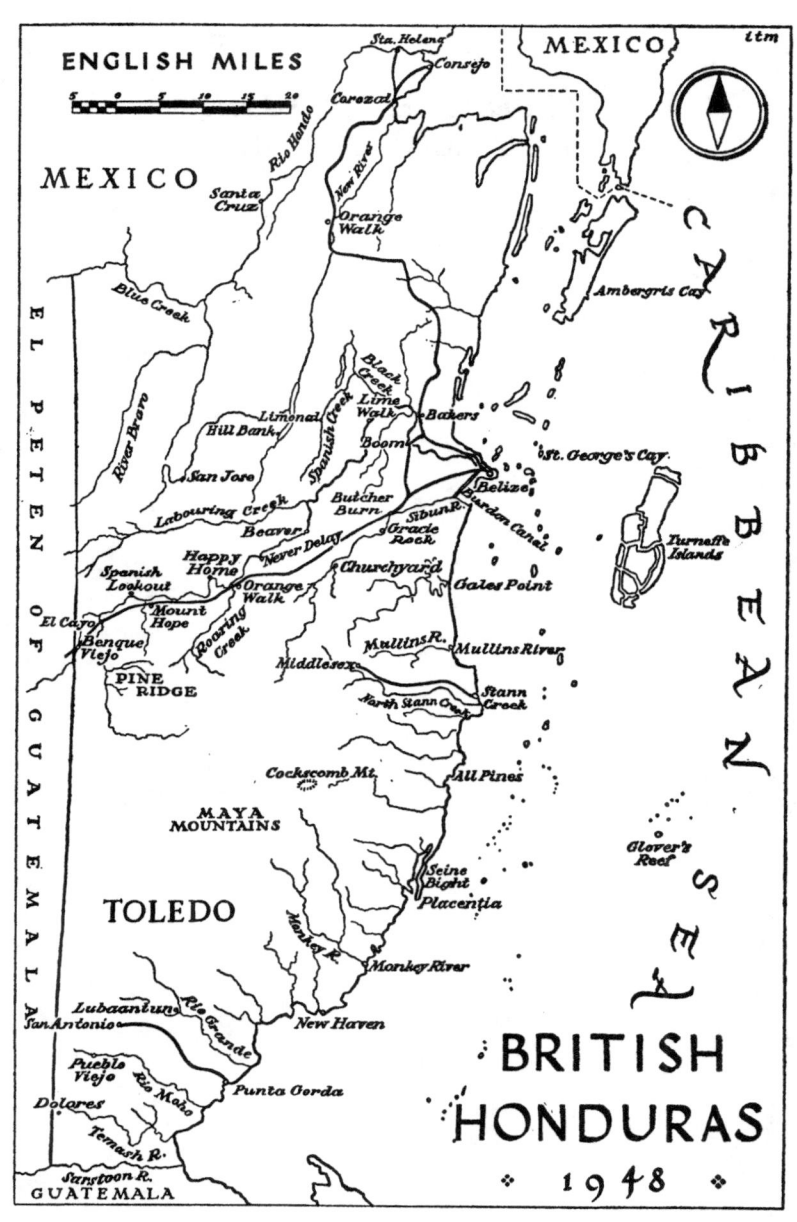

BRITISH HONDURAS
PAST AND PRESENT

By
STEPHEN L. CAIGER

> 'No greater ornament or dignity can be added to History, either human or natural, than truth. All other embellishments, if this be failing, are of little or no esteem; if this be delivered, all are either needless or superfluous.'
>
> Introduction to Esquemelin's *Buccaneers of America*

London
GEORGE ALLEN & UNWIN LTD
Ruskin House   Museum Street

FIRST PUBLISHED 1951

This book is copyright under the Berne Convention. Apart from any fair dealing for the purposes of private study, research, criticism or review, as permitted under the Copyright Act, 1911, no portion may be reproduced by any process without written permission. Enquiry should be made to the publishers.

PRINTED IN GREAT BRITAIN
in 11/12 *pt. Garamond type*
BY THE RIVERSIDE PRESS, EDINBURGH

To
THE MOST REV. EDWARD ARTHUR DUNN
Placentia, British Honduras
(Bishop 1917–43, Archbishop of the West Indies 1936–43)
whose devotion to the Colony was the
original inspiration of this book.

AUTHOR'S PREFACE

*

My main source of information about the early history of the Colony has been, of course, Sir John Burdon's massive three-volume work *The Archives of British Honduras*, 1670–1884 (published 1931). Sir John was Governor of British Honduras for nearly eight years, 1925–32, and intensely interested in everything that concerned the Colony. With the help of a like-minded group of research workers he examined every relevant record he could find, both in Belize and in London. His book as we have it now is a series of the more important extracts from the original documents printed in chronological order, and giving in every case the most scrupulous references to them. I had the honour of Sir John's acquaintance in Belize at the time when he was engaged in this research, but make no claim to have consulted the originals from which his *Archives* are drawn. Nor was it necessary. The heavy spadework of intensive research has been done once and for all by those who had the best facilities for it under the best possible leadership: all I have attempted here is to render Sir John's monumental treatise down, as it were, to a more accessible handbook for the general reader, though I have ventured to add a little from other sources too.

In one respect Sir John's researches were as disappointing as they were arduous. Original records of the earlier and in some ways the most interesting period of the Colony's history turned out to be fewer and more meagre than he had hoped. This paucity of records was, of course, natural in a buccaneer settlement more handy with the cutlass than the pen. But even after some sort of organized community had grown up in Belize, and it became the practice to keep regular State Records, there were all kinds of enemies, human, insect and climatic, to imperil their preservation. The city of Belize became the custodian of all documents relating to the Colony and to the outlying settlements in those parts, but it was no safe deposit for such things. As Sir John himself remarks,[1] 'The archives of the Colony are unfortunately too

---

[1] Burdon, i, xv.

fragmentary and defective to make the history of the early period clear; and even in regard to the later struggle with the Spaniards, it has been impossible to collect full documentary information.' And again,[1] 'British Honduras has been particularly unfortunate in the preservation of its archives. Besides all the ravages caused by decay, damp, and the insect pests which abound in a tropical climate, both fire and tempest have been particularly destructive.' Next to Jerusalem, Belize must be one of the most often 'utterly destroyed' cities in the world. The Spanish razed it to the ground again and again. Great fires have ravaged it. Several times it has been overwhelmed by hurricanes. In our own day (1931) it was almost wiped out by one such hurricane accompanied by a tidal wave, which very nearly destroyed the irreplaceable documents and the manuscript of the *Archives* which Sir John Burdon and his Committee had been collecting for years.

'On the day of the completion of his task (September 10, 1931),' writes Professor Newton in his Introduction to volume ii, 'Sir John took from the file the copy intended to be sent to London for the publishers, and placed it in a tin box. A few hours later Belize was struck by one of the worst hurricanes in its history, the office building was blown over, the papers which remained in their usual drawers and cupboards were scattered broadcast by the violence of the wind and soaked by the torrential rain beyond the possibility of recovery. Many of the original documents themselves suffered a like fate, and had it not been for the providential accident of their storage in the tin box, the whole of the labours of the Committee would have been in vain, and historians would never have had the opportunity of reading these papers. During a lull in the storm, search was made for the precious box among the ruins and luckily it was found intact. But a worse danger was to come, for while the Governor was shielding the box as best he could from the soaking of the rain, the floods poured over the ruined town and completely submerged it. By Sir John's care the box with its precious contents was kept just above the rising waters, to yield up the manuscript in due course to the printers. These details are worthy of recall, perhaps, as giving some indication of the dangers to which earlier papers must have been exposed in the course of history.'[2]

I have tried to fill up some of the gaps in Sir John's story by

---

[1] Burdon, ii, x. [2] *Ibid.*, ii, xi.

consulting other books, as noted in the bibliography, of which E. O. Winzerling's *Beginnings of British Honduras 1506–1765* (published by the North River Press of New York in 1946) and C. H. Haring's *The Buccaneers in the West Indies in the XVIIth Century* (Methuen, 1910) are the most important. The latter is an authoritative work on the subject, where every statement is verified by a careful reference to its source. Winzerling has added much that is quite new, especially with regard to the connection of the Colony with Providence Company, and where this writer has been followed, acknowledgement has been made to him by name.

For the twentieth-century period of the Colony's history I have relied on various official publications, as noted in the list of books.

As to the diplomatic situation, an endeavour has been made to present a fair statement on the controversial issue of the Colony's international status by comparing British official publications with J. L. Mendoza's fierce assertion of Guatemalan claims in his *Britain and her Treaties on Belize* (official English translation) published in Guatemala in 1947. No doubt if the matter is brought up before an international court of arbitration, as has been proposed, every possible avenue will be explored in the search for information about British Honduras and her relationship to the rest of Central America, and much new material will probably come to light. In the meantime, the present volume may shed a ray or two.

I should like to thank the Colonial Office Library staff for their invaluable help, the Rev. F. Kelly for reading the proofs, and Miss E. P. Biffen for compiling the Index.

STEPHEN L. CAIGER.

July 1951.

NOTE ON PRONUNCIATION

Honduras is accented on the u.   *Cay* is pronounced Kee.
Belize is pronounced Beleeze, with the accent on the last syllable.

CONTENTS

*

		page
	AUTHOR'S PREFACE	11
I.	*A Legacy of the Buccaneers*	17
II.	*Captain Wallace*	31
III.	*The Buccaneers turn honest*	40
IV.	*The British Logwood Settlements*	50
V.	*The Baymen of Belize*	60
VI.	*Spanish Aggression*	69
VII.	*The Navy to the Rescue*	79
VIII.	*The Battle of Belize*	89
IX.	*The Mosquito Shore*	101
X.	*Belize becomes a Colony*	120
XI.	*From Heyday to Hard Times*	137
XII.	*Between the Wars*	150
XIII.	*British Honduras To-day—and To-morrow*	168
XIV.	*The Controversy with Guatemala*	188
XV.	*Devaluation and Federation*	210
	ADDITIONAL NOTES	231
	CHRONOLOGICAL TABLE	233
	BIBLIOGRAPHY	236
	INDEX	237

MAPS
1. The Colony of British Honduras — 6
2. Central America — *at end*

Chapter I

*

A LEGACY OF THE BUCCANEERS

THE story of British Honduras seems almost too romantic for the pages of sober history. The long drawn-out, perilous, often well-nigh desperate, but finally triumphant struggle of a few English buccaneers to establish a foothold on the Spanish Main, and of their descendants to win recognition of their tiny holding as a Colony of the British Empire, makes as colourful a record of adventure as any work of fiction, yet it is a record of historic fact. Apart from all this, it deserves more attention from historians than it has yet received. The circumstances by which the various parts of the Empire have become attached to it are almost as diverse as the parts themselves, but among them all the experience of British Honduras has a quality of its own, and is indeed unique. Nor is it irrelevant to the Imperial situation now. After three hundred years, the story is still alive, the struggle is not ended, the embers of long-smouldering controversies are liable to be fanned to flame. By what title is this part of Honduras British?

It is not by Right of Discovery that we hold the Colony.

Admittedly it was not the British who first set eyes on the coastline of British Honduras. Columbus came very near to it on his fourth and last voyage in 1502, when he touched at Guanaja, afterwards called Bonacca, one of the Bay Islands in the Gulf of Honduras. Overtaken by one of the hurricanes for which these eastern waters of the Caribbean Sea are still notorious, but weathering the storm, he gave Thanks to God (*Gracias à Dios*) off the cape whose name still recalls his escape from the perils of The Deep (*Las Fonduras*, or *Honduras*). From that day to this, the Gulf and its adjoining shore have been called Honduras. Four years later (1506) two Spanish navigators, Vicente Yanez Pinzon and Juan Diaz de Solis, sailed westward from Bonacca to the Golfo Dulce, and thence northward along the Toledo Coast of what we now call British Honduras, leaving the lofty Sierra de Caria

(Cockscomb Range) on their port bow, and so threading their way through the cays, or little islands, off Belize until they reached Cozumel at the northernmost point of Yucatan. After this, the coastline was roughly charted by the Spanish, but none of them ever landed, so far as we know, upon the shore. None of them certainly ever occupied or settled upon it.

The first European to set eyes on British Honduras from the land side was also a Spaniard, in fact it was the great Hernando Cortés, Conqueror of Mexico, himself. In 1524 he made his memorable march almost in a straight line from Vera Cruz to Truxillo in order to punish the rebellious Cristobal de Olid, who, thinking himself safe at such a distance, had proclaimed the independence of Spanish Honduras. During this almost incredible journey through the trackless jungle, Cortés must have seen the sun rise over the jagged peaks of the Cockscomb Range. One of his captains, Dernal Diaz de Castillo, seems to have crossed them. He describes them as 'not very high, but consisting of stones which cut like knives'. In that case, he must have come close to the stupendous ruins of Lubaantun in the extreme south of the present Colony. Even in those days, the mighty temples, pyramids, and carved obelisks of the ancient Mayan city were in ruins, for the Mayas had long ago moved northwards to Chichen Itza in upper Yucatan and to Peten Itza near Lake Flores in Guatemala, where the Conquistadores massacred them almost to a man. Their descendants, still wearing the original tribal costumes and speaking the old agglutinative Indian dialects, have re-entered British Honduras in modern times, but in the sixteenth century the country seems to have been virtually uninhabited. Neither the Spanish when they crossed it, nor the British when they eventually settled in it, met with any opposition from native tribes.

But it was not by Right of Conquest, still less by Right of Occupation, that the Spanish claimed possession of British Honduras from the beginning. It was by the Divine Right of the Papal Donation of Pope Alexander VI, who in 1493 (the year after the discovery of the West Indies by Columbus) had made a present of the whole of this part of the New World, whether as yet discovered or not, to their Most Catholic Majesties Ferdinand and Isabella of Spain. From May 3, in fact, of that epoch-making year, the whole of the western hemisphere, beyond a longitude running 300 miles to the west of the Azores, was granted by the Pope and accepted by all loyal Catholics as belonging both by sea and land to Spain and Portugal. In many places, of course, this title was afterwards confirmed by discovery, exploration, conquest, and colonization. The story of the Spanish Conquest is indeed one of amazing courage, endurance, and resolution, dazzling in those days and dazzling now. Their achievements had also remarkably permanent results, as Maderiaga has justly pointed out. After four hundred years, that part of the New World which was actually conquered and occupied by Spain remains Spanish in everything but name to-day. Where, however, the Spanish claim to ownership rested solely upon the naïve assumption of the Papal Donation, time has a very different story to tell, as we see in Newfoundland, Canada, the United States, the West Indies, and, last but not least, in British Honduras itself.

The Papal Donation had barely thirty years in which to set its stamp on the New World before the Protestant Reformation began to call it to account, and it was British seamen who did it. The first recorded appearance of English freebooters in the West Indies occurred as early as 1527. Some Spaniards were loading cassava at the Isle of Mona, off Hispaniola, when they sighted a strange craft, well armed with cannon, bearing down upon them. Curiosity rather than alarm was the natural reaction in those days, so the Spaniards at once rowed out to discover who the stranger might be. It was an English vessel sailing from London to discover a north-west passage round the world to the land of the Great Khan of Asia. After many adventures, including a clash with icebergs off Newfoundland (already discovered by Cabot in an English ship), the captain of this strange vessel had turned south to the warmer waters of the Spanish Indies, and completely lost his bearings. The episode ended as sweetly as it had begun. The Englishman, supplied with a chart and provisions, set sail at once for London, and was heard of no more.[1]

But no doubt he had a tale to tell the mariners at home, and it was not long before other adventurers launched out for Westward Ho! with less innocent intent. In 1530 William Hawkins, father of the more famous John, came trading with the Indians off Brazil. In 1567 John Hawkins and Francis Drake were smuggling slaves into the West Indian plantations. In 1569 Drake sailed again, this time (as Haring puts it) 'with the sole unblushing

[1] Haring, 34.

purpose of robbing the Don'. From that moment the War of the Privateers was on. Henceforward for over two hundred years a thousand lesser Drakes were 'singeing the King of Spain's beard' wherever they found him, but most often of all in the West Indies and on the Spanish Main. 'The highways and byways of the Caribbean became to the Armada heroes what the playing fields of Eton were to those of Waterloo.' [1]

It was about this time that the English discovered in their turn the coast of British Honduras. Hawkins, Drake, Oxenham, Lovell and others all sailed on occasions through the Yucatan Channel to the Gulf of Amatique on their way to Truxillo, Nombre de Dios, and the rest. The Cockscomb Mountains became a familiar landmark, the cays and creeks a useful hiding and careening resort. Where they landed, there they sometimes lodged awhile. Where they lodged, there in time they settled. For their voyages were not always or solely for the purpose of 'robbing the Don'. The ambition to occupy and colonize some of these desirable spots had already entered their minds, ever since they had noted with some envy the easy prosperity of the Spaniards. There was plenty of land still unexplored, unoccupied, and (unless one acknowledged the validity of the Papal Donation) belonging to no civilized nation. Why should not England have a share of this wonderful New World?

Queen Elizabeth, for one, could see no reason. It must have given great joy and encouragement to her bold seafarers when she put into words the very thoughts they had been thinking. In 1587, incensed by Spanish claims to the monopoly of trade and colonization in the west, she uttered her famous Declaration of Policy:

> 'The Queen of England understands not why her or any prince's subjects should be debarred from the Trade of the Indies, which she could not persuade herself the Spaniards had any just title to by the Donation of the Bishop of Rome, to whom she acknowledges no prerogative much less authority in these cases. Nor yet by any other claim than as they had here and there touched upon the coasts, built cottages, or given a name to a river or cape, which things could not entitle them to a propriety, and this imaginary propriety cannot hinder other princes from trading in those countries, or from transporting colonies into those parts thereof where the Spaniards do not inhabit.' [2]

---

[1] Winzerling, 22.   [2] Quoted in Burdon, i, 48.

This Declaration of Policy was the Charter of the British Empire, signed, sealed and delivered by our victory over the Armada in the following year. It was a policy which had already been pursued in Newfoundland (1583): hereafter it would be our justification for the planting of many settlements and colonies in North America and in the West Indies. Some fifty years later, it was felt to be particularly applicable to our occupation of British Honduras. By no conceivable right could the Spanish claim 'Propriety' in that uninhabited and uninviting shore, where not even the names of the rivers or capes were Spanish, and where every 'cottage' was built by English hands.

After Elizabeth's forthright statement of policy, every incentive —patriotic, religious, mercenary, and adventurous—egged her subjects on to try their fortunes on the Spanish Main. Men sold all they had to buy a barque, quickly filled their forecastles with hardy seamen from the dockside taverns of London, Bideford, or Bristol, and returned home (if they returned at all) to be greeted as heroes, and to live the rest of their lives in affluence. The Queen herself commended, sometimes even knighted them. It was a cheap way of raising a navy, when her brave privateers at their own charges fought the battles of England on the high seas, and at the same time brought so much grist to the national mill. So the privateers became an institution, and their looting of Spanish vessels a legitimate Trade. They were no mere pirates, playing a lone hand for personal gain, but a kind of volunteer naval reserve. Without State pay, without provision of any sort from the national purse, and often enough even without those Royal Orders or Letters of Marque which were supposed to lie in the Master's locker, these British sea-rovers became the pioneers of Empire in the Far West. And they preferred the new name 'buccaneer' to any other, for it distinguished them from less reputable adventurers. Their peak period was the first sixty or seventy years of the seventeenth century.

The name itself was derived from the 'buccan' meat, or *boucan*, which became their staple provender while away from home. Perhaps the biggest problem for seafarers in the Tropics was that of food. Voyages were long in those days, and one could never be sure of a friendly reception when attempting to revictual on an unknown shore. The only method of preserving meat was to salt it so heavily that it became uneatable. It was the discovery of the 'buccan' method of curing flesh which gave the buccaneers their extended range of action and the physical sustenance necessary for their extraordinary feats of endurance. It was like that invention which enables a modern submarine to charge its batteries without surfacing—epoch-making in the annals of maritime warfare. Having caught and killed some of the wild cattle which roved over the islands (especially Tortuga), they cut the meat into long strips and dried it over a slow wood fire fed with bones and trimmings from the hides of the animals, by which means a fine red colour and a succulent flavour was given to the flesh. The place where it was smoked was called by the Carib Indians, from whom they learnt the practice, a 'buccan', so the men themselves became known as buccaneers. There were of course many who were not of British blood. The French were perhaps the most numerous in the early days of the 'Trade', being recruited afterwards by many Huguenot adventurers escaping from the long arm of Catholic persecution to the freedom and safety of the West Indies—Gueux de la Mer (Beggars of the Sea) they were often called. There were also many Dutch, escaping from Spanish persecution in the Netherlands, as well as 'Portuguese, Danes, Swedes, Courlanders, and all other nations' (Esquemelin).

The Dutchman Esquemelin, who lived amongst them from 1668–74, towards the end of their main period, has left us a most entertaining account of the buccaneers he knew so intimately:

> 'Being all come aboard they join together in council, concerning what place they ought first to go wherein to get provisions—especially of flesh, seeing they scarce eat anything else. Having got provisions of flesh sufficient for their voyage, they return to the ship. Here their allowance twice a day to everyone is as much as he can eat without either weight or measure. Neither does the steward of the vessel give any greater proportion of flesh or anything else to the Captain than to the meanest mariner. They then agree upon certain articles, which are put in writing by way of bond or obligation, wherein they specify what sums of money each particular person ought to have for that voyage, the law being "No prey, no pay!"'

Esquemelin goes on to specify the various amounts payable to the Captain, the Carpenter, the Surgeon, and so forth. Also the amount of compensation to be awarded for the loss of a right arm (600 pieces-of-eight), a left arm (500), a right leg (500), a left leg (400), an eye (100), a finger (100)—a curious estimate, the latter! He continues:

> 'They observe among themselves very good orders. . . . Yea, they take a solemn oath to each other not to abscond or conceal the least thing they find amongst the prey. . . . Among themselves they are very charitable and civil to each other, insomuch that if any wants what another has, with great liberality they give it one to another. As soon as they have taken any prize of ship or boat the first thing they endeavour is to set on shore the prisoners, detaining only some few for their own help and service, to whom also they give their liberty after the space of two or three years. From time to time they put in at one island or another. Here they careen their vessels, and in the meantime go to hunt, others to cruise upon the seas in canoes, seeking their fortune.'

It may be asked how were these highwaymen of the sea in their small and often ill-equipped vessels able to capture much bigger and better armed ships, such as the galleons of Spain? Esquemelin describes their method thus:

> 'Their first approach was made with great judgement, their tiny craft being so steered as to avoid the direct fire of heavy artillery, while their picked marksmen attempted to shoot down the helmsman and the sailors at the rigging. Then they got under the stern, proceeded to wedge up the rudder, and boarded the ship from several boats at once. The deck once reached, their personal dexterity, activity, and courage were so marked that they rarely failed to overpower their opponents.'

'Careening' (*i.e.* driving the vessel ashore and hauling it over on its side by ropes from the mast head) often proved a dangerous as well as a tedious occupation, but it was very necessary in those seas where barnacles, fungus, seaweed, and all sorts of underwater growths so fastened upon the wooden sides of the ship that the speed of chase and manœuvre upon which the buccaneers depended for their lives and livelihood was seriously diminished.

In appearance the buccaneers must have been more picturesque than æsthetic, although no doubt on a well-appointed ship with a fastidious captain such matters were probably more punctiliously ordered. An average buccaneer, as described in Haring's authoritative and well-documented work, wore 'a dress of the simplest —coarse cloth trousers and a shirt which hung loosely over them, both pieces so black and saturated with blood and grease of slain animals that they looked as if they had been tarred. A belt of undressed bull's hide bound the shirt and supported on one side three or four large knives, on the other a pouch for powder and shot. A cap with a short-pointed brim extending over the eyes, rude shoes of cowhide or pigskin made all of one piece bound over the foot, and a short large-bore musket, completed the hunter's grotesque outfit. Often he carried wound about his waist a sack of netting into which he crawled at night to keep off the pestiferous mosquitoes.' Such was his normal working dress. His holiday attire, however, when he landed after a successful voyage on the quay of Port Royal or Plymouth (if he dared) was very different—though possibly no less 'grotesque'. Here he would swagger into the taverns arrayed in the silks and sables looted from the cabins or stripped from the backs of his victims, matted locks adorned by a feathered hat, greasy neck half-hidden in a rumpled ruff, shirt encircled by a silken sash, bright hosen on his legs, rings on his fingers, and golden hoops in his ears, but still with his trusty dirk and pistol at his side. A lady-killer indeed, a swashbuckling hero to wide-eyed youths, a brilliant advertisement of the pleasures and profits of the noble calling of buccaneer. There was seldom any difficulty in enlisting a crew for the next voyage to Westward Ho!

Yet it must be granted they had their sinister side. There are bloodcurdling stories of their cruelties, ruthlessness, and sadistic humour, especially towards their mortal enemies, the Spaniards. The latter, indeed, had started it. Their inhumanity to the native Indians, despite honourable exceptions like Fra Bartolomeo de Las Casas, had disgusted the British even in that brutal age, and when the same inhumanity was practised against English seamen it was bound to lead to reprisals. As early as 1604, for instance, the Venetian ambassador in London reported that a Spanish warship in the West Indies had captured two English vessels, cut off the hands, feet, nose, and ears of the crews, smeared them with honey, and tied them to trees to be tortured to death by the flies.[1] On many occasions captured buccaneers were condemned to the galleys, committed to the mines, or just hanged outright as 'pirates'. Such practices explain, if they do not excuse, the cruelties perpetrated in return.

Yet incongruously enough, as it seems to us, many of the most typical buccaneers were deeply religious, even puritanically strict

---
[1] Haring, 54.

in their outlook. The 'solemn oath' referred to by Esquemelin was usually sworn upon the Bible which every captain carried in his locker. They buried their dead at sea with bared heads and a prayer. Indeed they often carried a Ship's Chaplain for this special purpose, and for the purpose of 'saying Mass' before going into action, after the example of Drake. Haring gives one or two typical instances:

> 'In March 1694 the Jesuit writer Labat took part in a Mass at Martinique which was performed by some French Buccaneers in pursuance of a vow made when they were taking two English vessels near Barbadoes. The French vessel and its two prizes were anchored near the Church and fired salutes of all their cannon at the Beginning of the Mass, at the Elevation of the Host, at the Benediction, and again at the end of the service.'

On another occasion Captain Daniel, a celebrated buccaneer, once landed on an island near Dominica, and kidnapped the Curé on board his ship, requesting that his captive should celebrate Mass. The priest dared not refuse, so the necessary vessels were sent for and an altar improvised on deck, salutes of cannon taking the place of church bells. Such was the respect of Captain Daniel for the Sacred Mysteries that when one of the buccaneers neglected to genuflect at the Elevation he whipped out a pistol and shot him through the head. After which the service proceeded without incident, though the priest was detained a little longer to give the dead man a decent burial.

A more Protestant type of buccaneer (killed 1722) was the pious Captain Bartholomew Roberts. According to Snow, he was a strict teetotaller who made his crew retire to their bunks every night at nine o'clock and punished by death any buccaneer who brought a woman on board. Betting, card-playing, and dice were forbidden on his vessel, and the Sabbath Day most strictly observed. Actually, many of these early buccaneers were Puritans of the 'Pilgrim Father' type nosing about among the islands of the Caribbean and the shores of the Spanish Main for some uninhabited yet fertile spot where they might settle down to work and the practice of their religion. Though frequently compelled to fight the Spaniards in self-defence, and often enough perhaps reduced by the attractions of the chase to make buccaneering a career, this was not their primary purpose. Even when they did for a while adopt the 'Trade' they still preserved many of their old scruples. It is on record that in 1637 the British settlers on Providence Island were severely taken to task by the Home Government for the sin of betting and gambling then rife among them and were ordered to send home to England all their dice, playing cards, and other gaming apparatus, 'which they presently did'. We shall notice later on that the very first enactment of Burnaby's Code (1765) in Belize, based on the long-standing customs of the buccaneer settlements in the Gulf of Honduras, prohibited 'Profane cursing and swearing in disobedience of God's Commands and the derogation of His Honor. Anyone guilty of the same shall on proof on Oath by one Evidence or more before any one of the said Justices of the Peace, forfeit and pay for every such offence the sum of Two shillings and sixpence Jamaica currency.' One of the first Police Magistrates appointed to enforce this regulation was the Reverend William Stanford, the Chaplain of the Settlement.

'Brethren of the Coast' these buccaneers often called themselves in their more responsible moods, and the title was not without justification. Rough, rude and wild though many of them were, yet a strong sense of brotherly loyalty did bind them together both afloat and ashore, ensuring the observance of a common code of decency—without which, indeed, the continual perils and hardships of their lot would have been insupportable. They were noted, as we have seen, not only for fidelity to contracts made one to another, and for common honesty in the distribution of their profits, but also for uncovenanted kindnesses and liberality. When the time came for them to possess African slaves of their own, they became no less celebrated for their humanity, indeed their egalitarianism, as masters. It was said that the slaves of the logwood-cutters around Belize were better off and better treated than most free men elsewhere. Though ruthless enough on occasion, nothing excited their anger more than cruelty or injustice to their own folk. Their women were forced to none of the hard work of hunting or wood-felling, being expected only to look after the home. And this, whatever colour their 'wives' might be, some of them having been shipped from home for the express purpose of marrying the settlers, others being wooed among the passengers of captured ships, but the majority being Negro women from the plantations.

Such were the 'bold buccaneers' of history and romance, who

played so large, though usually anonymous, a part in the founding of our West Indian Empire. And such in the main were the first settlers on the shores of British Honduras. Their blood flows in the Colony to this day.

The colonization of the country began, indirectly, with the Earl of Warwick's emigration scheme in 1629, the so-called Providence Company, a few years after our occupation of Barbados. There was nothing hostile to Spain in the plan to settle British colonists in such parts of the West Indies as were not in the occupation of any Spanish or other Christian prince. Warwick was neither swashbuckler nor land-grabber. His ship, the *Seaflower*, sailed from England in much the same spirit and with the same hopes as the *Mayflower* had set out ten years earlier, and its passengers included many of the same type—Puritans desirous only of building a free Protestant empire overseas. After touching at Tortuga, then a buccaneer stronghold, they sailed on through the straits between Hispaniola and Cuba, then, leaving the Spanish island of Sant Iago (Jamaica) on the starboard bow, steered for the Mosquito Gulf and the Spanish Main. Here they found a small island called Santa Katarina, occupied only by the famous Dutch buccaneer Captain William Blauveldt, or Bluefield, who explained that he had no intention of staying permanently, and suggested that the island would be an advantageous spot for Warwick's projected settlement.

It would be necessary, however, to fortify the place, advised Bluefield, who had few illusions about the Spanish. He foresaw that before long the new British Settlement would have to fight for its life, and that a change would come over the spirit of the settlement, for even Puritan principles would not be strong enough to resist the lure of Spanish gold. To encourage them, he offered the help not only of his own Dutch buccaneers, but of his friends and allies on the mainland, namely the Mosquito Indians. This is the first time we make contact with these Indians, who were to prove such faithful friends to the British for the next two hundred years. Bluefield had taken pains to conciliate them, and to convince them that there was a world of difference between Spanish Conquistadores and Dutch or English buccaneers. The Indians were worth cultivating. Braver and more warlike than any others on the Main, they boasted with truth that they had never been conquered by Spain. But they had suffered for their contumacy, and now hated the Spanish with an undying hate. Any enemy of Spain was a friend of Mosquitia.

So the Earl of Warwick landed on the island, calling it henceforth Providence Island.[1] So successful was the landing, and so promising the venture, that in the following year (1630) it is on record that 'Robert Earl of Warwick was made Governor in Chief and Lord High Admiral of all those islands and other plantations belonging to any of His Majesty's subjects within the bounds and upon the coasts of America, with a Committee to be assisting of him for the better governing of the said plantations, but chiefly for the advancement of the true Protestant Religion.'[2]

But Captain Bluefield's forebodings were soon fulfilled. In 1635 a Spanish fleet from the Main made a strong attack upon the infant settlement. After a five days' battle it was beaten off, but the experience left its mark. Obtaining from Charles I the liberty to 'right themselves' by making reprisals, the settlers became a thorn in the side of the Spanish, working hand-in-glove with the buccaneers, and themselves often yielding to the attractions of the 'Trade'. In 1639 the Spanish Ambassador protested hotly against the depredations of Providence Company, but the Lords refused to call Warwick to account. In any case, they said, 'no agreement or armistice arranged in England or Spain was ever much regarded by either nation in the West Indies', which was only too true. In 1641, accordingly, Don Francisco Diaz Pimiento swooped suddenly upon the island with a formidable armada, razed the fortifications, burnt all buildings to the ground, and made prisoners of all the settlers who had not perished or escaped. This was the end of Warwick's colony on Old Providence Island. It had lasted only twelve years.

But it was not the end of the British adventure. Unfortunately for Spain, the Colony had already thrown off shoots, which by this time had taken root on the mainland further up the Gulf. Under the shadow of the Cockscomb Mountains, in what is now the south of British Honduras, a Captain Daniel Elfrith was already cultivating potatoes, pumpkins, silk grass, and the like, and marketing them from the two trading stands, or *stanns*, of upper and lower Stann Creek.[3] On Tobacco Cay they grew the

---

[1] Not to be confused with the island of New Providence in the Bahamas.
[2] Quoted from State Papers by Winzerling.
[3] An alternative derivation from S. Anne has been suggested.

fragrant weed which every buccaneer smoked in his pipe. In 1634 a Captain Axe is named as in charge of the defences, armed with cannon from England. The largest plantation was run by a Philip Bell at Placentia Point, consisting of 600 Puritans, 200 Indians, and 100 slaves. Commis Bight still preserves by its name a memory of the commissary or agent, a Captain Camock, who looked after the produce. A study of the place-names in these parts would be full of interest, if we had space for it. Queen Cay, for instance, was named after the Queen of Bohemia, James I's daughter. Grass Cay, Silk Grass Creek, Freshwater Creek, Water Cay (where the buccaneers filled their kegs), Snake Cay, Ambergris Cay, Tobacco Cay, Samphire Cay are fairly obvious, but what episode of history is enshrined in such names as Bluefield Cay, Columbus Cay, Colson Cay, Ellin Cay, Goff's Cay, Hontin (Haunted) Cay, Jenkins' Creek, Mullins' River, Pork and Doughboy Point, Stuart Cay, Spanish Lookout, Swallow Cay, and scores of similar names which have come down to us from the old buccaneering days? At any rate the names show that this part of the Colony was very soon stamped as British. 'The Cockscomb Coast in fact has been for over three hundred years in unbroken British occupation', declares Winzerling in his American-published book on the subject.[1]

Whatever may have been the fate of the Cockscomb Coast settlements, the real nucleus out of which the present Colony of British Honduras developed was by common consent the Belize River area, among the low-lying logwood forests in the north. Here our first record of a British landing is in 1638, some three years before the sack of Providence Island, when a party of English seamen in search of logwood was shipwrecked near the mouth of the Old River, or Belize River, as it is now called. While awaiting rescue or reinforcements 'they started to cut and pile the precious timber, which they found there in abundance', and to build themselves rude huts. They unconsciously founded, in fact, the first embryo settlement in Belize. The authority for this statement is the *Honduras Almanack* of 1829,[2] a periodical official survey of the Colony based on original records no longer extant.[3] This is the earliest mention of a British landing in the

---

[1] To the present writer, this seems a somewhat extravagant statement, but Winzerling, on whose authority the whole of the foregoing paragraph depends, seems to have evidence unknown to Burdon or other historians of the Colony.
[2] Quoted in Burdon, i, 2.   [3] See Preface.

Belize area. No more information is given, but it would seem likely that these shipwrecked sailors were either exploring from a base on Providence Island, or else were seeking their fellow-countrymen on that island from one of the British settlements in Campeachy, of which more hereafter. The latter hypothesis would explain better, perhaps, how they knew logwood and its value when they saw it.

Such are the earliest records of British occupation in the Colony. There is no mention of conflict or encounter with any Spanish settlers ashore, no suggestion that any effort had been made to develop the logwood or other resources of the country before the arrival of the British. The Spanish authorities resented this trespassing, as they regarded it, upon Spanish territory, but their protests were so obviously of the dog-in-the-manger variety that even the early Stuarts, despite their desire to live at peace with Spain, rejected them in the spirit of the Elizabethan Declaration, and Cromwell followed suit. Nevertheless the nettle was never really grasped, and the diplomatic story of the next two hundred years is of a continual clash between the theoretical title to territorial possession of the country awarded by the Papal Donation to Spain, and the practical title claimed by England in virtue of actual occupation and use. In early editions of the *Encyclopædia Britannica*, when the question was being hotly discussed between England and Guatemala, Squier neatly sums up the situation thus:

However Great Britain's rights in Honduras might be questioned, it cannot be doubted that the enterprise of her subjects rescued a desolate coast from the savage dominion of nature, and carried industry and civilization where none existed before, and where, if left to the control of the Spanish race, none would exist to-day.'

Chapter II

*

CAPTAIN WALLACE

As to the city of Belize, the founder was a certain Captain Wallace, after whom it was named. It appears in the archives of British Honduras as Valys, Bullys, Bellise, Belice, and finally Belize (pronounced Beleeze).[1] The alternatively suggested derivation from the Spanish *balisa*, a buoy or beacon, seems unlikely, for the city was exclusively of British origin and would most naturally have received an English name from its inception.

Little is known about this Captain Wallace, despite considerable research. This is probably to his credit, for the fame (or notoriety) of a buccaneer was usually in proportion to his crimes and cruelties rather than to his virtues. We may assume, accordingly, that Wallace never rivalled L'Ollonois, Blackbeard, or Harry Morgan in villainy. The *Honduras Almanac* for 1839 informs us that his Christian name was Peter, that he was a Scotsman, born at Falkland, in Kinross, and that he settled in Belize in 1640, when he founded the city and had it called after his name. It is at any rate a fact that a Scottish strain has always traditionally characterized the Colony. At one time the Scottish Presbyterian Church was established and endowed by law in Belize simultaneously with the Church of England: Scottish words have survived in the local vocabulary side by side—after all these years!—with words of West African origin: and Scottish names are not uncommon among the people and places round about.

Various historians add further information about Wallace. Thus, the Mexican writer Justo Sierra asserts that he was 'a daring and enterprising Scotch buccaneer, who was moved by the reputation for riches in this region [*i.e.* the Gulf of Honduras, with its rich prize of Spanish galleons to be chased and looted]. In association with the most resolute of his comrades he determined to search for a site where he could establish his lair. So

---

[1] Up to 1840 the name Belize was applied both to the capital city and to the Colony as a whole—a usage which still obtains in Spanish-American circles.

he made a thorough survey of those reefs and shoals, and then found a river entirely protected by cays [*i.e.* small islands] and shallows. At the mouth of this river he landed with some eighty buccaneers, and started to build some houses, surrounding them with a palisade or breastwork—in short, a rude fortress. The place was called Wallace (Belize) after him'. This statement would not be inconsistent with the assertion of another historian, that Wallace first explored Turneffe Island, and then landed at the mouth of the Belize river for the purpose of cutting logwood. Wallace might easily have combined the 'Trade' of buccaneering with that of logwood-cutting as a side line. The date of his landing at Belize is given as 1640, that is to say two years after the first recorded landing of the shipwrecked British sailors mentioned in our last chapter. These men had spent their time ashore in cutting logwood, as we have seen, and may well have remained ashore and initiated Wallace into the secrets of this profitable industry.

A French record, for what it is worth, describes him as a capable and resolute man, 'un homme de tête et résolution'. Esquemelin, writing thirty years later, does not seem to have heard of him. Haring makes no mention of the name Wallace, but speaks of the exploits of 'an English adventurer sometime after 1638', clearly to be identified with our hero.[1] Winzerling has accumulated a good deal of information about his early life, which we shall give below. Finally, Asturias, the Guatemalan historian, states that he was Sir Walter Raleigh's First Lieutenant on the ill-starred expedition of 1617 in search of Eldorado on the Rio Orinoco in Guiana. He adds that after the failure of that enterprise, Wallace with his great captain tried to recoup the situation by chasing Spanish treasure ships in the Gulf of Honduras and the Yucatan channel, which brought them within sight of the mouth of the Belize River. If that is so, Wallace must have been about middle age when he returned to Belize some twenty years later, in 1640.

It is worth pausing at the mention of Raleigh to reflect on the last exploit of that enterprising but unfortunate pioneer of our Caribbean Empire, for it throws much light on the diplomatic situation of the early privateering period, and explains some of the factors in British foreign policy which for many generations impeded our efforts to build an empire on the Main.

[1] Haring, 63.

Raleigh had spent the best years of his life as an incorrigible Elizabethan in outlook. Of strong Protestant sympathies—he had been present in Paris at the Massacre of S. Bartholomew in 1572—he looked upon the Catholic Spaniards as *Demonios* whom it was a Christian man's duty to despoil. With the accession of James I to the throne, however, the political atmosphere became somewhat too rarefied for men like Raleigh to breathe easily. At first King James—the first King, by the way, of 'Great Britain'—followed boldly on the line of foreign policy laid down by the Tudor Queen. In 1605, for example, he repudiated the King of Spain's claim to call himself Lord of all the Indies.[1] But later, especially after Cecil's death in 1612, James's craving for peace at any price, and for power even at the price of Protestantism, led him to adopt a policy of appeasement with regard to Spain, which was little to Raleigh's taste. Raleigh was thrown into the Tower for *lèse majesté*, but thirteen years of confinement failed to break his spirit or change his views.

Ultimately it was the King's sore need of money, and more money, which obtained Raleigh's conditional release. He had succeeded in convincing the worried monarch that he knew a land where gold abounded thick as leaves in Vallombrosa, a land he called El Dorado, which was on the upper reaches of the Rio Orinoco in Guiana. He knew how to get hold of this fabulous treasure-trove, too, and assured the King that if he were given his freedom and a fleet of British privateers he could fill the royal coffers to the brim. So Raleigh was set free, and got his fleet. But there was a catch in it. What must have been his bewilderment when he opened his Sealed Orders! For James, torn between cupidity for the gold of Eldorado and an earnest desire to avoid trouble with Spain, had given Raleigh an impossible task. First, he was to ascend the Orinoco, find the mines, and bring home the gold. But secondly, he was on no account to trespass on Spanish territory, nor be drawn into conflict with its Spanish custodians. This was not the Tudor way of doing things, and Raleigh, though he promised to obey, could have had no intention of doing so, nor any hope of avoiding trespass on Spanish territory. Doubtless he argued that, in the canny King's eyes, success would be its own best justification. Unfortunately, he did not succeed. He could neither find the gold, nor avoid the clash with Spain.

[1] Haring, 56.

In desperation, he seems to have indulged in a little buccaneering up and down the Caribbean Sea outside his contract. This may have been the occasion of his visit to the coast of British Honduras, with Lieutenant Wallace on board, of which Asturias speaks. Incidentally, Raleigh would have been interested to know that the wool dyers of England would one day look to Belize for their logwood, for he himself had been engaged in the wool trade in his earlier years. However, his buccaneering enterprise was no more successful than the former. He had to return to James at last with empty hands, and was executed in the following year, 1618.

After this, the King was more than ever confirmed in his policy of appeasement. Raleigh's execution, indeed, was intended as an offering on that altar. Unfortunately for the buccaneers of the seventeenth century, as well as for their successors in later years, this policy of tenderness to Spanish susceptibilities continued to blur the outlines of British foreign policy in the West Indies long after James had gone. Again and again we shall find it throwing its shadow over British Honduras, and the Mosquito Shore, to say nothing of the British settlements in Campeachy. Nothing must be done to offend the Spaniards. The territorial claims of the Spanish king must be recognized, if he could show the slightest title to ownership. Any British settlement in such places, whether for logwood-cutting, mahogany, plantations, or any other industry, must be regarded, if Spain so desired, as a concession worked only by Spanish permission. In any clash with Spanish authority the British were to be subject to Spanish laws. The settlements were to have no independent government of their own. On the high seas Spanish ships must have the right of way and the monopoly of trade, except in so far as they granted special licences to other Powers. Any resistance to search by a Spanish commander, still more, any attempt to interfere with a Spanish ship, would be punished as an act of piracy.

On the other hand it was expected, as of Raleigh, so of the buccaneers at sea and the settlers on land, that they would continue to bring profit to the British Exchequer. They were to exploit every opportunity by land and sea, yet to avoid a *casus belli* with Spain! If they succeeded, well and good: the offence would probably be overlooked. The Governor of Jamaica at all events could be relied upon to pigeonhole complaints by the Spanish

Ambassador, if the defendant buccaneer could call sufficient pieces-of-eight as witnesses in his defence. On one occasion, at least, the logwood-cutters were ordered publicly to cease cutting as Spain demanded, yet secretly to continue cutting on the quiet. The most striking example of this kind of thing was Harry Morgan's raid on Panama in 1670. Peace had just been declared between England and Spain, and it had been agreed that all buccaneering should forthwith cease, yet such was Morgan's success that he not only escaped punishment, but was actually knighted by King Charles II. Such were the inconsistencies and ambiguities which continually affected the official British attitude towards the pioneers of empire in the Caribbean. No man knew, when he returned home, whether he would be garlanded as a patriot or hanged as a pirate. Yet the Empire grew.

To return to Lieutenant Wallace. Undeterred by Raleigh's misfortunes, Wallace seems to have continued his seafaring career. He reappears in history some twenty years after Raleigh's execution as captain of a small fleet of buccaneers in the West Indies. Somehow or other he had got together a band of three hundred Scottish and English adventurers of his own kidney who had recently been expelled from the island of Nevis, near S. Kitts, by the Spaniards. Included in his band were some of the Providence settlers, who had found that island too remote and dangerous for their liking, and had decided to get away from it while the going was good. With this company he sailed to the island of Tortuga, then occupied by about forty French settlers. After living amicably side by side with them for about four months, Wallace suddenly turned upon them, marooned them on the coast of Hispaniola, and hoisted the English flag.

Some of his victims, however, made their escape to S. Kitts, where they reported their injuries to a Huguenot merchant named Levasseur. Obtaining a commission from the Governor of S. Kitts, de Poincy, to subdue Wallace by force of arms—for most West Indian merchants were quite capable of meeting force by force in those days—Levasseur sailed a barque with fifty men to the northern shores of Hispaniola, whence in August 1640 he made a sudden descent upon Wallace's settlement in Tortuga, capturing the Governor of the Island himself. The English rallied and besieged Levasseur in his rocky fortress for ten days, till, finding they made little impression on the doughty Huguenot, they manned their boats and sailed away *en masse* to the Island of Providence.

On arrival, Captain Wallace found but a cool reception. The island, not particularly fertile at the best of times, was already overcrowded, and over the heads of the settlers the political sky was continuously thundering with menaces of Spanish commanders from the mainland burning to expel this hornets' nest once and for all from the Honduranian Gulf. Wallace, it seems, quickly made up his mind to move on. He already knew the shores of British Honduras, as we have seen, and perhaps had heard something of the shipwrecked sailors and their logwood camp. So one day in the autumn of 1640, just in time to escape the annihilation of the Providence Island settlement in the following year, Captain Wallace got together eighty of his best men, sailed off to Turneffe, and thence landed on the beach at the mouth of the Belize River. After which we hear no more of him for good or ill.

Wallace must have known that according to Stuart policy his exploit might be regarded at Court as 'trespassing on Spanish territory', despite the fact that no Spaniards had ever landed there, and that there were no visible signs of Spanish possession. But no doubt he had inherited, through Raleigh, the Elizabethan outlook. Since not even the building of an odd cottage or the naming of an isolated river or cape could entitle the Spaniard to propriety in lands which they had not actually occupied (see Elizabeth's Declaration of 1587), how much less could Spain claim propriety in a desolate uninhabited spot like the Belize River estuary, where the only human beings were a few shipwrecked Englishmen! As Captain Wallace stepped on to the low-lying mangrove-covered beach, hacked his way through the spiny bush, waded up to the waist in endless swampy savannahs, or drove his canoe up the rapids of the Belize river, tormented by flies, menaced by snakes and alligators, and with no human being in sight, he must have felt that here indeed was No Man's Land, a land which only the toughest of the tough could stomach, a land which was his for the taking, by every natural right.

If put to it, however, he could plead a more formal title to possession, namely, that the country was within the scope of the Providence Company's Charter of 1629, and could be held for the Crown by the same right as Providence Island. 'It must be remembered', writes Winzerling, 'that Wallace was no low adventurer. He was one of Warwick's Puritans, possibly a relative of Wallace, the first Governor of Connecticut, or the son of that Captain James Wallace who was ransomed by Sir Anthony Shirley from the Spanish near Truxillo in 1597.' Who can say? Yet a third possible title to the coast is said to have been given him by the King of the Mosquitos, who claimed the whole of the Honduranian shore as his own. Indeed Winzerling affirms that Wallace actually bought the land around Belize on contract from that sovereign, and that many Mosquito Indians assisted the settlers in cutting the logwood.

Thus in the year 1640 the British Settlement of Belize, although as yet only a tiny logwood-cutting encampment on the banks of the Old River, became a *fait accompli*. His Britannic Majesty King Charles I had all unwittingly been presented with a new jewel in the crown he was so soon to lose.

Logwood has been so often mentioned that it is time we explained what it was.

The uses of logwood, or Campeachy wood as it was called, after the place of its first working by Europeans, had been discovered by the Spaniards on the Mexican Gulf about the middle of the sixteenth century. A leguminous tree, *Hæmotoxylon Campechianum*, with scented yellow flowers and reddish timber, it yields a glucose sap which in fermentation provides (or provided, for it is now obsolete) the most effective dyes then known, especially for woollen goods. At the beginning of the seventeenth century it had become a major article of export from Campeachy, selling at the almost incredible price (for those days) of £100 per ton. It was not long before the French corsairs and British buccaneers, accustomed to chasing the *flotas* of Spanish galleons laden with gold and silver, found it almost equally profitable to pursue the logwood convoys, cut out a laggard or two on the high seas, and compel their crews to make for an English port.

Another way of getting hold of logwood, at more trouble but less risk, was to cut it for oneself ashore in the places where it was to be found. Early in the seventeenth century British adventurers discovered the prolific logwood forests of Campeachy. By the middle of the century, apparently with the full consent of the Spaniards, many firmly established British logwood-cutting settlements had grown up, especially at Laguna de Terminos and the

Island of Trist, together with the near-by villages of San Paulo, Post Real, Champetone, and others.

We have an interesting contemporary description of the logwood-cutters in Dampier's *Two Voyages to Campeachy*. Dampier as a young man in search of profit and adventure sailed from Jamaica in 1675 to Trist Island, in the Bay of Campeachy, anchoring at One Bush Cay, so called for 'having only a little crooked tree growing on it'. 'The logwood-cutters', he writes, 'were then about 250 men, most English, that had settled themselves in several places hereabouts. Our cargo to purchase the logwood was rum and sugar: we took no money for it, nor expected any. The rate was £5 per ton to be paid at the place where they cut it, and we went with our long boat to fetch small quantities. I made two or three trips to their huts, where we were always very kindly entertained by them with pork and pease, or beef and doughboys.'[1] Dampier afterwards voyaged to Campeachy a second time, evidently attracted by the life and its rewards, and on this occasion better furnished with the requisite equipment, *e.g.* 'hatchets, axes, macheats,[2] saws, wedges, a pavilion to sleep in, a gun, with powder and shot, etc.' 'The logwood trade', he observes, 'was grown very common before I came hither.'

Dampier continues with a description of the actual method of log-cutting and its transhipment. He enlisted in a group of cutters whom he had met on his first voyage.

> 'There were six in company, who had a hundred tons ready cut, logged, and chipped, but not brought to the creek's side, and they expected a ship from New England in a month or two to fetch it away. When I came thither they were beginning to bring it to the creek, and because the carriage is the hardest work, they hired me to help them at the rate of a ton of wood per month, promising me that after this carriage was over I should strike in to work with them, for they were all obliged in bonds to procure this 100 tons jointly together, but for no more. This wood lay all in the circumference of 500 or 600 yards, and about 300 from the creek side, in the middle of a thick wood impassable with burthens. The first thing we did was to bring it all to one place in the middle and from thence we cut a very large path to carry it to the creek's side. We laboured hard at this work five days in the week, and on Saturdays went into the savannahs and killed beaver. When my month's service was up, in

---

[1] For years afterwards the British cutters all over the Caribbean were known as the 'Pork and Dough Boys'.

[2] *Machetes*, or long sword-like knives.

which time we brought down all the wood to the creek's side, I was presently paid my ton of logwood.'

Logwood-cutting in Campeachy, however, was by no means all work and no play.

'Many of the cutters being good marksmen thought it a dry business to toil at cutting wood and so took more delight in hunting. But neither of these employments affected them so much as privateering. Therefore they often made sallies out in small parties among the nearest Indian towns, where they plundered and brought away the Indian women to serve them at their huts, and sent their husbands to be sold at Jamaica. Besides they had not their old drinking bouts forgot, and would still spend £30 or £40 at a sitting aboard the ships that came hither from Jamaica, carousing and firing off guns three or four days together. And though afterwards many sober men came into the Bay to cut wood, yet by degrees the old standers so debauched them, that they could never settle themselves under any civil government.'

To be fair to the logwood-cutters of Captain Wallace's early settlement in Belize, we should remember that Dampier's description applies to a date some thirty years later, when the morals and manners of the camps had been contaminated by the advent of the demobilized buccaneers of whom we shall speak in our next chapter. Yet by and large it is probable that Dampier's picture of the Campeachy settlements would apply to most of the logwood camps set up in British Honduras during the seventeenth century—a kind of tropical Wild West, including the saloon bars, gambling hells, music, loose women, and shootings-up with which most of us are familiar on the screen. But the torment of the heat, the fevers, the flies, the tarantulas and scorpions, the occasional hurricanes, the top-gallant floods and sluicing rains of the wet season were something the cowboys never had to contend with.

Such, one may suppose, were the living conditions of those early settlers under Captain Wallace, and their descendants, for another century in the adolescent colony of Belize.

Chapter III

*

THE BUCCANEERS TURN HONEST

WALLACE and his eighty buccaneers had scarcely settled in Belize, when news came to them that the original colony on Providence Island had been annihilated by the Spanish (1641), as already related. Captain Bluefield's settlements on the Mosquito Shore, however, remained intact, defended as well by the Indians as by such colonists as escaped thither from the Island. A party of refugees sailing north-west towards the Gulf of Amatique established themselves also in the island of Rattan, or Roatan, off the coast of Spanish Honduras. We shall hear of Rattan again, but on this occasion the British occupation was short-lived. In 1642 the Spanish under Don Francisco de Villalba y Toledo quickly drove out the intruders. Rather surprisingly, Villalba refrained from attacking the recently founded settlement in Belize, so that the wood-cutters were allowed to consolidate their position in that district undisturbed. The coast near the Belize river estuary is not easy of approach by vessels of any great size. Apart from the numerous sudden small cays and coral reefs which stand on guard, the waters inshore are tideless and shallow, while the beach affords poor landing for small boats owing to the tangle of interlacing mangrove roots descending to the water's edge. Even if they land, the jungle presents an almost impassable barrier to those who would penetrate further. These natural advantages, added no doubt to the vigilance of the buccaneers themselves, deterred the Spanish from any resolute attack upon the Colony until it was too late to extirpate it easily.

Nor was Belize without protection from her buccaneer friends at sea. In 1642 Captain William Jackson set sail, armed to the teeth, on an expedition of revenge for the destruction of Providence Isle, having been commissioned by the Earl of Warwick, now Admiral of the Fleet, to try to retrieve it. Although Jackson failed to recover Providence Island, he made his presence felt among the Spanish shipping off the mainland of the Honduranian Gulf, even to the extent of harrying their chief port of Truxillo. In the following year (1643) he had the audacity to drop anchor in Port Royal, Jamaica (then in Spanish possession), and extort a ransom for the city of Santiago de la Vega to the amount of 7000 pieces-of-eight and a cargo of provisions. This exploit had an unexpected sequel. Jackson's privateers were so delighted with the lovely island that twenty-three of the crew refused to leave it, and the others determined to secure it for England at the first opportunity—which came in no more than twelve years' time (1655). Jamaica was thus in effect a payment of compensation to the British for the loss of Providence Island, and everyone will agree we got the better of the bargain.

At the same time a determined attempt was made to consolidate our settlements on the Mosquito Shore. A large number of runaway Negro slaves, revolting against the cruelty of their Spanish masters in the West Indies, had been making the Mosquito Coast their chief sanctuary for some years. These Cimarrones, as they were called, had heard of the anti-Spanish feeling as well amongst the Mosquito Indians as among the British and Dutch buccaneers, so that the Shore seemed a natural place of refuge, from which they would be neither repulsed nor extradited. Intermingling with the natives, these hybrid Afric-Indians became known to the buccaneers as Sambos, congregating chiefly on the northern part of the Mosquito Coast between Cape Gracias à Dios and Castillo Point. A glance at the map will show the strange un-Spanish names which still commemorate the alliance of those invaders with the seventeenth-century buccaneers—the River Wanka, Black River, Brewer's Lagoon, Cape Cameron, Turtle Bight, Salt River, and the rest. Sambo-land remained, of course, a province of the Mosquito Monarchy, which thus stretched from just east of Truxillo, including the Bay Islands of Rattan, Bonacca, Utila, Barbareta, Mosat, etc., in the Honduras Gulf, down to Bluefields, Monkey Point, and San Juan del Norte (Greytown) in Nicaragua, with the islands (circumstances permitting) of Old Providence, Henrietta, S. Andrew, and Roncador. The claim of the Mosquito King may have resembled in its grandiose unrealism that of our own kings to the sovereignty of 'Great Britain, France, and Ireland', but it was based on the historic fact that the Mosquitos were the aboriginal inhabitants of these places, and still clung ideally to their ancient patrimony. That they came very near to realizing this ideal with the help of British arms, and only failed to do so through the non-cooperation or negligence of the Home Government, will be seen as our story progresses.

It is worth giving passing notice to one of the best-known characters and writers of this period in the history of the Spanish Main. It was about 1641, the year of the fall of Old Providence, that the Dutch buccaneer Captain Lucifer, shipmate and friend of the Captain Jackson mentioned above, captured in the Bay of Honduras an Englishman named Thomas Gage. Gage had been brought up as a boy in the British logwood settlements of Campeachy, but had gone over to the Spaniards, and become a Dominican friar. Returning now to England he soon announced his conversion to Protestantism, joined the Roundheads, and became a Minister of Religion. In 1648 he published a lively narration of his experiences among the Spaniards in Central America, denouncing the enormities of the Papists, and painting a seductive picture of the wealth of the Spanish possessions in the Caribbean, which might be seized with profit by his own countrymen.

In 1654 Gage laid before Cromwell personally a scheme for the expansion of the British Empire in the West Indies. The Spanish colonies, he said, were but sparsely populated by whites, and weakly held. The plum was ripe for the picking.

> 'To my countrymen I offer a New World, to be the subject of their future Pains, Valour, and Piety, desiring their acceptance of this plain but faithful Relation of mine, wherein the English Nation may see what wealth and honour they have lost by the oversight of King Henry VII, who living in peace and abounding in riches did notwithstanding unfortunately reject the offer of being the first Discoverer of America. I know no title the King of Spain hath to these parts but force, which by the same title, and by a greater force may be repelled.'

There was a fine Elizabethan ring about this—none of your pedantic Stuart diplomacy with its nonsense about 'trespassing on Spanish territory'. Cromwell was deeply moved. Where kings had failed, a commoner should succeed. He thereupon declared war on Spain, and in the following year (1655) made himself master of the rich and extensive island of Sant Jago (Saint James), henceforth to be known to all ages as Jamaica.

With the British occupation of Jamaica, a new era begins in

the history of the British West Indies. Here at last was a possession big and wealthy enough for the Home Government to take a lively interest in. Jamaica thus became the Headquarters of our West Indian Empire, with full status as a British Colony, a regular armed guard by sea and land, and an almost plenipotentiary Governor of its own. No need was there any longer for the other Caribbean colonies to wait many weary months for instructions to come from Whitehall, no longer was it necessary to send every major criminal all the way to England for trial, no longer would the buccaneers and settlers in the West Indies feel infinitely remote from their Base. Ideally placed between the Spanish Main and the British islands of the Bahamas and Antilles, Jamaica stood like a hen among her brood, spreading over them protective wings.

From the Spanish point of view, Jamaica more resembled a spider in the heart of its web, ready to dart out at the slightest quiver on the circumference. Port Royal indeed became a veritable nest of privateers, or licensed buccaneers armed with Letters of Marque commissioning them to rove the seas in the King's name, and challenge the King's enemies wherever they might be found. Often enough the Governor of Jamaica was sufficiently broad-minded to overlook the absence of such papers in return for a percentage of the spoils which some enterprising buccaneer might bring into port. Sometimes he would even conveniently forget that peace had been declared in far-away Europe, and that technically the victims were no longer enemies at all. So from Jamaica sailed a constant stream of well-armed, bravely manned barques, brigantines, schooners, or even pinks, flying the Jolly Roger or the English flag as the mood took them, chasing Spanish ships at sight, as a dog chases cats, and captained by such noted seamen as Colonel Morgan, Harry Morgan, Jackman, Morris, Mansfield, Dampier, Sharp, Coxon, Sawkins, Harris, and the rest.

Nor were their exploits confined to the high seas, for the buccaneers were amphibious fighters, expert at landing on unlikely beaches, hacking their way through jungles, even storming apparently impregnable fortresses defended by every known instrument of war. Thus in 1665 the celebrated Harry Morgan, Morris, and Jackman with 107 men, in two barques, attacked the town of Campeachy, coasted along the shores of Belize, and sacked the Honduranian port of Truxillo. Joining forces with the Mosquito Indians in Monkey Bay, they ascended the San Juan River as far inland as Lake Nicaragua, and took by assault the great city of Granada. The Indians had to be forcibly restrained from slaying the hated Spanish prisoners out of hand.[1] In the spring of 1666 Sir Thomas Modyford, Governor of Jamaica, got Captain Mansfield, one of the most notorious buccaneers of the day, to assemble a fleet of his own kidney at Bluefield Harbour on the Mosquito Coast, with Harry Morgan as his second-in-command. With this force Mansfield recaptured Old Providence Island, which had been in Spanish hands since the destruction of Providence Company in 1641, and established it as a self-governing buccaneer colony, with James Modyford (brother of Sir Thomas) as Governor. On returning to Port Royal, Mansfield was received with open arms, although England and Spain at the time were striving to negotiate peace.[2]

The new colony was soon extinguished, however. Towards the end of the same year the President of Panama, Don Juan Perez de Guzman, forced the settlers to capitulate after a three days' siege. They were thereupon subjected to the most inhuman tortures, being maltreated until 'their corpses were noisome to one another', and cast chained into the oven-like dungeons of Panama.[3] Modyford and his buccaneer friends were furious. No reprisals could be too merciless for the perpetrators of such atrocities, and plans were laid to make the Spaniard pay dearly for his crimes. The Home Government, however, was in no mood to continue the war. The English Navy was in a poor state, and Pepys allows us to see how little appreciation was felt at the Admiralty for the naval enterprise of the privateers. 'Lord Bellassis', he writes on February 20, 1667, 'tells us as a grand secret that he do believe the peace offensive and defensive between us and Spain is quite finished. . . . We have done the Spanish abundance of mischief in the West Indys by our privateers from Jamaica, which they lament mightily, and I am sorry for them to have done it at this time.'

Despite these forebodings, however, peace was made at last in the Sandwich Treaty of Madrid (May 23, 1667). One of the first stipulations made by Spain was the prohibition of all buccaneering whether by sea or land. Article II of the Treaty provides that 'Neither of the said Kings of Great Britain or Spain . . . shall do or procure to be done, anything against the other in any place

---

[1] Haring, 137. [2] Ibid., 135. [3] Ibid., 140.

by sea or land'. Article III, that 'They shall take care that their respective People and Subjects from henceforward do abstain from all force, violence or wrong'. Article IV, that 'There shall be free Trade and Commerce in such a way and manner that without Safe Conduct and without general or particular Licences, the Peoples and Subjects of each other may go freely as well by land as by sea, navigate, and go into their said countries'. This mutual non-aggression pact, therefore, was the death knell of all buccaneering, at any rate in theory, and from 1667 onwards it became the duty of every Government official to see that the 'Trade' was duly outlawed and suppressed.

Modyford understood this perfectly well, of course, but felt it was one of those occasions when a blind eye should be put to the telescope. The buccaneers with his connivance ignored the Treaty, and continued with their preparations for revenge upon the Spaniards. Early in the following year Harry Morgan took and looted Porto Bello, and in 1669 did the same to Maracaibo, sailing from Port Royal with the full knowledge of the Governor. In 1670 a second Treaty with Spain was signed by Lord Godolphin at Madrid, a Treaty of great importance to British Honduras, as we shall see hereafter. But neither did this second agreement put the most famous of all buccaneers out of business. In fact it was in the very year of the Godolphin Treaty that Harry Morgan perpetrated that most amazing and profitable feat in the history of buccaneering, the sack of Panama, of which Esquemelin has left so circumstantial an account. On Morgan's return to Port Royal, the Governor and Council of Jamaica accorded him a hearty vote of thanks! Spain naturally protested in the strongest terms, and Charles II found himself obliged to placate her by disowning Morgan and discharging Modyford. Despite a huge petition in their favour, they were clapped into irons, brought home to London, and imprisoned in the Tower.

The new Governor of Jamaica, Sir Thomas Lynch, was determined to enforce the recent treaties. A general amnesty was proclaimed to all freebooters who, though late in the day, should surrender themselves and their vessels at Port Royal, and by 1672 Lynch felt able to report home that 'this cursed Trade, which has been so long followed, is now ended'. The age of the buccaneers, in the true sense of the word, had passed. The age of the pirates begins—pirates who chased, fought, and looted friend and enemy alike, with no pretence at legality, no longer patriots but criminals, the lawless highwaymen of the sea. Most relentless of all in ferreting out and 'liquidating' the ex-buccaneers was now, ironically enough, that old lag Harry Morgan himself. Brought for trial before Charles II, his glamorous personality had made such an impression upon the Merry Monarch that, instead of hanging, he found himself actually knighted for his exploits. In 1675 he was back again in Jamaica as Deputy Governor, where he remained till his death in 1682.

It now became a problem for the ex-buccaneers—such of them as did not become pirates—to turn their somewhat unusual gifts and experience to honest uses. Neither by training nor temperament were they adapted to the arts or restrictions of peace. Many returned home to England, bringing with them as much of their booty as had not been squandered or lost. Others settled down as best they could on plantations of the various West Indian islands, or signed on before the mast on merchant ships. Some of them, more successful or more thrifty than the rest, had accumulated considerable fortunes through the 'Trade', and before surrendering themselves to the authorities took the precaution of burying their treasure chests full of gold, silver, costly ornaments, and precious stones on some uninhabited island of the Caribbean or lonely spot on the shores of New England to which, in more settled times, they intended to return with their rough map, a spade, and a boat in which to carry the treasure home. Stevenson's *Treasure Island* is certainly founded on fact. Some of the treasure seekers were successful and lived in affluence happily ever after. Some returned to find that other spades had been at work before them, and nothing but an odd piece-of-eight or two remained. Some mislaid their maps or lost their lives before the treasure could be recovered, and left a legacy to three hundred years of treasure hunters in the search for 'Pirate Gold'.

Several such buried treasures have actually been found—probably more than have ever been published by their fortunate discoverers. To give but one example. One day in the year 1900 young George Benner of Boston happened to see a very old unopened seaman's locker in his aunt's lumber-room. On forcing it open he found among an assortment of sailors' trinkets a folded vellum chart showing the estuary of the Kennebec River in Maine, with a star drawn over a small bay. Underneath the star was a faded note, 'Stand abrest gurtsbolder bring top in line with hill N ¼ m it lise 12 fathom N E near big trees under stone.' Benner and a friend excitedly followed up the clue, found the spot indicated, with a boulder and the remains of a big tree marking the site, and eventually located a large flat stone buried about a foot beneath the ground. Under the stone lay a rotted wooden chest filled to the brim with golden coins, pearls, and diamonds. Carrying their treasure away in canvas bags to a bank in Boston, the fortunate youths had it valued at over 20,000 dollars. Edward Rowe Snow, who tells the story,[1] adds that 'George Benner still is alive and active on the streets of Boston to-day.'

But perhaps the chief single avenue of employment for the discharged buccaneers was the trade of logwood-cutting. By this time logwood was more than ever welcomed in English markets, where it continued for nearly two centuries to be a valuable article of commerce. The occupation was ideally suited to the buccaneers. They were used to hard physical toil, long experience had inured them to the discomforts of life in the tropics, there was an exhilarating spice of danger in the defence of the settlements against prowling enemies, their skill with weapons could still be of use in hunting for their food on the savannah or in the bush, good fishing in sea and river abounded, and the life was pleasantly free from those restrictions and conventions which put such a damper on high spirits in the streets of civilized towns. Moreover very little financial capital or special technique was needed for the craft of logwood-cutting. The precious timber was easy enough to recognize. All that was needed was an axe, a sword or machete, saws, wedges, and ropes for hauling the timber down to the waterside. The strong current of the stream would do the rest, floating the logs down to the haulover near the estuary, where they could be assembled on the *barcadero*, and so shipped for home. The rough discipline and customs which had been observed aboard ship could very conveniently be transported to the settlements ashore, where the method of allotting shares in the profits of the business under the superintendence of an elected ganger would follow the model of distribution aboard ship. Thus the buccaneers very naturally and cheerfully abandoned, if they were law-abiding, their freebooting on the high seas, landing here and there among the logwood settlements of the Caribbean coast

[1] *Pirates and Buccaneers*, 1944.

which had been planted, as we have seen, some thirty or forty years earlier, especially on the Mosquito Shore and in British Honduras. As buccaneers on the high seas they had played their part in the discovery and conquest of Empire: as honest hardworking logwood-cutters ashore they continued to play an equally important part in consolidating that Empire.

It is probable that the Treaty of 1667 added indirectly to the importance and prestige of Belize. No stretch of coast in all the Caribbean was so suitable a hiding-place for such buccaneers as chose to ignore the Treaty. The coastline was fretted with innumerable tree-grown estuaries invisible except to a direct view, the beaches on the cays were admirably adapted for careening barnacled vessels, there was plenty of good fresh water and natural food everywhere and, to cap it all, the residents ashore were by tradition favourably inclined towards their old Brethren of the Coast. For obvious reasons most of these ex-buccaneers, or pirates as we must now call them, have remained anonymous and their misdeeds unrecorded, but from time to time a brief shaft of light illuminates the scene. Thus in 1677 we hear for the first time of the little island of S. George's Cay, then known as Isla de Casinas. It was on this Cay that Fr. José Delgado made the acquaintance of the celebrated buccaneer Captain Bartholomew Sharpe. Delgado and his missionary companions had been captured and ill-used by some English buccaneers on the mainland. One night the buccaneers, sated with their sport, fell into a drunken stupor and could easily have been killed, but Delgado persuaded his companions to spare their lives. He was shortly afterwards rescued by Captain Sharpe, who was a very religious man—his ship was called the *Most Blessed Trinity*—and would not stand by to see a minister of religion, even though he were but a Spanish friar, maltreated. Sharpe took Delgado aboard his vessel to S. George's Cay, and there, after a brief examination, sent him on his way rejoicing. This happened in the year before Sharpe and Coxon, from their headquarters among the Honduranian cays, made their famous raid upon Porto Bello, and in company with Dampier marched across the Isthmus to the Pacific after the example of their hero, Harry Morgan.

A few years later, 1682, S. George's Cay is again in the picture. Coxon by this time had given up buccaneering, to take up the trade of logwood-carrying from Campeachy and Belize to Jamaica.

While watering on the cay, his men, or some of them, mutinied, intending to steal the ship, and make off on their own account as pirates. Coxon, however, got the better of them, arresting the three ringleaders, and bringing them back in irons to Port Royal, where they were tried and hanged by Sir Harry Morgan. In the following year (1683) the Dutch privateer Nicolas van Horn assembled a fleet of ex-buccaneers at Ruatan and among the cays off Belize, with which he made a successful raid on Vera Cruz, the chief port of Mexico. He was afterwards killed by another pirate, Graff, and buried on Loggerhead Cay, near Cape Contoy. Other pirates associated with these parts were Banister and Christopher Goffe, who have bequeathed their names to two cays off Belize. Banister, after having been sentenced to death for piracy at Port Royal, escaped and took refuge in Belize. A fine seamen, he eluded for years, and on one occasion actually defeated in action the naval vessels sent to capture him under the command of Captain Spragg, R.N., but he was brought to the yard-arm at last, in 1687.

As an appendix to the story of the buccaneers we may note that their last great exploit was the capture of Cartagena in 1697. On that occasion the Sieur de Pointis with a force of 4000 men, many of them ex-buccaneers under Ducasse, laid siege to Cartagena, reduced it to an honourable capitulation, and sailed away for France. The buccaneers, however, secretly dropped behind the rest of the fleet, and returning to the city put it to a merciless sack, squeezing several millions more out of the citizens in gold and silver. Most of these pirates were captured eventually by a British fleet under Admiral Nevill, losing the bulk of their treacherously gotten treasure; and it was driven home upon the sea-rovers that the forces of law and order were too strong for any further 'Trade' of that description. 'With the capture of Cartagena in 1697 the history of the buccaneers may be said to end. More and more during the previous years they had degenerated into mere pirates, or had left their libertine life for more civilized pursuits.'[1]

Among these civilized pursuits was the logwood industry in Belize, where the settlements from now onwards grew apace.

[1] Haring, 266.

Chapter IV

*

THE BRITISH LOGWOOD SETTLEMENTS

WITH the signing by England and Spain of the Treaty of 1667, outlawing all buccaneering, those who cared about England's glory or had an eye to her future in the West Indies must have realized the enormously increased importance of the British logwood settlements. To put it at its lowest, it was obvious that unless the buccaneers could find employment in some honest occupation sheer necessity would drive them back to their old manner of life.

Sir Thomas Modyford, Governor of Jamaica, enterprising, far-sighted, Elizabethan-minded as ever, pleaded hard with the Home Government to devote a little more attention to this embryo empire in the new world—'these new sucking colonies',[1] as he called them. The superannuated buccaneers, he said, were a fine 'soldierly' lot of men of whom England might stand in need in 'any new rupture', when they could be depended on to be 'always ready to serve His Majesty'. In addition to the military advantage which might accrue through having these expert mariners and doughty fighters settled in the West Indies, they were also bringing considerable grist to the Imperial mills through commerce. Already there were about a dozen logwood vessels, formerly privateers, selling the wood at £25 to £50 a ton, and making a good profit. Nor were they doing anyone any harm. 'They go to places uninhabited or inhabited only by Indians', said Modyford, doubtless having in mind Belize among other places, 'in no way trespassing on the Spaniard.' He adds that, with a little encouragement from Home, the 'whole logwood trade will be English and be very considerable, paying £5 per ton custom'.

It was probably with some such consideration in mind that the Godolphin Treaty already mentioned was agreed with Spain,

[1] Burdon, i, 49.

1670—an important landmark in Imperial history. It was the first attempt of Stuart diplomacy to clarify our territorial position in the New World and to obtain from Spain a black-and-white admission that her monopoly of empire in those regions was at an end. The Godolphin Treaty, in fact, was England's somewhat tardy follow-up of Elizabeth's defiant Declaration made a hundred years earlier. By Article VII of the Treaty it was agreed that England should henceforth hold and possess without question 'all those lands, regions, islands, colonies, and places whatsoever, being situated in the West Indies or in any part of America, which the said King of Great Britain and his subjects do at present [*i.e.* in 1670] hold and possess'. So far so good. Having made this unusually virile gesture, however, King Charles and his advisers found themselves too exhausted to compile that detailed schedule of British Possessions up-to-date without which Article VII would always be open to misunderstandings. One could be quite certain that well-established places like Barbados, S. Kitts, Jamaica, and the North American colonies were included, but what about less explicitly held possessions? Of Godolphin's refusal to grasp this nettle firmly, Burdon remarks: 'The result was over a century of ineffectual diplomatic effort on the part of England, a European War, and a century of desperate strife and misery for the unfortunate settlers in Belize.'[1]

Candour, however, compels the historian of British Honduras to admit that, while the 'unfortunate settlers in Belize' were probably *in the mind* of the negotiators of the Godolphin Treaty, they are not in fact *named*. It was too early, apparently, for the name Belize to have impinged upon officialdom, and the boundaries of the region called 'Honduras' were still ambiguous. The Wallace settlement at this time must have been comparatively small, for the only colonies to be actually named are those around Campeachy, although allusion is made vaguely to similar communities in the phrase 'Honduras, the Mosquitos, etc.'[2] Possibly we are to understand 'etc.' as including Belize, but the most prominent logwood settlements at this time were those to the north of British Honduras, in upper Yucatan—that is to say, Campeachy, Cape Cattock, Cozumel, Port Real, San Paulo, and

---

[1] Burdon, i, 9. Had Sir John Burdon lived to see this Treaty disinterred with all the old ghosts resuscitated by Guatemala in 1948, he might have written not *one* century, but nearly three!

[2] Burdon, i, 51.

Champetone, as named by Modyford in a letter to Lord Arlington in 1672.[1] As these Campeachy logwood-cutters were the forerunners, and perhaps the original inspiration, of the camps in Belize they are of great importance in our story, and must be dealt with in this chapter, especially as many of the arguments used on behalf of the Campeachy settlements apply by the same token to those on the Belize river.

We have seen how Modyford pleaded with the Home Government for recognition of the ex-buccaneers who had taken up the honest trade of logwood-cutting. His successor as Governor of Jamaica, Lord Lynch, fortunately adopted the same line, at any rate to begin with. Lynch was troubled by the fear that the Godolphin Treaty of 1670 might be interpreted to the disadvantage of the British in Campeachy, especially at Cape Catoche (Cattock). The question was, whether the settlement here could count as one that was already in British possession at the time of the signing of the Treaty. If so, by the terms of Article VII, it would remain British. But already the ambiguity of that indolently framed Article was creating confusion. The Spaniards were claiming that the logwood in those parts had never been *possessed*, but only *exploited* by the British. In which case, the camps were still on Spanish territory, and worked by Spanish permission. This ambiguity was to poison the Anglo-Spanish atmosphere in Belize a few years later, and even to the present day, so it is worth while pausing to examine it.

With regard to Cape Catoche, Lynch claimed that it was a British possession under the terms of the Treaty, for the following reasons: 1. The British have been cutting there for many years. 2. It is a desolate and uninhabited place. 3. The practice of cutting seems to argue possessory rights under the Treaty. 4. If the British claim is established, the Dutch and French can be excluded. 5. The Spaniards have never made any complaint hitherto. 6. The encouragement of wood-cutting makes it easier to reduce privateering. 7. 'It would employ 100 ships a year, and bring more into His Majesty's customs and the Nation's trade than any colony the King hath.' 8. 'I know there's so many places, islands, and cays where Strangers hunt fish and cut wood, and where the Spaniards seem to have no right, especially since the Treaty, having no mark of dominion or sovereignty there.'[2]

[1] Burdon, i, 53.   [2] *Ibid.*, i, 51.

We may conjecture that among the 'many places, islands, and cays' mentioned by Lynch, the Belize river and its coastline were included. At any rate, there is little in Lynch's argument about Cape Catoche which would not apply equally to the Belize settlement. The Spanish, however, contested his claim, and the Council of Plantations in Whitehall dithered in a way only too familiar at some periods of British foreign policy, so that Lynch was moved to appeal again 'for God's sake give your commands about logwood', lest the uncertainty and Spanish insolence should set a 'new war' ablaze.[1]

A little while later Lynch reported that the Spanish Governor of Campeachy had gone so far as to hire a Dutch privateer named Yallahs (Yellows) to attack the British logwood ships in the Yucatan passage, and to raid the settlement in Trist. The Queen Regent of Spain issued a Royal *Cedula* that any British traders sailing from ports in the West Indies without a licence from Spain should be proceeded against as pirates,[2] and from this time it became part of Spanish policy to confiscate all logwood cargoes. In the year 1672 over a dozen such cargoes, with their ships, were seized off Campeachy alone. The Spanish evidently considered the Godolphin Treaty as more honoured in the breach than the observance, and Lynch's 'new war' seemed not far round the corner.

The men on the spot did all they could. The logwood-cutters themselves showed such a bold front on land that the Spanish did not dare to attack their settlements. But at sea off Yucatan they were hopelessly outnumbered and outgunned by Spanish men-of-war from the Mexican Bay, and, though they organized a system of protected convoys with help from Port Royal, their losses were considerable. Lynch continued to try his best to interest the Home Government, begging them at least to settle one way or the other the question of the 'propriety', British or Spanish, of the Yucatan settlements.[3] Modyford, now under a shadow in London, but still loyal to the West Indies he had served so well, continued his advocacy of the 'new sucking colonies', begging the Government to recognize them as British. 'This possession in the West Indies is held by the strongest that can be, namely, falling of wood, building of houses, and clearing and planting of ground.'[4] Lord Vaughan, Governor of Jamaica

[1] Burdon, i, 52.   [2] *Ibid.*, i, 52, 53.   [3] *Ibid.*, i, 55.   [4] *Ibid.*, i, 53.

from 1675, urged that the settlements should be annexed to Jamaica.[1] Lord Carlisle, who succeeded Vaughan, added his voice to the same effect. Instances of Spanish injury and insults were reported at frequent intervals to Whitehall. But it was all to very little effect. The Home Government expressed sympathy, but was clearly either powerless or disinclined to risk a rupture with Spain. In particular, there was no real attempt to settle the fundamental question as to the ownership of the territory where the logwood camps were working.

In 1674 Lord Arlington, Secretary of State, went so far as to urge upon Godolphin, the Spanish Ambassador at Madrid, that the complaints of the settlers should be dealt with. 'His Majesty is so sensible of the sufferings of His Subjects in those parts that you must endeavour to procure some liberty for the cutters of logwood in those remote parts where the Spaniards have none, and His Majesty's subjects have had long abode and residence.' At first sight this looked as though Whitehall meant to take the matter up at last. But it was worse than nothing. It contained the implied admission that the territory was to be recognized after all as Spanish, and that the settlers would have to sue for Spanish permission to continue their trade. It was, in effect, a renunciation of our territorial rights in Yucatan, and by implication those on the Spanish Main, including Belize itself—a repudiation by a Government official of the Treaty of Godolphin solemnly agreed four years earlier by his own Government. It made nonsense of Article VII in that Treaty, and threw away the fruits of victory won in the late war. For the sake of an uneasy spell of personal peace and quiet, the diplomats of Whitehall had rejected the protests of the men in the front line, humiliated their overseas representatives, thrown away a flourishing source of trade, and betrayed their fellow-countrymen to the tender mercies of the most notoriously arrogant and inhuman power in the West Indies. The repercussions of this careless note of Lord Arlington's were to last for centuries.

Its effect on the Yucatan settlements was eventually to wipe them out altogether, although it took longer than might have been expected, owing to the courage and tenacity of the settlers. Five years after Arlington's declaration of policy, conditions in Campeachy had so far deteriorated that the Board of Trade was

[1] Burdon, i, 54.

urging all British logwood-cutters, not only in Yucatan but throughout the Spanish Main, including presumably those in Belize and the Gulf of Honduras, to evacuate the settlements as quickly as possible and 'apply themselves to the planting upon the islands of Jamaica'.[1] Three years later (1682) poor frustrated Governor Lynch had to abandon his defiant attitude. 'I have forbidden', he writes sadly, 'our cutting of Logwood in the Bay of Honduras and Campeachy, your Lordships having justly declared that the country being the Spaniards', we ought not to cut the wood.' He comforted himself by pretending that it was of little consequence, since by that time logwood had become a drug in the market—a statement which Burdon points out was by no means true to fact. Nor were the British settlers in the least disposed to obey either the Board of Trade at home or the Governor of Jamaica. They had their own interpretation of the Godolphin Treaty. It had given them the right to continue in possession of what they had already possessed, and they meant to stick by it, not only in Campeachy but elsewhere. In British Honduras, for example, the *Honduras Almanac* of 1828 remarks that the Treaty was 'very properly read as allowing their title to the possession of Belize', and they were prepared to enforce it against both the oppression of Spain and the defeatism of the British Court.

This somewhat truculent attitude on the part of the ex-buccaneers naturally caused the Home Government considerable embarrassment. Although not prepared to fight Spain on their behalf, Godolphin could hardly expect his Government to fight the buccaneers. His next proposal was typical of the period. While officially accepting the Spanish claim to territorial possession of the Central American continent, he privately urged upon the Spanish authorities in 1672 that they might well refrain from asserting the letter of their rights. To the settlers themselves he threw out the suggestion that they should continue with their logwood-cutting, but do it as unobtrusively and secretly as possible. 'Although we have no shadow of a claim in those parts', he said, 'let our settlers cut the wood surreptitiously, not avowedly, whereby to give example and pretence to other nations, but underhand and without making depredations on the country.'[2] He hopes to persuade Spain to 'connive' at the practice. Burdon

[1] Burdon, i, 56.   [2] *Ibid.*, i, 53.

comments severely on this disingenuous suggestion. It was indeed the nadir of Stuart diplomacy, the Munich of the West Indies. And of course it settled nothing.

It must be admitted that the Spanish, in Campeachy at all events, had some cause for complaint. It was to that district that Dampier went in 1674 and 1675, so that we have a fairly clear picture of the sort of people these early British logwood-cutters really were. Dampier, as we have seen, has a sad tale to tell of the corruption of manners and morals caused among the older settlers by the incoming buccaneers—of their potations, slave-raiding, kidnapping, quarrelling, and violence. In short, they were looked upon as undesirables of whom the Spanish Government wished to be rid as soon as possible, or whom at least they must keep within the strictest control. The Archives of this period are full of records of clashes between the logwood-cutters and the Spanish, especially when it became clear that the former had no intention of evacuating their camps either for Godolphin or anyone else. In 1680, for example, the settlement at Trist was exterminated by a strong Spanish force, which imprisoned the survivors in dungeons at Campeachy and Vera Cruz. There were also many incidents at sea, as when a British ship was captured off the cays of Yucatan (probably meaning British Honduras), and the captain with eight hands were marooned on Turneffe.[1]

Constantly attacked by land and sea, and with no hope of succour from England or even from Jamaica, it might be supposed that the Yucatan settlements had at last heard their death knell. If they did hear it, they refused to lie down and die. They may on the contrary have rejoiced at the excuse for brushing up their buccaneering, and have re-entered the arena with relish. The celebrated buccaneer Laurence Graff, whose blushing bride had gone to the altar with a brace of pistols bulging under her wedding veil, signalized his return to active service by attacking, looting, and burning the Spanish capital of Campeche itself. The exploits of his celebrated brig *The Big Trompoose* (La Grande Trompeuse) were the theme of seamen's yarns from Charleston to the Rio Grande. The waters of the Mexican and Honduranian Gulf in particular became about as safe for Spanish shipping as a pond full of goldfish with a pike let loose in it. Among the famous, or notorious, buccaneers who 'infested' the Gulf at this time were

[1] Burdon, i, 56.

Sharp and Coxon, returning to Port Royal with Dampier on board, together with huge quantities of indigo, cocoa, cochineal, tortoiseshell, money and plate looted from Spanish bottoms. This was in the year before they forgathered with Harris and Sawkins at the Golden Isle for the raid on Darien so vividly related by Basil Ringnose in Dampier's *Voyages*.

Somehow or other the British held on through it all, with that grim tenacity which earned them the name of 'Bulldog'. From beginning to end, they retained their footing in the enemy-encircled peninsula of Yucatan for all but a hundred years. Looking ahead, we shall find that in 1704, when Spain and England were once more at open loggerheads in the War of the Spanish Succession, the settlers are still in possession. Plans were being made to protect them against assault by the erection of stockades made out of the cut logwood awaiting shipment, and by 'building a galley or two' to defend the coast. Even Whitehall woke up, to the extent of recommending the establishment of a formal constitution in the Colony. But—how typical of our vacillating policy!—a month later the officials were informing the Governor of Jamaica that 'there seemed very little chance of establishing any Governor at Campeachy at this time', and the idea was abandoned. That the settlement was able to hold out during the whole of that long war (1702–13) was surely a remarkable achievement, cut off as it was from any assistance by land or sea.

It seems strange that the Treaty of Utrecht (December 9, 1713), which brought the war to an end, did not deign to mention the logwood-cutters or logwood-cutting rights after all this. Yet although restoring to Spain all territorial conquests made by England during the war, the Treaty of 1713 did add the salient proviso that this clause should be interpreted 'without prejudice to any liberty or power which British Subjects enjoyed before the outbreak of War, either through right, sufferance, or indulgence'. This the Government doubtless considered sufficiently explicit, seeing that by common knowledge British logwood-cutting in Campeachy, Belize, and elsewhere on the Main had been permitted long before the outbreak of War. Logwood-cutting, long established by precedent and tradition, was not to be prohibited: that was clear. The Treaty therefore could be welcomed by the settlements as a further confirmation of their right to the unmolested practice of their trade, even if it left ambiguous their right to territorial possession.

Four years later (1717)—the nonchalant Stuart regime having been displaced by that of George I—we find British Foreign Policy a little more definite. The Board of Trade and Plantations now openly expressed the view that the Campeachy settlements were *not* included among those British conquests which were to be returned to Spain. 'The English settlements at Cape Cattock, Laguna de Terminos, and Trist were effectively occupied by British subjects before the War, so are not to be restored by the Treaty of Utrecht.'[1] By implication it was assumed at once that this decision obtained also in the case of the settlements around the Mosquito Coast and the Belize river. They too had been 'effectively occupied' before the war. It was a pity they had not been actually named in the Pact.

Actually it was the latter settlements which most interested the logwood-cutters in the early eighteenth century. Though the Home Government seems not to have realized it, Campeachy was no longer in the foreground of the picture. 'The centre of gravity of logwood-cutting was shifting at this time from Campeachy to the Belize district', observes Burdon.[2] As late as 1732 the Spanish were, it is true, protesting fiercely against the continuance of British pretensions in Northern Yucatan, claiming that the logwood-cutters were trespassing on Spanish soil, and Whitehall, grown stiff rather too late in the day, was countering that in this matter the onus of proof lay upon Spain. But by that time the Campeachy settlements were almost deserted. The cutters, apart from being weary of interference, had already gathered in all the most accessible timber. As they penetrated deeper into the forests, the labour of hauling the logs down to the seashore had grown intolerable. In short, the logwood of Campeachy was 'worked out'. The cutters had heard great stories of the comparatively virgin forests further south beyond the Rio Hondo, in the Belize river district, where swift streams and creeks lay at the edge of the clearings ready to carry the timber down to the sea. There were also rumours of another kind of tree, even more valuable than logwood, growing down to the water's edge, a hard, smooth wood called mahogany, which made a fine timber for shipbuilding and furniture-making.

[1] Burdon, i, 64.   [2] *Ibid.*, i, 67.

On the whole the logwood-cutters were glad to see the last of Campeachy.

We have dealt with the Campeachy settlements at some length, because their experience both of Spanish aggression and of British diplomacy was repeated almost *pari passu*, except for their final abandonment, in the case of British Honduras. In Belize, as in Campeachy, the Spanish claimed territorial possession, the settlers contested the claim, and the British Government vacillated. In Belize, as in Campeachy, the local cutters were left almost unaided to fight their own battles, and to settle by force of arms an argument which was making no progress one way or another in the wordy council chambers of Europe. And when Campeachy had fallen, it was in Belize that the struggle was continued, and brought to a successful end.

Chapter V

*

THE BAYMEN OF BELIZE

THE ex-buccaneers were not the only source from which Wallace's settlement on the Belize river was recruited. In its early years it was regarded as a more or less experimental offshoot of the extensive logwood-cutting British communities previously established, as we have seen, by pioneers from Providence Island along the Mosquito Shore of the Bay of Honduras. After the capture of the island by the Spaniards, in 1641, we may safely assume that many of the dispossessed colonists found their way to the comparative security of the Indian Shore, and to the still more promising logwood settlements in far-away Belize.

The territory of the Mosquito (Mesquito, Mesekito) Indians, or Mosquitia as it was often called, stretched from the outskirts of Truxillo on the coast of what is now called Spanish Honduras to almost as far south as Bocas de Toro in Panama. Since the Indians were completely independent of Spain, and firmly attached to England by every tie of sentiment and mutual advantage, the British logwood-cutters in their midst looked upon the whole of the coast from the Rio Hondo in Yucatan to San Juan de Norte (afterwards called Greytown) as a kind of informal extension of the Empire. True, there was an unfortunate break in the British continuity between Truxillo and the Golfo Dulce—but here no worthwhile deposits of logwood were to be found, so it made no matter. Thus they looked upon the Gulf of Honduras as a British sea, and called it familiarly 'The Bay'. The islands in it, from the fair-sized Rattan and Bonacca to the innumerable little cays that stretched along the shore to the northwards, were called the 'Bay Islands', and the British settlers known generically as 'Baymen'.

The story of British Honduras, therefore, is interlocked with that of the Bay and of the Mosquito Shore, and so remained until the latter half of the nineteenth century. One of the earliest references in our diplomatic records of the Mosquito Shore connection appears in a letter from Governor Lynch to the Council of Plantations in Whitehall in 1671, when he argues that the Peace of Godolphin (1670) should not be deemed to prohibit our trade with the Mosquito Indians.[1] He points out that there is no mark of Spanish sovereignty in these parts, and adds 'it will not do any harm to conciliate the Mesikitos by a little trading'. Ten years later Lynch was forced, as we have seen, to change his tone and even to forbid any further log-cutting in 'the Bay of Campeachy and Honduras'. But he could hardly have expected to be obeyed. Ultimately he had to admit that, on sending a certain Captain Coxon with vessels to the Bay of Honduras to enforce the evacuation of the logwood-cutters, the crew had mutinied, while Coxon himself had joined the cutters![2] At this very time Dampier was on the Mosquito Shore. His account of the logwood settlements and their friends the Mosquito Indians helps one to realize how deeply embedded were the British in this part of the Main.

Dampier's description of the Indians, so long our allies on the Spanish Main, is worth quoting:

> 'They are tall, well made, raw-boned, lusty, strong, and nimble of foot, long visaged with lank black hair, look stern, hard favoured, and of a dark coffee-coloured complexion . . . inhabiting on the Main between Cape Honduras and Nicaragua.'

After describing their skill in fighting, hunting, and fishing, and their extremely keen vision, he continues:

> 'For this they are esteemed and coveted by all privateers, for one or two of them on a ship will maintain 100 men . . . it is very rare to find privateers destitute of one or more of them when the commander or most of the men are English; but they do not love the French, and the Spaniards they hate mortally. When they come among privateers they get the use of guns, and prove very good marksmen. They behave themselves very boldly in fight, and never seem to flinch or hang back . . . they will never yield nor give back while any of their party stand. I never could perceive any religion nor any ceremonies or superstitious observations among them, being ready to imitate us in whatsoever they saw us do at any time.'

(Perhaps this last remark explains why they very soon adopted the Christian religion *en masse*.) 'They marry but one wife with

[1] Burdon, i, 51.   [2] *Ibid.*, i, 57.

whom they live till death separates them.' The wife is left to manage their small plot of land after the man has once cleared it of jungle, while the husband goes hunting or fishing. Their chief delight is in carousing over potations of spirituous 'pine-drink' made out of pineapples. 'While among the English they wear good clothes, and take delight to go neat and tight. But when they return again to their own country they put by all their clothes and go after their own country fashion, wearing only a small piece of linen tied about their waists hanging down to their knees.' The buccaneers found these Indians very useful as guides in their incursions inland against the Spaniards. Everywhere the Mosquito villages *en route* gave food and shelter to the British invaders when they knew they were marching against the common enemy. Dampier has much more to say about them in the celebrated account he wrote of his passage from Cape Gracias à Dios to Bluefields and Bocas de Toro, whence he sailed to the Straits of Magellan and so round the world.

Not many years later (1698) Dampier was followed by a 'privateer' or pioneer of a very different type. William Paterson, one of the founders of the Bank of England, was fired by the idea of planting a British colony on the Spanish Main in Darien, with the ultimate purpose of cutting a canal to the Pacific. The possibility of using the San Juan river and Lake Nicaragua as a waterway across the isthmus had been mooted as early as the sixteenth century, and its commercial possibilities were obvious. Organized by Paterson, a band of over 2000 adventurous Scotsmen sailed to a place still called Punto Escoces (Scotch Point) to found the colony of 'New Caledonia'. Maderiaga remarks:

> 'The commercial acumen of this enterprising intruder seems to have been less keen than might have been expected of the founder of the Bank of England, for the cargo which he sought to sell to Popish Spaniards and tropical Indians was mostly composed of cloth, shoes, stockings, hats, wigs, and 1500 copies of King James Authorized Version of the Bible!'[1]

The expedition was a complete and piteous failure. The Spanish, the climate, disease, and hunger took such toll that barely 300 were able to get back to Scotland.[2]

British enterprise further north, however, had better fortune.

---
[1] S. de Maderiaga, *Rise of the Spanish American Empire*, p. 121.
[2] For Admiral Benbow's part in this affair, see p. 232.

The earliest recorded mention of Belize *by that name* appears in an 'Account of the Sea Ports belonging to the Spaniards in America' presented by one John Fingas to the Council of Trade in September 1705.[1] In this he describes the coast of Yucatan as 'a great part drowned'—meaning swampy and low-lying—and adds: 'Sixty leagues from Porto Caballo [now Puerto Cortéz, in Spanish Honduras] lyeth the River of Bullys, where the English for the most part now load their logwood.' The settlement, as we have seen, was then over fifty years old, but there were many obvious reasons why the logwood-cutters had been backward in advertising its existence. The experience of Spanish aggression and of diplomatic exchanges with a not too reliable British Government at home had warned them of the dangers of publicity. The advice of Lord Godolphin to get on with their work 'surreptitiously' and 'underhand' had been well laid to heart, while the coral barriers and shoals of the approaches to Belize had formed a natural 'iron curtain' shutting them off from the world. That this policy of self-effacement had been successful is shown by the fact that while in all the diplomatic exchanges of this period Campeachy, northern Yucatan, and the Mosquito Coast were frequently named, the thriving logwood settlements around Belize were still able to blush unseen and unheard of by the Powers-that-be. Like Robinson Crusoe (Alexander Selkirk), who was cast on his desert island (Juan Fernandez) this very year (1705), the Baymen of Belize were 'monarchs of all they surveyed'. And they were making good use of their freedom. By 1717 we learn that they were exporting as much as 4000 tons of logwood per annum at an average of £40 per ton, and were wealthy enough to buy African slaves on the open market.[2]

The Treaty of Utrecht (1713) has already been mentioned.[3] It will be remembered that although logwood-cutting is not explicitly authorized by the terms of this Treaty, nor are the British settlements named, yet the Spanish agreed not to deprive British subjects in Spanish America of any privileges 'through right, sufferance, or indulgence' which they had enjoyed before the war of 1702–13. This applied as much to Belize as to Campeachy or the Mosquito Shore, and the claim which the Council of Trade made for Campeachy that it had been effectively occupied before

[1] Burdon, i, 60. [2] *Ibid.*, i, 7. [3] See page 57.

the war, and therefore was not to be restored to Spain, applied with no less force to the region round Belize. The Baymen at all events took this for granted. Nor did the Spanish authorities protest—as yet.

These were exciting days for the young settlement. In 1717 the notorious pirate 'Blackbeard' (Edward Teach), having joined forces with 'Gentleman' Stede Bonnet, and defeated His Majesty's man-of-war *Scarborough* off Barbados, sought sanctuary in the labyrinthian waters off Belize. Making a course for Turneffe Island, he spent a week provisioning and filling his kegs at Water Cay. Then he sailed to Sapodilla Cay, preying upon the Spanish and other foreign ships that hove in sight. Though a fearless fighter and a skilful seaman, Blackbeard was not a pleasant character, with his fourteen wives, and his practical joke of shooting with two pistols under the cabin table when losing at cards. He was killed in the end by Naval Lieutenant Maynard after a terrific struggle in which the pirate received twenty sabre thrusts and five pistol wounds before collapsing on the deck of his ship. There was rejoicing in Charlestown when Maynard sailed home with Teach's blackbearded head dangling from the yard-arm. His bo'sun was named Israel Hands (the original of the Israel Hands in *Treasure Island*), who is said to have buried an enormous chest full of treasure on one of the cays off Belize. At least one search-party has tried to locate it. In 1867 two Americans with an old map found, or thought they had found, the hiding-place on Turneffe. It is unknown what success they had, but the deep hole they dug is still to be seen. Similar search-parties were scouring the cays as late as 1906.[1]

A few years later (1722) we hear again of Israel Hands as mate aboard a pirate barque captained by the infamous Edward Low. Low's career as a pirate began one day when loading logwood in the Bay of Honduras. Resenting what he considered an unreasonable order from his captain, he discharged a musket at him and decamped with twelve other seamen in the ship's long boat. To seize a slightly larger boat was no great trouble, and with that a larger vessel still, until he was strong enough to join forces with another pirate, Captain Lowther, and so to hoist the Skull and Crossbones at the mast of the brig *Ranger*, with no less than eighteen cannon as her armament. Despite his courage and

[1] Burdon, iii, 291.

resource, it is difficult to see anything romantic in Low's sadistic humour. It was Low who, on learning that the captain of a rich Portuguese prize had dropped most of the treasure overboard, cut off his lips, ears, and nose, broiled them, and forced him to eat them piping hot. After which he slaughtered in cold blood every officer and man on board. In the end his own men sickened of him, turning him adrift on the tropical high seas in a small open boat. By a chance in a million he was picked up by a French warship, only to be hanged for his crimes in the harbour of Martinique. Truly there was a difference between the old buccaneers and the new pirates!

It was Low's custom in his more genial moods to maroon those who offended him upon some deserted beach or island. One of those so treated was the American, Philip Ashton, captured by Low while fishing in Nova Scotia. On Ashton obstinately refusing to join the pirates, he was tortured and threatened with death, but managed to escape to a small desert island near Rattan. This was in 1723. For two years this Honduranian Robinson Crusoe lived alone on the island, subsisting on coconuts, mammy apples, wild hogs, turtles, fish and other provender fortunately plentiful. His chief trouble was with alligators, snakes, and flies —as anyone who knows those parts can readily believe—and the lack of shoes on his feet. One day Ashton found a canoe washed up on the beach, in which he paddled to the island of Bonacca, not far away. But on a boatful of Spaniards approaching he hid in the bush, escaping back to his desert island under cover of night. Seven months later, however, two large canoes approached the beach filled with rough-looking men, who shouted to him to stay. 'They told me they were Baymen from the Bay,' runs Ashton's narrative. 'This was confortable news to me, so I bid them pull ashoar, there was no danger.' The Baymen, horrified by his 'poor, ragged, lean, wan, forlorn, wild, miserable' appearance, brought him in their arms to the boat, and after a while to Bonacca, where he was picked up by an English man-of-war, the *Diamond*, and so returned to his home after an absence of nearly three years.

The Spaniards were now becoming alarmed by the increasing number of British logwood-cutters on their shores, and both by land and sea were watching every opportunity to expel the intruders. The *Honduras Almanac* of 1828 speaks of a raid from

Peten as early as 1718, which penetrated some miles into the settlement, to a spot on the Old River still called Spanish Lookout.[1] It is stated that the Mosquito King sent assistance to the Baymen on this occasion. The Spanish also cruised up and down the Bay with hostile intent. War or no war in Europe, the hatchet was seldom long buried in the Gulf of Honduras. The records mention many instances of British logwood ships attacked and burnt 'under frivolous pretences' since the signing of peace. 'In time of War', complained the settlers, 'if taken we were treated as lawful enemies, but now as pyrates and thieves.'[2] In 1722 the Spanish were threatening to send all Englishmen apprehended in Yucatan or the Bay of Honduras to the silver mines in Mexico. In 1724 they made a determined effort to expel the Sambos or Cimmarones from the mouth of the Rio Colorado, with the assistance of Guatemalan troops, but had little success, complaining that 'the Sambos had advantages over the Spaniards in a strong navy, good arms, and free trade with the world'—the navy referred to being the British. In 1728 Spain imagined herself strong enough to put forward the ancient Donation of Pope Alexander VI (1493) as her title-deeds to the country:

> 'With all the islands and seas adjacent from the time of the discovery, conquest, and aggregation of them, which comprehend all the islands and continents found out, discovered, or that shall be discovered, between the Arctic and Antarctic Poles, 100 leagues westward of the Islands of Azores.'[3]

The claim was too fantastic to be taken seriously or to be soon repeated, but in all the long controversy between Spain and England (smouldering even to this day) the dead hand of this Papal Charter is apt to make itself suddenly felt.

In 1730 the Spanish proceeded from protests and pinpricks to offensive action on a considerable scale. Figueroa, Governor of Yucatan, took it upon himself to send a brigantine to the Belize river, where he captured and destroyed seven British logwood vessels. This offensive by sea was followed almost immediately by a raid from Bacalar, in Southern Yucatan, overland by way of the Rio Hondo and the New River down to the settlement at Belize itself. These two attacks are the first organized acts of Spanish aggression against the 'sucking colony'. There is no

[1] Burdon, i, 5.   [2] *Ibid.*, i, 63; i, 66.   [3] *Ibid.*, i, 67.

doubt they were made in grim earnest and with success from the Spanish point of view. During the campaign the invaders captured 16 Englishmen, 2 women, and 20 Negro slaves. In addition to the damage done by the attack from the sea, the land forces burnt thirty ranchos or logwood villages up-country, and four ships on the quayside at the Haulover, near Belize. The settlers appear to have been caught completely unawares: they had no stockades, forts, or weapons worth mentioning, still less armed vessels. For the Spanish it was a glorious victory, and one that cost them nothing at all in loss of men or ships. Shortly afterwards (1732), a sharp diplomatic exchange is reported between the Spanish and British Governments. England sent in a bill for compensation for the recent damage and evictions in Belize. Spain demanded that 'the huts on the River Vallis be removed and never again inhabited, and that no wood for dyeing be cut'.[1] England quoted her ancient rights, the Godolphin Treaty of 1670 and the Treaty of Utrecht (1713). Spain described the cutting of logwood as 'a notorious and detestable abuse not allowed by any of the Treaties'. And so the battle of words went on.

The dispute became more and more acrimonious. Spain realized that the British logwood settlements were daily growing in strength, and becoming more than ever inclined to demand as of right what they had once besought as a concession, while England at last was awakening to the commercial and perhaps to the political importance of these far-flung outposts of Empire. Neither side, looking up past documents relating to the points under discussion, could quote clear precedents or agreements. Too long the diplomats had either ignored or had shied away from a head-on collision on what seemed at first so negligible an issue. Both sides had made shortsighted and deliberately evasive declarations, and their policy had wavered. If Spain could quote Pope Alexander, England could reply with Elizabeth. When Spain dragged up the pusillanimous admissions of Godolphin, England bethought herself of Modyford, Lynch, and of many statements of claims made by the settlers themselves. From the military point of view, on the Spanish side were accessibility by sea and interior lines of communication by land: on the English side, virtual command of the Caribbean with the help of a stronger navy than Britain had yet known, and the dogged tenacity of the logwood-cutters

[1] Burdon, i, 67.

themselves. The controversy dragged on. In 1737 the Governor of Yucatan, Salcedo, ventured another raid on Belize, and England made a last attempt to secure an explicit agreement with Spain about log-cutting rights. But in the end all remained unsettled, and there was nothing for it but the arbitrament of war.

Chapter VI

*

SPANISH AGGRESSION

WAR is not caused by a trifle, as Aristotle somewhere observes, but it may be started by one. The stories of Spanish arrogance in the Caribbean had long created an explosive atmosphere, when a certain Captain Jenkins fresh from the West Indies appeared before the bar of the House of Commons with a shrivelled human ear in his hand. Lifting the flap of his wig before the eyes of the horrified members, he explained that it was his own ear which the Spanish, after torturing him, had cut off to the accompaniment of curses and insults against his country and his King. This brought matters to a head, so to speak. Walpole was forced by public clamour to declare War against Spain and her ally, France. Unfortunately this long war, 'The War of Jenkins' Ear', as it was called (1739–49), entered upon without conviction and fought without energy, brought little glory to England's arms, nor much comfort to the English settlers on the Spanish Main. Admiral Vernon opened with a successful attack upon Porto Bello, but was badly beaten shortly afterwards at Cartagena, and very soon the repercussions of the war in Europe were diverting attention from those on whose behalf it had been originally declared.

Among the allies of England in this struggle, few historians trouble to mention the Mosquito Indians, without whose loyal support the Bay settlements might easily have been annihilated and there would have been no British Honduras on the map to-day. News of the outbreak of hostilities had scarcely reached the New World when Edward, 'King Elect' of Mosquitia, sent the following letter to Governor Trelawney of Jamaica. It is worth quoting in full:

> "Sir, we your lawful subjects do thank you for your care and assistance to us in offering us commissions and assisting us in any lawful occasion. We humbly beg you will help us with the following things: a Commission for Edward King of the Mosquitos: a Commission for William Britton, Governor: General Hobby now lying

dangerously sick we desire a blank for, in case of his death, to make his son general: a Commission for Thomas Porter and Jacob Everson, being captains of His Majesty's perriaguas (shallow-draft gunboats): as likewise your assistance in sending us some Powder, shot, flints, small arms and cutlasses, to defend our country and assist our Brother Englishmen: and a good schoolmaster to learn and instruct our Young Children, that they may be brought up in the Christian Faith. All we beg that he may bring with him is Books and a little salt: as for anything else we will take care to provide for him and a sufficient salary for his pains. We likewise promise him that he shall have no trouble to look for victuals, nor any provisions; for we shall take care to provide for him such as our country can afford. These necessaries we humbly beg you will assist us with, and we shall always be ready upon a call to serve you, and take care of any of your lawful subjects and our own country. We humbly beg leave to title ourselves Your true subjects and loving brothers,

EDWARD KING ELECT.

THOMAS PORTER } *Captains.*
JACOB EVERSON

Dated Moskito Shore May 19, 1739".

No doubt the Indians sent similar assurances to their sister colony in Belize, which must have been extremely heartening to the encircled and outnumbered settlers.

A year or two later Governor Trelawney forwarded the Indian King's letter to the Society for the Propagation of the Gospel in England,[1] with the remark that a missionary would now be safe among the Mosquitos as 'the Spaniards have for a long time given over the thoughts of conquering them'. He added that 'to speak his own thoughts of it, these Indians have a demand in justice upon our Nation, as they have learnt most of their vices, particularly cheating and drinking, from the English, so they ought in recompense to receive some good and learn some virtue and religion too'. The way had already been prepared for a Christian missionary in Mosquitia. A Mr. Robert Hodgson had previously been sent with thirty soldiers to the Shore to organize the resistance of the Indians against the Spanish foe, and this Mr. Hodgson had combined his military duties with some elementary instruction in the Christian religion. It is on record that the S.P.G. sent £50 for the Mission in 1742.

This Mr. Hodgson, it may be noted, had been commissioned

[1] *Two Hundred Years of S.P.G.*, 1901, pp. 234, f.

originally along with a Mr. William Pitt to report upon and exercise authority over all the British logwood settlements in Central America. Landing in Belize they had found little need of their presence in the growing capital of that colony, so had moved on almost at once to the Mosquito Shore and the Bay Islands of Rattan and Bonacca.[1] They remained for many years in the district, partly with an eye to the possibility of surveying for a canal across the Isthmus. 'There is still to be seen upon the Honduranian coast a little cluster of graves, with a carved stone over the last remains of 'BILLY PITT', which mark this forgotten attempt at colonization.'[2]

In the meantime, the defeat of Vernon before Cartagena and the disappearance of the British Navy from the Gulf had seriously alarmed the Baymen of Belize, as well it might. What chance, humanly speaking,· could a handful of half-armed English logwood-cutters expect to have against the encircling might of Spain—Mexico, Yucatan, Quintaroo, Guatemala, Honduras, Nicaragua, and shoals of Spanish gunboats out at sea? There was serious talk of evacuating Belize and moving in a body to the Mosquito Shore and the Bay Islands. A Mr. Gerrard of Belize wrote strongly, however, against such a counsel of despair, particularly as 'a settlement on Rattan would be very expensive and more vulnerable than the settlement on the Belleze River.'[3] So the logwood-cutters elected to stand at bay, praying only the Privy Council that a Governor might be appointed and some force sent to their aid (1743). In this same year, nevertheless, some of the children of the principal families of the Mosquito Coast were evacuated to Jamaica. The demand from Belize for a Governor commissioned by the King grew more insistent and the plan more detailed. In 1744 the settlement felt strong enough to ask for the status of a formal Colony, with a Governor and elected Council of twelve leading citizens, who should be empowered to enact local by-laws and adjudicate in civil and criminal cases, with statutes based upon the laws of England. The request, now that the war had blown the policy of Spanish appeasement sky-high, did not seem unreasonable. It got as far as an Order in Council recommending that Belize be made a Colony and a legislative body be formed to draw up a Constitution (1744).[4]

[1] Burdon, i, 69. [2] L. E. Elliott, *Central America*, 1924.
[3] Burdon, i, 70. [4] *Ibid.*, i, 71.

Unfortunately the news of this defiant Order in Council came to the ears of the Spaniards, who realized of course that it meant the deliberate annexation by England of what they still claimed to be Spanish territory. Their reaction was immediate and violent. In 1745 we read of a Spanish raid up the New River with 6 boats and 60 men burning and destroying all before them, as well as capturing many Negro slaves.[1] A threatening message was sent that soon they would do the same to Belize itself. Again the wood-cutters begged for help, this time from Major Caulfield stationed on Rattan. This officer promptly reconnoitred the military position. Three forts at least would be required, he adjudged, which would take too long to build, but 'much might be effected by a man-of-war with perriaguas manned by 25 men in each perriagua, which would always be in readiness to pursue the Spanish crafts up Rivers and into little Creeks. The Baymen, on being consulted, had agreed with this opinion'. After this, it is astonishing to learn that the number of men in Belize was now no more than 50 whites and 120 Negro slaves. With this small force the settlement proposed to hold its ground against all the might of Spain! In the end, all that Major Caulfield was able to send to the beleaguered log-cutters, so far as we know, were thirty muskets, with some ball and flints. Details are lacking, but somehow or other the Baymen managed to stand their ground, and when the war ended, in 1748, the settlement in Belize was still on the map, and still flying the English flag. No wonder Sir John Burdon waxes enthusiastic about his 'heroic' Baymen, and Sir Charles Metcalfe, Governor of Jamaica, could write in 1842, 'I regard the History of British Honduras as affording one of the most remarkable instances of British enterprise and energy.'

Yet the Treaty of Aix-la-Chapelle, which brought the 'War of Jenkins' Ear' to an end in 1749, found no room in its clauses for the logwood settlements on the Spanish Main. On the other hand it said nothing about abandoning them. During the war any lingering traces of the once extensive British settlements in Campeachy and northern Yucatan had been blotted out, but the settlements in Belize and on the Mosquito Shore emerged stronger than ever. The Indians were now in a fair way to becoming Christianized. The Rev. Nathan Price had already done useful work along Black River before his death at Rattan in 1748—the

[1] Burdon, i, 72.

Mosquito Royal Family itself had embraced the Faith. In 1749, Robert Hodgson, now Captain, was appointed the first official Superintendent of the British settlements on the Nicaraguan Coast, and the Spanish, as observed by Governor Trelawney in the letter quoted above, seemed to have given up all hope of conquering the district. In Belize the logwood industry had even extended its operations, no less than 8000 tons of the precious timber being cut and sold at £20 per ton in 1750.[1]

But it soon appeared that the Peace of Aix-la-Chapelle was not intended by the Spanish to affect their attitude to the logwood-cutters. The lights of peace had scarcely been turned on, before they had to be put out. The arrogance and aggressiveness of the neighbouring Spaniards indeed took on a new lease of life, and the weary business of negotiating with them over the rights of the cutters had to be started all over again. The war in this respect had settled nothing: the Treaty, as usual, had shirked the issue. A contemporary statement of the position records renewed Spanish attempts to dislodge the British from Belize, and urges the Home Government to see that the settlement should be supported: 'Such a Body of season'd Men as are at present there may hereafter prove a very great support to the New Settlement established by some of His Majesty's Forces at Rattan Island, the North-West End of which is but one Hundred and Seventy Miles from the English Town in Honduras'.[1] This appeal, however, seems to have proved ineffectual, for shortly afterwards our troops were withdrawn from Rattan, which was thereupon fortified by the Spaniards and made a base of operations against the wood-cutters and their trading ships, both of British Honduras and of the Mosquito Coast.[2] At the same time orders were sent from Madrid to the Captain-General of Nicaragua, Honduras, and Costa Rica to eject or destroy the settlers once and for all. Whatever might be thought of this in Europe, it meant a local declaration of war against the Baymen, and by them the challenge was fearlessly taken up.

Not content with attacking the British by land, and robbing their cargoes at sea, the Spanish hit on the device of enticing from them the Negro slaves without whom their industry could scarcely be carried on. From this time forward we hear a great deal of this mischief, whereby the slaves were promised emancipation

[1] Burdon, i, 77. [2] *Ibid.*, i, 78.

if they could effect their escape to Spanish territory. The wood-cutters countered it, not by attempting to terrify or invigilate their slaves, but by redoubling their efforts to win their personal affection and loyalty. The Negroes for the most part became more like comrades than slaves, until the good relations between them and their masters became universally known, and the time came when it could be said that slaves in British Honduras had a higher standard of life and a happier lot than any free Negroes in the West Indies or the world. We shall have occasion to refer to this again, and shall see how the bread thus cast upon the waters returned after not so many days to the Baymen of Belize.

The settlers, however, were deeply angered by this Spanish trick, and not surprisingly (for those days) took their revenge as and when possible. In 1753 the Governor of Jamaica felt obliged to apologize to the Spanish for certain 'Barbarities said to be committed by the English at Tobacco Cay and the River Valis', declaring his readiness to punish the offenders; but he added: 'I should not wonder if the cruel treatment by many of your *Guarda Costas* to the English has given rise to their Revenge—tho' cruelty is not the characteristick of the People of *my* Nation.'[1]

So the Battle of the Bay went on, while the rest of the world was enjoying a few years of uneasy peace. In 1754 Billy Pitt of the Mosquito Shore, whose name has already been mentioned, reported a twofold invasion of Belize from Guatemala (El Peten) and the sea. Spanish warships had seized a number of British logwood ships in the Bay, while an army of 1500 had cut a path from Peten to the upper River Belize, penetrating as far as Labouring Creek to places 'where it was thought impossible they ever could come'. The British logwood-cutters, hastily gathered in from the surrounding creeks to the number of 250, engaged the enemy, killed many of them, and, having checked the advance, sent to Belize for reinforcements. Then with a force of 500 whites and their slaves they in turn took the offensive. But the Spanish had already withdrawn to the forests of Peten.[2]

Both the Spanish and the British had orders from their home governments to terminate this irregular cat-and-dog fight, but the little war went on. In the following year (1755) the Spaniards made a still more formidable attack in force upon Belize itself.

[1] Burdon, i, 79. [2] *Ibid.*, i, 80.

On this occasion they were completely successful. The Baymen were compelled to evacuate the town, fleeing in every vessel, boat, dorey, and canoe they could lay hands on with their wives and children to the safety of the Mosquito Shore, where Billy Pitt and the Indians received them with open arms. The Spanish burnt Belize to the ground, and went off, remarking that the place was not worth occupying, as 'it was only fit for the English'. They hoped that the wholesale destruction they had wrought would discourage forever any fresh attempt of the 'intruders' to establish themselves in Belize. The Governor of Jamaica, however, on hearing of this set-back to the Colony, reported to Whitehall that the logwood-cutters had been expelled from Belize 'but he had no doubt they would soon repossess themselves again according to their usual custom'. Which leads one to suppose that Belize had suffered at the hands of the Spanish more often than the extant archives admit.

The Governor of Jamaica was right in his supposition. Within a few months the 'resettlement of the Baymen had been effected without any opposition, the Spaniards having entirely forsaken it, after they had burnt the Houses and destroyed the Indian Provisions which they found planted there'. Fortunately they had been unable to fire the great heaps of logwood on the barcadero 'as it happened to be the Rainy Season, and most of the wood was under water'.[1] The spectacle of their burnt-up huts and ruined gardens, far from discouraging the Baymen, only made them more determined to dig themselves in upon the swampy fever-stricken soil of their beloved Belize, and so to fortify the place that this sort of thing should never occur again. Engaging an expert military engineer, named Jones, they proceeded to build a stockaded fortress a few miles up the river at Haulover, which they furnished with nine six-pounder cannons and nine mounted swivel guns provided from the Mosquito Shore arsenal. Twenty regular soldiers from the Shore stood guard while the fortifications were in course of erection, and the settlers all signed a Memorial asking for a permanent garrison of 40 privates under 2 officers, together with an occasional visit by a gunboat, the soldiers to be 'appareled like Baymen in Frocks and Trousers in order to give as little Umbrage as possible to the Spaniards'. The request was granted, and the Invoice of Expenses charged

[1] Burdon, i, 81.

to the logwood-cutters for this service is still on record. It amounted to £470/13/5. In those days one had to pay for the privilege of building the Empire not only with blood and toil and tears, but in hard cash!

Spain, when she heard of it, was furious at this—the first—attempt to fortify and defend by a regular force of arms what she still persisted in describing as her territory. In 1760 William Pitt (the Prime Minister—not 'Billy') observed that the Spanish were now pressing their claims with 'uncommon vehemence and warmth', and in the following year it became obvious that this long-standing question of English rights in the Caribbean was becoming a *casus belli*. There were many other causes of dispute, of course, but in the end they seemed to narrow down to the tiny problem of the Bay settlements, so that the British Minister in Naples was moved to exclaim that of all the points in dispute, that of Honduras was the only one of importance to the King of Spain. 'Thus', observes Burdon, 'the little Settlement on the Bay of Honduras was once the principal cause of a European War'.[1]

The Seven Years War (1756–63), between England on the one hand and Spain in alliance with France on the other, began badly for England in Europe, but prospered exceedingly in the western seas. Rodney's spectacular victories at Martinique, S. Lucia, Grenada, and the rest soon convinced the enemy that Britannia ruled the waves, however ill her armies might fare ashore. Within two years the signing of the Peace of Paris (1763) seemed to settle the immediate question as to the log-cutter's rights. In Article XVII of the Treaty, England for her part undertook to demolish the offending fortifications in Belize, but Spain promised not to molest or interfere in any way with the peaceful industry of logwood-cutting, loading and carrying away, 'under any pretext whatsoever'. For this purpose 'the log-cutters may build without hindrance and occupy without interruption, the houses and magazines (warehouses) which are necessary for them, their families, and their effects'. The British victory had won for the long harassed settlers the right to go about their work in peace and safety, and to practise their ancient trade by right, no longer of mere local custom, or unwritten law, but by the express terms of a regularly signed Treaty between their Home Government and

[1] Burdon, i, 12.

Spain. Strange as it may seem, the Treaty of 1763 secured the first plain black-and-white statement of the legitimacy of this important British industry, although logwood-cutting had been in operation for a hundred years! In a sense, it was a victory for Belize.

So far, so good. But when the Baymen had sobered up sufficiently to read Article XVII to the end, they perceived that the Treaty was not all it had seemed at first sight. First, although Madrid had promised on paper to allow them the unimpeded right of logwood-cutting, experience had shown that the Spaniards on the spot were not always too ready to obey their own Home Government. It seemed therefore, rather premature of the Treaty, to order that 'His Britannic Majesty shall cause to be demolished all the fortifications which His Subjects shall have erected in the Bay of Honduras and other places of the Territory of Spain in that part of the World'. These fortifications had been built and equipped at considerable expense only a few years previously, and the solid fact of their existence had been very comforting to the settlers as they went about their business. Henceforward, it seemed, they would have to rely on the more flimsy protection of a scrap of paper.

Secondly, the Treaty still left unsettled the vexed question of ownership of the logwood territory, or rather it had settled it in favour of doctrinaire Spanish claims, and very much to the chagrin of those settlers who for over a hundred years had worked, argued, pleaded, and shed their blood to establish their territorial right. The statesmen at home had basely betrayed them in speaking of the logwood camps as being in the 'Territory of Spain', and talking of 'His Catholic Majesty's permission'.

Thirdly, the Treaty had shirked the problem of deciding upon the limits of the areas where logwood-cutting was to be permitted. No actual place-names had been mentioned beyond the vague 'Bay of Honduras and other places in that part of the World'. The clause, in fact, could be read in two ways. The cutters could claim the right to cut logwood wherever they found it, while Spain could interpret the Treaty as permitting only those boundaries which had already been in existence before the war.

Finally, the Treaty was very explicit about the rights of cutting *logwood*, and logwood only. According to the exact wording of

Article XVII, the cutting of any other kind of growth for commercial purposes would be outside the law. Now the fact of the matter was that the logwood industry, though still important, had begun to take second place to that of mahogany. Those were the days of Chippendale, the famous furniture designer and manufacturer, soon to be followed by Sheraton, under whose magic touch this beautiful timber became, and remained for 150 years, the favourite material for household furniture. It was also largely used in the beams and stanchions of shipbuilding and later on of railway carriages. Mahogany, in short (*Swietenia Mahogani*), was almost worth its weight in gold, and the kind of mahogany that grew in the Belize settlement was as good as any in the world. Moreover, while the logwood forests were becoming worked out in the more accessible places, mahogany-trees still remained an almost virgin crop, growing conveniently near to rivers and creeks, to which they could be easily rolled and so floated down to the loading stage. The settlers therefore noticed with dismay that the Treaty of 1763 carefully made no mention of anything but logwood. In fact it really settled very little at all, and the cutters saw breakers ahead.

Chapter VII

*

THE NAVY TO THE RESCUE

TROUBLE began almost at once. Waiting only for the destruction of the fortifications around Belize, and for the withdrawal of all English troops and military stores from the settlement, the Governor of Yucatan opened the new Spanish offensive at the end of 1763 on the very lines which had been feared by the cutters. He complained that they had already broken the Treaty: they had started logwood-cutting 'without waiting to settle limits with the necessary solemnity that should have secured the British establishments'. He demanded that all logwood-cutters between the Rio Hondo and the New River should retire to the Belize river at once. If the settlers persisted in 'such irregular and excess of logwood-cutting' he would not be responsible for the 'fatal consequences' which might ensue.[1] But the settlers, who had recently evacuated Campeachy without demur, were not equally ready to clear out of the Rio Hondo district. Tacitly they had come to regard this wide river as the boundary between Yucatan and the British concessionary area. The logwood forests from the Rio Hondo down to the New River being particularly extensive and easily worked were not lightly to be relinquished, and were certainly not expropriated by the Treaty. When, therefore, the Commander of Bacalar proceeded to march troops into the Rio Hondo and New River districts, and to blockade the mouths of those rivers with armed vessels, the Baymen were immediately up in arms again.

A Public Meeting of the Baymen 'in Council' (they had already some sort of civic organization) at once sent an urgent petition to the Governor of Jamaica, pointing out that the long-established British settlements in the Rio Hondo district had been molested in defiance of the recent Treaty. The settlers had withdrawn peaceably to the New River, but even there had been pursued by Yucatan troops, and 'ordered to evacuate every river except

[1] Burdon, i, 89.

the Belize, which it is admitted them to stay a little while, but as your Petitioners believe, not to have the privilege of logwood-cutting even there'. After speaking of the 'miseries which your Petitioners experience from the inhumanity of the Spaniards', they ended with the usual appeal for speedy reinforcements.

The Governor of Jamaica, more realistic than the periwigged politicians at home, reacted promptly and with decision. The Hon. Sir William Burnaby, Knight, Rear-Admiral of the Red, and Commander in Chief of Her Majesty's Squadron at Jamaica, on being informed of the plight of his fellow-countrymen, also reacted strongly. A tart exchange of despatches, beginning with the Governor of Yucatan, spread to the Embassies in London and Madrid. England spoke of the Spaniard's 'inexcusable action'. The Spanish Ambassador in London wrung his hands, and spoke of War; the King of Spain ordered the Governor of Yucatan to stick to the Treaty; the Governor of Jamaica demanded £27,097/8/5 compensation for the maltreated logwood-cutters. There followed a perfect spate of letters and language.[1] But nothing much was *done* till Admiral Burnaby, respectable modern version of the old-time buccaneers who had founded the settlement, took action early in 1765 with four ships of the line and 400 soldiers to make a demonstration off the threatened coast, and 'reinstate the Logwood Cutters in the Bay of Honduras'.

Sir William Burnaby is one of the major heroes in the history of British Honduras. The despatch which he indited on board his flagship H.M.S. *Active*, anchored off Belize on March 25, 1765, is still extant. 'The Governor of Yucatan had ordered the Commandant of Bacalar to give possession to the Baymen in form. They were now reinstated on Rowley's Bite, the New River, and the Rio Hondo. The Governor of Yucatan who started all the trouble was dead. His successor had expressed the highest regard and esteem for all Englishmen, and had given assurances of better behaviour on the part of the Spaniards in future.' Burnaby added drily that he had nevertheless arranged for a warship to be stationed permanently in the Bay.[2]

It is of interest to note that with Burnaby on this expedition to British Honduras was the (afterwards) famous explorer James Cook, then serving his apprenticeship in the Royal Navy, but soon to survey New Zealand and Australia and to circumnavigate

[1] Burdon, i, 93–99. [2] *Ibid.*, i, 99.

the Globe. A few years later (1769) he published perhaps the earliest literary work on British Honduras: *Remarks on a passage from the River Balize in the Bay of Honduras to Merida in Yucatan*, by Lieutenant J. Cook.[1]

It was possibly on the suggestion of Admiral Burnaby that the Baymen about this time decided to occupy the islet of Las Casinas, a few miles off Belize. It is recorded that, 'invited by the healthfulness of its air and the convenience of its situation, it having a good harbour for shipping, they cleared the ground upon the island for plantations and erected comfortable houses there'. It was henceforward renamed S. George's Cay, in honour of the Patron Saint of England—possibly with some allusion to the Spanish Dragon so recently discomfited ashore. Did Admiral Burnaby, one wonders, foresee how useful that little island would prove to be for the defence of the Colony, or that its name would one day be given to the final victory which once and for all made British Honduras our own?

The Admiral was not satisfied with merely reinstating the log-cutters. He saw that the time had now come when they should be banded together in some more organized establishment than had hitherto prevailed, with a central Government and Judicature of their own. The Baymen had frequently asked for a Constitution. Before he left them he would see that they had it. Not that law and order were novelties in the settlement, nor some semblance of local authority unknown, but it had all been spasmodic, vague, and lacking in official sanction. It was Burnaby's intention to gather all their old case-law and custom derived from the buccaneering practice of former years, 'The Ancient Usages and Customs of the Settlement', into a consolidated Code. After considerable research and consultation with the older inhabitants, he succeeded, and the result became known as 'Burnaby's Code'.

Burnaby seems to have sensed the democratic atmosphere of the settlement from the beginning, and had the good sense to realize that the methods of the naval quarter-deck were not for such a community as this. Calling a public meeting of all the white settlers in April 1765, he hammered out with them a Code

---

[1] There seems to be some doubt, however, about the identity of this Lieutenant Cook. Apparently there were, by a strange coincidence, *two* lieutenants in the British Navy at this time, both of them called James Cook.

of Twelve Main Regulations to which they all (apparently) subscribed. Briefly they were to the following effect:

(1) Against 'profane cursing and swearing in disobedience of God's command and the derogation of His honour'—penalty 2s. 6d. for each offence.
(2) Against theft.
(3) Against 'enveigling' or harbouring any sailor deserting his ship in the harbour.
(4) Against hiring a servant without a written agreement.
(5) Against kidnapping anyone to act as a servant—except a steersman (pilot), and that only for a single trip.
(6) No taxation without representation.
(7) Justice to be administered by a Court of seven elected Magistrates with a Jury of thirteen Housekeepers.
(8) In emergency the commander of any warship sent to the Bay shall have authority to enforce the Code.
(9) Any disputes about its interpretation to be adjudicated by a panel of seven.
(10) Any crime not mentioned in the Code to be punished in accordance with the Custom of the Bay.
(11) All future legislation to receive the approval of the majority of the inhabitants.
(12) No distraint on property for debt, before first obtaining an order from a Magistrate.

It was also agreed that henceforward the Judiciary should normally meet not in Belize but on S. George's Cay, which thus became for a time the administrative capital of the Colony.[1]

Such was the famous 'Burnaby's Code', on which the Admiral was congratulated by the inhabitants, before he sailed away for the Mosquito Coast. It was an excellent system for the time and place, organically developed from long accepted custom, and expressed in simple forthright terms. But it contained one serious weakness—no arrangements were made for a standing police force which should ensure obedience in the last resort. Burnaby overlooked the fact that, as soon as his troops and sailors withdrew, there would be no legal executive in the settlement. Possibly he thought that, where every man had voted for the Code, every man would serve as a sort of voluntary special constable to see that the Code was kept. He was soon disillusioned. Returning to Belize at the end of the year (1765) he found the inhabitants once more 'in a state of anarchy and confusion'. Although they had

[1] Burdon, i, 100.

'all approved of, and all signed, and agreed to the Regulations, they had since dwindled (so he was informed) into the same state of confusion, complying with the Regulations so long as they prove favourable to themselves, but on the contrary refuse to submit their causes to tryal'. What is needed, he suggests to the Home Government, is the appointment by the Home Government of a Superintendent of the Settlement at £1000 a year.[1]

How much trouble and confusion would have been saved, had Whitehall agreed to this wise suggestion from the man on the spot, will be realized by anyone who studies Burdon's Archives of the Colony for this period. On several occasions it became necessary to send a naval vessel to enforce the law. One naval officer, after certain unpleasant experiences, reported hotly: 'There ought to be a Frigate at least stationed permanently off Belize'. And again: 'Their Government depends on the strongest arm'. As late as 1771 we find Burnaby still complaining of a 'state of anarchy' in the Colony, and shortly afterwards Admiral Rodney himself was compelled to intervene in a glaring case of piracy, where the Baymen looted a Spanish frigate driven ashore on the Northern Triangle reef off Belize, and refused to deliver up their loot even at His Majesty's command.[2]

Meanwhile the Spaniards were not showing conspicuous loyalty to the terms of the recent Treaty. Admiral Pavey in Jamaica had to report in 1767 that the 'Spaniards are again burning and destroying the log-cutters' houses, decoying their Negroes, and even imprisoning the Settlers themselves'. We hear a good deal about Spanish molestation in this period, especially in connection with the Negro slaves. In decoying and seducing the Negroes from their allegiance, the Governor of Yucatan had hit on a way of striking the Baymen in their tenderest spot, while yet keeping within the letter of the law, for the assistance of the Negroes, who considerably outnumbered the white settlers, was absolutely vital to the cutting, and still more to the heavy work of dragging to the river and loading up the heavy timber. The Baymen and the Government protested, the Governor of Yucatan promised amendment, or disowned the practice, but the loss of the Negroes became a serious cause of frustration and alarm. Worse still, the Spaniards succeeded in inciting the Negroes on at least one occasion to active revolt against their lawful masters.

[1] Burdon, i, 109.   [2] Ibid., i, 119.

In 1773 a large-scale Negro revolt took place on the upper reaches of the Belize river. Making a sudden attack on a group of wood-cutters, they killed six white men, and actually threatened to advance upon the capital. Once more it was a case of the Navy to the rescue. Captain Davey with a few sailors sailed up the river, only to find the rebels securely hidden in the bush. Next day fourteen of them surrendered, but a large body remained defiant. Three parties, each of forty naval men and Baymen, were organized to round them up, while all wood-cutting and trading in the Colony came to a standstill. Eventually Admiral Rodney sent a Captain Judd with a stronger naval force to put the rebellion down once and for all. But it was easy for the Negroes to cross over into Spanish territory, and the Spaniards, who had fomented the trouble, naturally refused to give them up. Eleven violent Negroes wanted for murder were traced to Yucatan, but were harboured by the Commandant of Bacalar. The great majority, however, in the end were successfully 'mopped up', and Judd returned to naval headquarters with the report that the rebellion was over. It had been an alarming episode, and led the Baymen to reiterate their demand that their title and status in the country should be more clearly defined. The time had come, they insisted, for the Home Government to recognize Belize openly as a British Colony. Fortunately for their peace of mind, they little knew how long they would have to wait for that!

The declaration of war against England by the North American Colonies on July 4, 1776, added a new complication to the Baymen's problems. In 1777, for instance, while the famous American privateer Paul Jones was harrying the British further north, Captain Hezekiah, of the American sloop *General Washington*, sailed into the harbour at S. George's Cay, threatening to burn Belize to the ground if he was not furnished with stores. The Baymen reported that they 'had no alternative but to meet his demands, which were limited chiefly to rum'. The enterprising Yankee then sailed southwards, capturing three British vessels on the way, and when H.M.S. *Cupid* came up from the Mosquito Shore, to deal with him, she had the ill luck to be wrecked on a coral reef, though 'the Baymen gave every assistance'. In the following year France joined with the 'United States' against England, in 1779 Spain and Holland lent their weight to the enemy coalition, and, with other European nations overtly hostile,

England stood alone against the world. Once more, after an uneasy armistice of only fifteen years, Belize found herself at war with her inveterate foe. In the struggle that ensued England and her 'sucking colonies' might well have seemed outmatched, especially in the outlying parts of her far-flung maritime Empire. But the British Navy was a host in itself. Those were great days for the 'wooden walls of England'. With Admiral Rodney in the Caribbean there was really not much fear from the Spanish or French fleets, even with the United States to help. Especially, had men realized it, with Nelson on board.

Young Horatio Nelson had been appointed by Admiral Parker to his first command in 1778—Commander of H.M. brig *Badger*, with orders to ply in the waters of the Bay of Honduras. No doubt on this voyage he made acquaintance with the coast of the Mosquito Shore, the Bay Islands and the difficult waters off Belize. This turned out to be very fortunate for the Baymen, as we shall see. In 1779, when the War with Spain broke out, he was officer in command of Port Royal (Jamaica), where 'Nelson's quarter-deck' still survives the earthquakes which destroyed the port. 'Here Nelson trod' is the inscription let into the brick wall. 'Ye who walk in his footsteps, follow in his glory.' On an adjoining wall are three memorial tablets, said to be those of his three Jamaican 'wives'.

But even the British Navy could not be everywhere, just when it was wanted. On September 15, 1779 (the very day, as it happened, that Paul Jones made his destructive raid on Scarborough, forcing H.M.S. *Serapis* to strike her colours to the *Bonhomme Richard*), the Governor of Bacalar made a surprise attack on the Baymen of Belize before they even knew that war had been declared. Swooping down with a fleet of nineteen perriaguas and a schooner upon the little community on S. George's Cay, where many of the leading citizens were now accustomed to reside on account of its salubrity and the presence of the civic buildings, the Spaniard had no difficulty in seizing the island. There followed a typical example of Spanish cruelty which long rankled in the memory of the Baymen. Over 140 Englishmen, with their wives and children, were taken prisoner, packed into perriaguas, and landed on the coast of Quintaroo. Thence they were marched through 300 miles of pestilential forest to the Yucatan capital at Merida, whence they were transported to the dungeons of Havana.

Most of the victims succumbed to their sufferings, and there were few alive to enjoy their liberation more than three years later at the end of the war. The conqueror of the cay was prevented, however, from occupying it or following up his success ashore by the timely appearance over the skyline of H.M.S. *Badger*, Commander Horatio Nelson. Although too late to overtake the Spanish convoy of prisoner-laden perriaguas on its way to Quintaroo, Nelson saved from destruction the many small craft loaded with refugees from the Cay and from Belize on their way to the Bay Islands.

A record of this disaster is preserved in the Archives,[1] signed by one Edward Hill, who was on the cay when the Spaniards landed, 'but escaped at 11 p.m. the same night with seven more in a dory which he had concealed in his back yard, and was so fortunate the next morning early to get on board a Schooner Boat belonging to Richard Hoare and Thomas Potts, lying at the Old River's mouth, from whence they immediately proceeded to the Mosquito Shore'. Many of the refugees fled to Rattan, where they were furnished with arms for the defence of the island, while on the Shore itself the British settlements were as usual under the protection of the warlike Mosquito Indians.

As to Belize, the catastrophe of the cay robbed it of its principal inhabitants for the time being, and the machinery of government ran down at once. For the space of a year or two the place was deserted, and once again the Spaniards had some reason to think they had dealt the British settlement its death-blow. But in quiet backwaters up the creeks, and in clearings where the Spaniards dared not or did not penetrate, the wood-cutters were still doggedly pursuing their occupation, confidently expecting one of Belize's many phœnix-like revivals. Their confidence was justified, for a year or two later Colonel Despard, of whom we shall hear a great deal more, sailed over from Rattan, and rebuilt several of the hutments in Belize. When Peace was declared, in 1783, the settlement had already recovered much of its vigour, and was able to benefit by the terms of the Treaty then agreed. But we anticipate.

During the war with Spain, the sturdy friendship of the Mosquito Indians had meant a great deal to the harassed settlers in Belize, and it was fortunate that they were strong enough to give

[1] Burdon, i, 128.

practical proof of it. The ties of amity had now been strengthened by those of religion, for the Mosquitos, who had always bitterly resisted the Catholicism of the Conquistadores, had no objection to joining the Church of England. We have already noted the S.P.G. Mission of 1742. A few years later a Mr. Christian Frederick Post took up his residence on Black River as a catechist, or lay preacher. Living among the Indians from 1768, he retired to America in 1784 owing to ill-health. He had already, however, been joined by another missionary, the Rev. Robert Shaw (1774), and by a Rev. William Stanford (1776), both of whom we shall meet later in Belize. A whole generation of Indians, therefore, had grown up in the British tradition, religion, and alliance.

As it was from the Mosquito Shore that the defence of Belize had been organized, so it was upon this shore that a speedy revenge was taken for the Spanish outrage on S. George's Cay. Nelson sailed straight from the cay to the Nicaraguan port of San Juan de Norte, which with Indian assistance he captured, together with the fortress of La Concepcion. Galvez, President of Nicaragua, counter-attacked with reinforcements from Costa Rica, but without success. The British, however, were compelled soon afterwards to evacuate the place owing to a disastrous epidemic of Yellow Fever among the troops.[1]

We now hear for the first time of a certain Colonel Edward Marcus Despard, who was destined to play a prominent part in the drama of British Honduras. Despard, a former shipmate and friend of Nelson, had recently been appointed Governor of Rattan, from which island he now sailed to the mainland with a crew largely composed of angry refugees from S. George's Cay, marched upon a Spanish fort up Black River, and destroyed it. Lastly a strong naval attack was made, on September 21, by a British fleet of four warships (*Charon*, *Lowestoft*, *Pomona*, and *Porcupine*) upon the Spanish Honduranian port of Omoa, near Truxillo, under Captain John Luttrell. The seamen, assisted by 250 Baymen, carried and fired the town at the first assault, but could not take the inner fort 'as the Baymen, who were carrying the scaling ladders, had dropped them in their eagerness to fight'. However, the place was eventually reduced (October 19), and booty to the extent of three million dollars carried away.[2] Further to the south an army of 14,000 Mosquito Indians was mobilized

[1] Villacorta, 129.   [2] *History of Royal Navy* (1899), iv, 44.

at the Sambo capital of Bragman Town, and a strong force of British troops garrisoned the British settlement at Bluefield, whence they made frequent incursions against the neighbouring Spaniards. It will thus be seen that the Mosquito Coast was a tower of strength to the British cause.

But the most crushing rejoinder to Spanish aggression on the high seas was Nelson's destruction of the Spanish fleet at Cape S. Vincent and Rodney's return to the West India station in 1780. During the rest of the war the Bay settlements were never in real danger, especially after Colonel Despard had been able to pay that first personal visit to Belize of which we have spoken. On that occasion he rebuilt Belize and S. George's Cay, secured the safety of the former by erecting a stockaded fortress at Haulover, and disembarked upon the quayside many of the Baymen who had taken refuge with him on Rattan. Despard returned to his post with a love for Belize in his heart which was soon to draw him back to it.

Hostilities in the West Indies ceased entirely with Rodney's decisive victory over de Grasse off Martinique in 1782, and in the following year the Peace of Versailles brought the war to an end.

Chapter VIII

*

THE BATTLE OF BELIZE

IN the Peace of Versailles (1783), which left her more firmly entrenched than ever in Gibraltar, Great Britain made little provision for the future of her far-western Rock on the Honduras Gulf. Strangely enough, in view of her growing Imperial ambitions, she did not even question the Spanish claim to territorial possession and sovereignty in Belize. All she demanded in 1783 was that the log-cutting privileges granted by the Treaty of 1763 should be reaffirmed, and that the boundaries of the concession should be more clearly defined. It will be remembered that the former Treaty through the absence of such definition had been construed by the log-cutters as permitting them to cut timber wherever it could be found, while the Spanish had construed it as applying only to the narrow territory between the New River and the River Belize, an area of 300 square leagues. Fox now pointed out that though 300 square leagues sounded generous, much of it was mere swamp or savannah. He therefore insisted on the northern boundary being fixed at the Rio Hondo.

In the end the British view prevailed. A map was drawn and coloured showing the British concessionary area as stretching from the Rio Hondo on the north to the Belize river on the south, and the frontiers of Peten Itza (vaguely indicated) on the west.[1] All logwood-cutters who might have strayed beyond these boundaries were to be immediately rounded up and gathered within the permitted zone. It was also agreed that the British fortifications, since they were on Spanish territory, were to be demolished, and that no other trade than logwood was to be permitted on a commercial scale. Furthermore the Treaty laid it down that the cays in the Bay were not to be permanently occupied by the settlers. So much for Article VI of the Treaty of 1783.[2] In the following year the Spanish and British commissioners on

[1] The map is reproduced in Burdon's *Archives*, i, 136.
[2] Burdon, i, 137.

the spot bilaterally agreed and delimited the boundaries thus defined.

Needless to say the settlers were profoundly disappointed by this meagre award. They were actually in a worse case than they had been before the war. If this was victory, they asked, what would defeat have meant! Hundreds of Englishmen with their families and slaves had penetrated into logwood areas beyond the Treaty limits—over the Rio Hondo, into the Peten district, and above all over the Belize river towards the River Sibun. From these profitable cuttings they were now roughly evicted by the Spaniards, and bundled into the narrow preserve coloured yellow on the map. Overcrowding and unemployment was the immediate result, those who turned to other occupations being warned that the Treaty permitted logwood-cutting and nothing else. Mahogany was still not mentioned in the concession. Even fishing as a trade and 'turtling' and market-gardening were forbidden. The final insult had been the clause demanding the evacuation of the cays, including the now famous S. George's Cay itself.

Against this intolerable position, the Baymen protested in no uncertain terms. They wrote in a memorial to Lord North of the 'diminutive extent and insufficiency' of the Spanish concession. 'All the inconveniences, difficulties, and hardships which formerly they laboured under are unremarked and unredressed.' 'No freedom of navigation is permitted.' They are 'as open and liable as ever to have their Negroes seduced and their property pilfered'. 'No security whatever is provided for them in case of rupture between the two Crowns.' They were excluded from all the cays, even S. George's Cay, 'which for health, convenience, and security was to them above all other situations on the Coast', and so on.[1]

Governor Campbell of Jamaica, writing to Lord North in the following year, supported the Baymen's protests. The frontiers laid down by the Treaty should most certainly be extended. Of the cays, S. George's, the Southern Triangles, and Turtle Fishing Cay should be secured to the settlers. He recommends a strengthening of the Constitution by the appointment of a Governor, approving the choice of Colonel Despard of Rattan for that position. Belize became the centre of almost continuous public

[1] Burdon, i, 139.

meetings for the combined purpose of strengthening its civic organization and voicing its detestation of the Treaty. Among other items, heavy damages were claimed from the Spaniards for their depredations on S. George's Cay, 'carried out in defiance of all the Laws of War and in contravention of Article 36 of the Treaty of Madrid (1667) and Article 18 of the Peace of Utrecht'.[1] Their indignation was not soothed by the gift of a shipload of convicts which the Home Government now proposed to make them. It was resolved that the landing of these convicts from the *Mercury* now in the harbour would 'damage the credit and character of the country', and that they should be re-embarked without delay. Two scoundrels who nevertheless got some of the convicts ashore, for the purpose of selling them as slaves, were speedily arrested, and the convicts rounded up. The troubles of the harassed settlers were further augmented by a severe hurricane (November 20, 1785) which lasted twelve hours and did much damage.

Eventually the Baymen secured at any rate one concession from the Government. Colonel Despard was summoned from the Mosquito Shore, and arrived in Belize in June 1786 to take up office as the first Superintendent of the settlement, fixing his residence at Haulover.[2] This implied the establishment in Belize of a formal Constitutional Government, with a Magistracy, Law Courts, Legislature, and Governor (in all but name) as in other recognized colonies, against which the Spanish had always protested as infringing their own sovereignty. But by then the whole question of the wood-cutting settlements was again in the melting-pot. Spain, anxious still to negotiate the restoration of Gibraltar by England, reopened negotiations on the Treaty of 1783, out of which emerged the epoch-making Convention of London.

The Convention of London (1786) marked a much more conciliatory approach on the part of Spanish diplomacy to the log-cutting question in British Honduras. This Convention, rather than the Treaty of Versailles, was the true harvest reaped by our victory in the war, and especially by the heroic success of Gibraltar's resistance in her three-year siege. Spain had come to the conclusion that she had everything to gain and little to lose by placating British feeling in the West Indies. She now agreed accordingly to modify the harshness of the Treaty of Versailles

[1] Burdon, i, 146.   [2] *Ibid.*, i, 153.

in the following important respects: (1) the boundaries of the logwood concession were extended as far as the Sibun (Jabon) river southwards; (2) the cutting of *Mahogany* was explicitly allowed, as well as the use of all *natural* fruits of the earth—though no plantations such as sugar, coffee, or cacao might be made; (3) the occupation of S. George's Cay was conceded—but there must be no fortifications or troops—and the other cays might be used for careening ships and so forth; (4) fishing was to be permitted. All this was very acceptable as far as Belize was concerned.

But the Spanish negotiators insisted on two drastic stipulations. First, that the British settlements on the Mosquito Shore of Nicaragua should be completely evacuated and abandoned for ever. Secondly, that the British in Belize 'must meditate no more extensive settlements, or the formation of any system of government either military or civil'.

In making the former demand, namely for the surrender of the Nicaraguan settlements, Spain made a serious diplomatic blunder. At first they could not understand why Great Britain agreed to it so readily. The Mosquito Shore settlements were the oldest British communities on the Spanish Main, they were the firmest held and the easiest to defend owing to the Anglophil Indians in that region, they were numerically and commercially important, readily accessible by sea, and had proved vital to the defence of Belize. It certainly seemed surprising that England should so lightly give them up. But it was not long before Spain realized that in this respect our diplomacy had been, whether by accident or design, extraordinarily astute. When Spain, after making what she considered the vast concessions of the London Convention, asked for the return of Gibraltar as a *quid pro quo*, England blandly pointed out that she had already received her *quid pro quo* in the shape of the evacuation by the British of the whole of the Mosquito Shore and its Bay Islands. Thus, in effect, the Shore was surrendered as an alternative to the surrender of the Rock, and no one can say it was a bad bargain. But there was more in it than that. Though England might evacuate her own subjects from the Shore, she had neither the intention nor the power to evacaute the Mosquito Indians, nor had she been asked to break off her alliance with those Indians. So that, in the upshot, the Mosquito Shore remained more firmly than ever in the British sphere of influence—a British Protectorate, in fact, in all but name.

The second stipulation, that the Belize settlement should have no civic organization of its own, was more troublesome, indeed impracticable. It resulted through no fault of his own in the ruin of the newly appointed Superintendent. Colonel Despard, an officer and a gentleman of the rigidly conscientious type, had strict orders from the Home Government to carry out the provisions of the London Convention in the letter and the spirit, and this he resolved to do, though it must have gone very much against the grain of a man who had fought so resolutely against Spanish aggression. Putting His Majesty's commands above both his private feelings and his beloved Baymen's protests, Despard quickly found himself in an impossible position. His worst problem was the evacuation of the settlers from the Mosquito Shore. It was bad enough having to evict one's fellow-countrymen from their ancestral homes against their will, to the number of 2250 white and black. It was worse to thrust this enormous number of 'displaced persons' upon the already somewhat overcrowded settlers in Belize, who bitterly resented the new arrivals, outnumbering the original Belisians as they did by two to one. Strict orders received from Whitehall to 'give preference to the Mosquito Shore arrivals' did not help very much to stem the rising tide of indignation and revolt. Despard had no police force, it must be remembered, and at times was compelled to ask assistance even of the Spanish Commissary and Spanish troops to enforce the law—which naturally made him more unpopular than ever.

According to the Treaty, the Constitution recently granted to the Baymen with all its legal and judicial apparatus, and with Despard as Superintendent, had been abolished by the Convention of London. Strictly speaking, Despard had now to regard himself not as the President of a democratic community, but as an officer specifically commissioned by the King to carry out the terms of the Treaty. Whitehall supported him in this interpretation of his duty, but Whitehall had no means of persuading Belize to take the same view. Inevitably Despard came to be looked upon as a tyrant, a self-willed autocrat, even as a traitor to his own countrymen. Both the general public and the Magistrates turned against him. On occasions it came to open rebellion, as when

Despard, strictly within the law, awarded one Joshua Jones from the Mosquito Shore a log-cutting allotment No. 69 then in the possession of a native Belisian, and the Magistrates 'armed with guns, pistols and cutlasses' turned the newcomer out and put him in irons.[1] Despard enforced his decision in the end, but there were countless such clashes.

At first Whitehall supported Despard up to the hilt. In February 1788 Lord Sydney wrote that the settlers have 'conducted themselves in a very unwarrantable and indecent manner, and His Majesty was much displeased at their conduct'. Despard, however, must excuse them: they 'misunderstood the fact that his authority overrides their old Regulations'. A hint of a slight cooling in the Home Government's regard for him appears, however, in the postscript: 'I am inclined to think that by good Management and a more conciliatory Demeanour on your part, you might, etc. etc.' The poor man's observations upon this are not reported.[2] In the following year the position had become no easier. Even Despard was moved to indignant protest against an over-zealous Spanish inspector who rooted up all the food gardens in Belize on the grounds that they were against the Convention. But the Baymen's protests against Despard's high-handed ways mounted in fury. The principal inhabitants wrote home about his 'visible spirit of self-importance and uncontrollable domination', declaring that 'Englishmen can never brook the despotic Government of an individual. We have tasted the sweets of liberty and hitherto have never forfeited our right and title to that valuable blessing'. His rule was 'too degrading for an Englishman to suffer'.

At length the volume of these unfair accusations, which ought to have been fired at the negotiators of the Convention, rather than at the subordinate whose duty it was to carry it out, induced the Home Government to order an Enquiry into Despard's administration. Lord Granville, Secretary of State, came to the damaging conclusion that the 'accused' had displayed a 'warmth of temper perhaps excusable owing to the conduct of the Settlers, but it was difficult to explain the irregularity of his proceedings with the Spanish Commissary, especially in supporting his destruction of the Plantations'—which was exactly what Despard had *not* done!—and so forth. Yet his Lordship adds that he 'dis-

[1] Burdon, i, 166. [2] *Ibid.*, i, 168.

approves of infractions of the Treaty by the settlers, and has no intention of encouraging anything resembling Colonial government in Belize'. Logically Despard had been vindicated, but diplomacy is not logical. In the spring of 1790 he was superseded, though not at once recalled, and Colonel Peter Hunter took his place.

The first public action of Colonel Hunter was to arrange a democratic poll for the election of a new body of Magistrates (May 3, 1790). To his own and Hunter's astonishment, Despard was returned at the top of it! [1]

But the man had had enough of politics by now. Brokenhearted and disillusioned he cast off the dust of Belize for ever and returned to England. He seems to have been permanently embittered. One is scarcely surprised to find him involved in a revolutionary plot in London against the Government in 1802. Despite a testimonial by Lord Nelson to his distinguished service in the Navy, he was hanged in the following year.

Perhaps it was providential for Belize that Despard left when he did. Trouble was again brewing between England and Spain, and Despard would have been far too punctilious in his observance of the Convention to take the necessary military precautions. It was not long before the Governor of Yucatan was complaining that 'things are not going half so smoothly now that Colonel Despard is gone'.[2] For his successor, Colonel Hunter, was a very different type of man. He had scarcely entered Belize before he began importing arms from England, and erecting illicit fortifications in preparation for the struggle he saw looming ahead. Hunter had no use for appeasement. One of his first regulations (June 16, 1790) was to order thirteen lashes to be repeated on three separate days together with amputation of the right ear as a penalty for enticing slaves to 'run to the Spaniards'. (We never hear of Despard ordering such punishments.) He also organized a militia of armed volunteers, and a system of espionage against the Spaniards. All this was a palpable infraction of the London Convention, but Whitehall made no objection. Nor did the settlers complain of a disciplinarian regime which, though sharp, was short. For in the spring of 1791 Hunter departed, leaving the settlement for over five years (1791–96) under the control of the seven magistrates without any Superintendent at all.

[1] Burdon, i, 188. [2] *Ibid.*, i, 190.

They were six years of uneasy peace in Honduras with complaints from both sides of infractions of the Convention, and various petty acts of provocation and aggression. Faintly from the distance came the grim tocsin of the *Marseillaise*. In 1793, the year when the Petit Caporal first attracted notice in the siege of Toulon, Revolutionary France declared war on England. In 1796 Spain joined forces with the French, and very soon England found herself standing alone with her back to the wall against the most powerful combination of enemies she had yet faced.

Timid councillors suggested compromise in an apparently desperate situation, but William Pitt the Younger had no use for appeasement. He was a great believer in the Empire, both in India and in the Far West. His spirit infected the new Superintendent, Colonel Thomas Barrow, who soon after the outbreak of war, suddenly appeared on the quayside of Belize (December 31, 1796). Barrow at once followed Hunter's example, put the settlement in a posture for defence, concentrated most of the population in Belize, evacuated S. George's Cay, and proclaimed Martial Law. Ably seconding him came the gallant young Captain John Ralph Moss in H.M.S. sloop *Merlin*, the only naval vessel which England could spare.

Barrow had no easy task to win the co-operation or confidence of the Baymen, long disillusioned and bewildered by the vagaries of British Diplomacy where Honduras was concerned. Many of the logwood- and mahogany-cutters refused to come into Belize. At a public meeting held on June 1, 1797, it was proposed that the whole Colony should be evacuated to the Mosquito Shore, where the Indians still offered a safe refuge. The resolution to stay and fight it out was carried by only a small majority—hardly surprising, when one remembers that the settlement at this time was scarcely bigger than Yorkshire, with a population of some three or four thousand, encircled by the hostile millions of Spanish America! Furthermore the call-up of men for military training prevented the cultivation of crops, so that there was a serious shortage of food. At one time the *Merlin's* crew had to live on local plantains! There were even signs of panic, until fresh troops from England arrived in the autumn. The leading citizens were not always as helpful as they might have been. Particularly obstreperous seems to have been the Rev. William Stanford,[1]

[1] See page 87.

Chaplain to the settlement, who, on being suspended for insubordination, chose this untimely moment to challenge the Superintendent to a duel, and continued for some years to make a nuisance of himself.

Fortunately the Spanish, who, had they known it, held Belize in the hollow of their hands at this time, kept putting off their attack, and the Colony was given time to improve its position under the whiplash of Barrow's and Moss's energetic exhortations. In January 1798 three companies of the 6th West India Regiment reached Belize, together with 171 Negro slaves enlisted on a promise of emancipation at the end of the war. A local Belisian, Thomas Paslow, recruited a large force of slaves, and fitted up his private scow as a gunboat. Other improvised gunboats were named, typically, *Towzer, Mermaid, Teazer, Swinger*, manned by the Baymen. Thomas Potts, a veteran Magistrate, who was old enough to remember Admiral Burnaby, fitted up and appointed himself captain of the *Tickler*, which was to win mention in Barrow's dispatches. His sculptured tombstone on S. George's Cay is in good preservation to this day. Captain Osmar, an American, offered his services and his ship. And among the 'Pork and Doughboys' of the settlement there were many unknown heroes ready to pull their weight in the hour of need.

Suddenly the Spanish struck. On September 3 (quoting Barrow's dispatch), a powerful armada of 32 vessels, 500 seamen, and packed with 2000 'land troops' under the command of Arturo O'Neill, Governor of Yucatan, was sighted sailing from the north, with the obvious intention of forcing a passage over Montego Cay Shoal towards S. George's Cay, and making that island the base of operations against Belize. This attempt was foiled by 'our little squadron' beating them off 'with great ease', and destroying all the buoys which the enemy had laid down to guide them through the narrows. On the 5th the attack was renewed from another direction, but again repulsed, though the Spaniards 'fired off an immense quantity of ammunitition to no manner of purpose, while our people fired comparatively little, but with a steadiness which surpassed my most sanguine hopes'. On the following day, Captain Moss in H.M.S. *Merlin*, and two armed vessels, sailed to S. George's Cay, thwarting yet another advance of the enemy by way of Long Cay. A landing at Belize river mouth itself was then threatened, but Barrow in command of the land forces made

G

suitable dispositions in the channel and at the Haulover stockade, which he planned to defend to the death if it came to the worst.

The threat on Belize was a feint, however, for the Spaniards had not abandoned their original intention of seizing S. George's Cay as an essential preliminary to further operations. On September 10 they were seen advancing in order of battle upon the island. The Baymen's little fleet of improvised boats and rafts was immediately drawn up for action, with H.M.S. *Merlin* in the centre. The engagement opened about 2.30 p.m. 'The enemy came down in a very handsome manner and with a good countenance in a line abreast using both sails and oars.' (It was discovered afterwards that they were so confident of victory, that they carried letters addressed to several people in Belize, which they expected to deliver before nightfall!) Captain Moss at once made the signal to attack, and his motley crews moved forward with an eagerness and courage 'which, to use his own expression to me on the occasion, would have done credit to veterans', wrote Barrow in his dispatch.

The action lasted about two hours, during which Captain Moss showed himself as 'an officer of very great merit'. He was ably supported by his improvised 'fleet'. Captain Osmar lost his vessel on a reef, but 'got command of a flat [raft], and sustained at one time an action against five of the Spanish gunboats, and at another time against seven, in both of which he succeeded in beating them off'. The logwood-cutters, out of their element but evidently with some of their ancestors' buccaneering blood still running in their veins, became 'impossible to restrain, hastening in canoes, dories, and pitpans with impetuosity to join their companions and share their danger'. The Negro slaves, armed only for the most part with 'Poke-'em-mo'' palm spears of fire-hardened wood, proved themselves particularly loyal and plucky. 'You will be astonished to hear that our Negromen who manned the fleets gave a hearty cheer on coming into action, and in the midst of firing of grape kept up upon them by the Spanish vessels, these Negroes in an undaunted manner rowed their boats and made every exertion to board the enemy.' About 3.30 p.m. the largest vessels of the Spanish flotilla surrounded and concentrated their fire upon H.M.S. *Merlin*, heart and brain of the British defence. Captain Moss fought gamely back at them, while seventeen small boats sailed or paddled to his assistance, with Barrow himself in the van. Suddenly, seeing the reinforcements approaching, the Spanish fleet broke off the action, and withdrew to the north. In the morning they could be seen on the horizon 'shaping a course for Baccalar'. It was all over.

The Battle of S. George's Cay had been fought and won against enormous odds by the smallest force, surely, ever to be engaged in one of the decisive battles of history. Captain Moss gives the exact figures. 'Our force, besides the *Merlin*, as follows: 2 Sloops with one 18-pounder and 25 men. One Sloop with one short-9-pounder and 25 men. 2 Schooners with 6 4-pounders and 25 men each. 7 gun-flats with one 9-pounder and 16 men each.' He adds that 'the behaviour of the officers and crew of His Majesty's Ship gave me great pleasure, and the spirit of the Negro slaves that manned our small crafts was wonderful'. This tiny armament was all that stood between us and the loss of our last footing on the Spanish Main. In the Battle of S. George's Cay, not only had the Spanish outrage upon the island twenty years earlier as well as a century of Spanish oppression of the settlement been amply avenged, but the Belize settlement had established its Right to Live. Never again were the Spaniards to attempt the forcible eviction of the colonists whether by land or sea.

The rejoicings and relief on shore and throughout the logwood camps of the interior may well be imagined. As time went on the tension wore off, and a new sense of security and self-confidence descended upon the settlers. For the victory of S. George's Cay, though the numbers engaged were few and its importance is minimized by Spanish and ignored by most English historians, turned out to be surprisingly conclusive. There were no further Spanish assaults—at least of such weight as to cause anxiety—and the settlers realized eventually that their own courage and resolution, combined with the loyalty of their Negro slaves, had succeeded where the wordy warfare of the diplomats had failed.

From that moment onwards they looked upon the settlement as British no less by the time-honoured Right of Conquest than by the previous right of occupation and use. Thus, a month after the victory Admiral Parker of the West India Station was speaking of Belize as 'part of His Majesty's Dominions'.[1] On October 29 of the same year a Public Meeting in Belize affirmed in so many words that 'the tenure and possession of the country is now

[1] Burdon, i, 265.

altered. His Majesty holds it by force, and it may in some degree be considered as a Conquered Country'.[1] From this time forward the Union Jack flew boldly on public buildings, and the right of the settlement to a Constitution of its own, with Judicature, Executive, Police, and Superintendent was taken for granted. Despite certain murmurs to a different effect from diplomatic quarters, the settlement was now regarded as a British Colony in all but name.

Napoleon secured a valuable breathing space by the Treaty of Amiens in 1802, but renewed the war in the following year. In 1804 the French Admiral Villeneuve raced with the Spanish fleet to the West Indies, only to turn east again without striking a blow, until the Battle of Trafalgar (1805) set its seal for a hundred years on British supremacy at sea. But the victory which is remembered most in British Honduras is the Victory of S. George's Cay. Each year its Anniversary is observed in the Colony to this day. September 10 is the greatest festival in its civic year. Everyone makes holiday, processions tour the streets, the bands play, the flags fly, banquets are spread for young and old, public orations and church services improve the occasion, and everyone smiles broadly at everyone else as Belize commemorates the Glorious Victory which liberated her for ever from the thrall of Spain.

[1] Burdon, i, 274.

Chapter IX

*

THE MOSQUITO SHORE

THE settlement's feelings of exultation and relief over the liberation of Belize were naturally shared by its old friends and allies the Indians of the Mosquito Shore, to whom we will now turn.

We have seen how the long-standing British logwood settlements on the Shore had been evacuated in 1786 under the terms of the Convention of London. The Shore could now no longer be regarded as British territory, nor as held in British occupation. It remained British notwithstanding both in sympathy and to a large extent in practice. The Indians refused to acknowledge themselves subjects of Spain, continued to assert their invincibility and independence, and still looked to the British as in an almost mystical sense their brethren by all the ties of tradition, gratitude, comradeship in arms, and unity of Faith. Although the British settlements had ended, there was nothing in the Treaty to terminate this ancient *entente cordiale*. The Mosquito Shore with its bay islands—especially Rattan—continued to afford strength and comfort to the Belize settlers, both by its markets and by the sanctuary it provided in the hour of need. Just before the Battle of the Cay, for example, some of the weaker sort in Belize had counselled flight to Rattan so persistently that Captain Moss had even to threaten that he would drop a shot across the bows of any boat attempting it.[1]

There is something rather touching in the Mosquitos' hero-worship of England. They tried so hard to become British subjects! For a long period their sovereign on his accession to the throne made a special journey to Port Royal, there to receive his crown at the hands of the Governor of Jamaica and to pay homage to the Great White King.[2] Afterwards they went to Belize for the same purpose. Their royal princes were educated in British schools. Over their public buildings flew the British flag. They liked to think of Mosquitia as a province of the British Empire.

[1] Burdon, i, 249.   [2] *Ibid.*, ii, 250.

It is all forgotten now, and few historians of the period trouble to recall it, but it is at least of interest to remember that there was once a time when the British Empire very nearly established a foothold on the bulge of the Central American mainland, and when the colony of British Honduras came within an ace of embracing both sides of the Honduranian Gulf from Yucatan to Costa Rica.

The Mosquito Shore, in effect, played such an important and co-operative part in the development of Belize that it is impossible to tell the story of the one without bringing in that of the other.

When England stood alone with her back to the wall against the armed might of Napoleon and his many satellites, when her Army and Navy had their hands too full of trouble in Europe to spare much thought for the West Indies, when Belize in particular found herself in deadly peril from encircling enemies both by land and sea, the Mosquito Indians never faltered in their allegiance. On the very eve of the Battle of the Cay, King George of Mosquitia showed his confidence in the outcome by sending his son and heir to Jamaica for education, and by asking the British Government for a supply of arms so that he could more worthily fight the common enemy. Immediately after the victory, although a Spanish counter-attack was expected at any moment, two Mosquito chieftains with their retinues voyaged to Belize to offer their congratulations, being followed a few months later by His Majesty of Mosquitia in person. The *Archives* record the gratification of the Public Meeting and its vote of £150 for his entertainment. It was not the last of many such royal visits to the Colony.[1]

On the renewal of Spanish hostilities in 1803, the Mosquito King again asked for a consignment of up-to-date muskets from England. He also begged for a Union Jack, 'as we mean', he said, 'to fight under English colours'.[2] On inquiry by Superintendent Barrow if all this were in order, the Commander-in-Chief of Jamaica replied that 'the importance of cultivating the friendship of the Mosquito Indians' had never been greater. He added that the young King John had been sent to school in Jamaica at the Government's expense in order to 'impress upon him the advantages of our alliance'.[3] In the following year the Indians were supplied with arms from England, and with these

[1] Burdon, i, 279.   [2] *Ibid.*, ii, 72.   [3] *Ibid.*, ii, 79.

were able to attack Truxillo itself, liberating certain British subjects made prisoner by the Spanish Honduranians. Such was the jealous interest we took in our Mosquito allies that the Navy was instructed to prevent any Yankees from reaching the Shore, lest their English appearance and language should make them 'dangerous rivals for the friendship of the Indians'.[1] Thus in many ways the steadfast loyalty and courage of the Mosquitos protected the flank, as it were, of our West Indian Empire at a time when we needed all the help we could get.

The victory of Waterloo (1815) had scarcely restored order in Europe before the stability of Central America reeled under the political earthquake of the Mexican rebellion against Imperial Spain. Revolution was in the air. After the French and North American revolts against their respective *anciens régimes*, it was now the turn first of Mexico and then of all the other Spanish provinces—Guatemala, El Salvador, Nicaragua, Costa Rica, Spanish Honduras, Panama—to throw off the yoke of the Motherland, and raise the banner of La Libertad. This diverted attention from the British settlements around Belize, which were enabled to consolidate their foothold accordingly with very little interference from their old enemies. It also enabled the Mosquito King to assert with added firmness the independence of his country from Spanish suzerainty. The Spanish authorities indeed were fortunate in not having to contend with a general uprising of Indians throughout the isthmus.

The upheaval in Central America had repercussions far beyond the Caribbean. On the Stock Exchange in London were business men watching the situation with interest, and hoping to rake chestnuts out of the fire. The Mosquito Shore, now virtually a British protectorate but inhabited mainly by 'untutored savages', seemed to offer a promising field for exploitation. The most important enterprise in view was, of course, the projected canal through Nicaragua to the Pacific, which, if it materialized, would bring the Mosquito Indians very much into the picture. But there were minor speculations too. It was about 1819 that a certain Gregor MacGregor secured from the Mosquito King a concession of land in Poyasia, near the mouth of the Black River, where there still survived some dilapidated huts, warehouses, rusty machinery, and other relics of the British settlements which had

[1] Burdon, ii, 84.

been evacuated to Belize under the Treaty of 1786. MacGregor sketchily surveyed the ground, parcelled it into lots, and issued an attractive prospectus of a new Gold Mine Company, a veritable Eldorado awaiting only a few British immigrants to convert the native Indians into willing workers, and the speculators into millionaires. The letterpress described the area as a subtropical paradise, not only beautiful and productive beyond belief, but already blessed with the amenities of civilization. It was spoken of as 'The State of Poyais', with an ordered government, and a 'well-established capital city at San Joseph'. The promoter of the company was called 'His Serene Highness Gregor, Prince of the Poyais, Cazique of the Poyer Nation, Defender of the Indians'. His business agent, or rather 'aide-de-camp', a Mr. George Augustus Low, wore the resplendent insignia of a 'Commander-in-Chief of the Poyasian Army'.

Hundreds of canny Scots and Englishmen with their wives and families gambled their life's savings, and—as it turned out—their lives on this Caribbean Sea Bubble. It was all a swindle, of course, yet just within the law: there was land, there were buildings, a little gold had been washed out of the river silt. But it was far from being the Golden Shore of their dreams. On disembarking after a long, uncomfortable voyage over the Atlantic (this was before the days of steamships, of course) they found—in the words of a contemporary report—'nothing but a few wretched huts, no one to receive them, no shoes, provisions, or even good water'. They were soon in desperate plight, many of them being delicately nurtured folk who had never done a hard day's manual labour in their lives. Several of them died of privation or disease. Eventually news of their condition reached their compatriots in Belize.

The Colony rose to the occasion with energy and decision. A Colonel Hall was dispatched at once to Poyasia, where he discovered 'an accumulation of misery beyond description', including the newly turned graves of over seventy dead. Picking up a few drums of oil and other stores which the expedition had brought with them, he shipped the survivors to Belize, where the Magistrates at once made themselves responsible for their maintenance. Some of them were settled at the expense of the Colony in the pleasant district of Stann Creek, with three acres of fertile land apiece, suitable tools for farming, and a gang of twenty coloured labourers under an overseer to give them a start in earning their own living. The sick were looked after in hospital. Others were given passage back to England at the Colony's expense. The total cost of these acts of mercy was estimated at £4290, 4*s*., but no bill was ever sent in. The *Archives* do not mention any particular expression of gratitude on the part of the immigrants, but there was a sequel in 1823, when Mr. George Augustus Low published a libellous attack upon the Magistrates entitled *The Belize Merchants Unmasked*. In this they were accused of having robbed the Poyasian Estate Company of a large quantity of oil and other stores, and of ruining a promising experiment!

All this drew the eyes of England to the hitherto almost unheard-of countries of Mosquitia and our settlement in Belize. Most people were astonished to learn that the Empire had a footing on the Spanish Main. To the diplomats the question of the 'Poyasian Company' gave much food for thought. Politically speaking, was this attempted Poyasian settlement an infraction of the 1786 Convention forbidding British occupation of the Mosquito coast? Or had that Convention lapsed on the recent break-up of the Spanish Empire in Central America? In that event, what was the precise status in international law of the *soi-disant* independent Kingdom of Mosquitia? Had the Mosquito King been within his rights in granting a concession to MacGregor? Thus many interesting points were raised, some of which had a direct bearing upon the status of Belize. It would have been well for the future of our holdings in Central America if these questions had been settled there and then: it would at least have saved a century of ambiguity over our position in Belize itself. But the nettle was not grasped. Superintendent Cobb of Belize reminded the Government that 'the Mosquito Shore is a territory over which the right of Great Britain is disputed', and that 'the surrounding republics have stated plainly that they would consider even a partial settlement of English people in Mosquitia as a hostile action',[1] but Whitehall never directly took up the challenge. The policy she pursued was a characteristically British compromise. Without definitely asserting any territorial rights either in Belize or on the Shore, she proceeded to act as though such rights had been assumed so long that there was no need to define them. So they were not defined. But while the politicians

[1] Burdon, ii, 280.

'cut the cackle', the men of action 'got to the horses' without more ado. Belize we determined to embrace within the Empire as a full-fledged Colony: in Mosquitia we would be content for the time being with a Protectorate, while feeling our way to the creation therein or thereabouts of another Colony. This was the policy we pursued for the next forty years.

It was now (1823) twenty-five years since the Victory of S. George's Cay. The independence of Belize had never been seriously threatened since then, and the settlement had grown so amazingly in prosperity that the formal grant of colonial status was clearly only a matter of time. In 1824 this was flatteringly acknowledged by the Indians of the Mosquito Shore, who in that year for the first time brought their new king with his crown for coronation in Belize, instead of in Jamaica as heretofore. On April 3 the Superintendent, representing His Majesty King George IV of England, carried out the ceremony in accordance with precedent, being authorized by his Legislative Assembly to expend £1000 on entertainments and presents 'in order to maintain the great attachment of the Mosquito Nation to the English'.[1] The religious part of the function took place in the newly erected Parish Church of S. John the Baptist.

The importance of the Mosquito connection was now being more acutely appreciated than ever, in view of the Nicaraguan Canal project, which might require a right of way across Indian territory. It was resolved by the Legislature to send an annual *douceur* of £300 to the King of Mosquitia, 'otherwise we shall lose his friendship, as the Spaniards and Americans are only too anxious we should do'.[2] On several occasions the King had to complain that payment of the subsidy was overdue, but his complaint was always effective. In this and in many other ways Mosquitia became more firmly attached than ever to the British 'sphere of interest'.

A vivid and informative account of the Mosquito Coast, as seen through English eyes at this period, provides a sequel, as it were, to Dampier's narrative of his landing on the same coast some hundred and fifty years earlier, and is written in very much the same spirit of eager curiosity and zest. It is found in a rather rare book called *A Narrative of a Residence on the Mosquito Shore during the years* 1839, 1840, *and* 1841, *with an Account of Truxillo and the adjacent Islands of Bonacca and Roatan*, by a certain Thomas

[1] Burdon, ii, 280.   [2] *Ibid.*, ii, 315.

Young, who sailed from London to Black River with a view to establishing trade relations with the Indians, and if possible with the Spaniards of the interior. After 'delivering his credentials' to the King of the Mosquito nation, Robert Charles Frederic, 'who looked remarkably well in the uniform of a post-captain in the British Navy', he travelled over the whole coast from north to south under His Majesty's protection. 'Any Englishman could traverse from one end of the country to the other, without the expense of a yard of cloth, for the king's orders to all were to feed and lodge them, and provide them with horses if they were wanted.' It was as well, however, to keep away from the interior, for the Columbians (Spanish) were always ready to attack foreigners, especially Englishmen, and occasionally gathered for an assault in force upon some Indian town. On such occasions, help was at once invoked from Belize, and the enemy was made to realize that the Mosquito King, protégé of the British Crown, was not to be molested with impunity.

Like Dampier, our author was greatly impressed by the loyalty and courage of the Indians of these parts. After a century and a half, they were still as hostile to the Spaniards, and as friendly to the English, as ever they were. Yet it must be admitted that the natives were not what they had been in the days of the buccaneers. Increased prosperity through trade with Europe had brought with it the evils which too often accompany the impact of 'civilization' on primitive peoples. It was disappointing to find that the Christian religion after all these years had made but little permanent impression on the Indians outside the better-populated centres and the Royal Court. There had been such a great increase in drunkenness and immorality that, with the increasing number of Caribs on the one hand, and the pressure of white men on the other, 'in a few generations there will be but few Mosquito Indians left to tell the tale'. The only hope, in Mr. Young's opinion, was that they might be lucky enough to find good leaders who would discipline and educate them, and so bring out all that was best in the blood of their ancestors to arrest the marked decline into which the race was falling.

For linguists and anthropologists Mr. Young's book will have a special interest, for it is perhaps our only source of information on the languages of the Mosquito Shore at this period. Fortunately for us he takes pleasure in 'showing off' his knowledge of them, and offering a rough translation as he goes along. There are three distinct groups, it appears: the aboriginal Indians of the Spanish interior, the Caribs of the coast, and the Sambos or Mosquitians also of the coast, as far west as Black River. It is these Sambos who interest him most. They are a fine, upstanding, energetic, pleasant-featured race of all shades, varying from the copper colour of the Indian to the dark hue of the Negro, but sadly addicted to fire-water, and with little religion save a dread of Oulasser, the Evil Spirit. He regards their racial origin as 'obscure', but gives many samples of their speech, which might enable a linguist to identify it. Thus: *Casak wop: arwaller barrossa* (Go straight ahead: there's the lagoon); *Yapte tarra—pine yapte* (Grandmother—good grandmother); *Ouplee, ouree polly i doukser* (Friend, I have a fever). He even attempts to set down one of their folk-songs *in extenso:*

> *Keker miren nane,*
> *Warwar paser yamine krouekan.*
> *Coope narer mi koolkun i doukser.*
> *Dear mane kuker cle wol proue.*
> *I sabbeane wal moonter moppara.*
> *Keker misere yapte winegan.*
> *Koker sombolo barnar lippun,*
> *Lippun, lippunke.*
> *Koolunker punater bin biwegan.*
> *Coope narer tanes i doukser.*
> *Coope narer mi koolkun i doukser.*

Which he translates: 'Dear girl, I am going far from thee. When shall we meet again to wander on the sea-shore? I feel the sweet sea-breeze blow its welcome on my cheek. I hear the distant rolling of the mournful thunder. I see the lightning flashing on the mountain-top, illuminating all things below. But thou art not near me. My heart is sad and sorrowful. Farewell, dear girl. Without thee I am desolate.'

What are the affinities of this strange language? The present writer can throw no light upon them, but would be grateful to any reader who could. Is it akin to the Red Indian group, or has it sufficient resemblance to some West African dialect to confirm the legend that these Sambos were descendants of Negro slaves wrecked upon the Mosquito Coast in the early eighteenth century? Perhaps it is a question which will never now be answered. There were only a few thousand of these people in Mr. Young's day, and their numbers were dwindling rapidly. 'My countrymen go wrong way,' said one of them. 'They drink English grog and mushla: they go after sookeahs [witch doctors]: they have bad chiefs: soon the English will take all the country, and my people will be dead.'

A new feature which had appeared on the Mosquito Coast since the days of Dampier was the large and increasing number of Carib 'Indians'. As these still compose an important part of the population of that coast, and of British Honduras, it will be interesting to trace their somewhat complicated origins. The first Caribs of whom we have any knowledge seem to have migrated from the Orinoco district of the South American mainland somewhere in the fifteenth century to the islands of the Antilles and the West Indies generally. These were the people, well-built, brave, and ready to put up a fierce resistance to the invader, whom the Spanish Conquistadores and other European adventurers found in occupation of the islands in the sixteenth century, and who were so ruthlessly decimated that when it became necessary to secure labourers for the new plantations of the Caribbean, the slave raider was invited to supply the need from the teeming Negro hordes of West Africa. The original 'Red' Carib Indians thus became virtually extinct, abhorred by the Spanish both for their untameable ferocity and for their inveterate cannibalism. They bequeathed their name, however, to the Caribbean Sea.

The last island on which they survived in any number was S. Vincent, in the Windward Isles, where both the English and the French endeavoured to enlist their support in their respective claims to ownership of the place. The history of the 'Black' Caribs begins in 1675, when a vessel carrying a cargo of some hundreds of West African slaves was wrecked upon the island, and the delighted Negroes were assisted by the Caribs in the most co-operative manner to exterminate their European oppressors. As the Peace of Utrecht shortly afterwards (1713) deliberately left the international status of S. Vincent in abeyance, the Carib population, Red and Black, were able to manage their own affairs in their own way, and learnt to live together and even to intermarry in perfect harmony for some years. Eventually, however, the greater vitality and fertility of the Negro element excited the apprehensions of the Indians, and by the time that the English had regained the island, in 1760, there had grown up a marked animosity between the Red and the numerically superior Black Caribs, the Reds supporting the British interest, and the Blacks that of the French. On the outbreak of the French revolutionary war against Great Britain, a French adventurer named Victor Hagues roused the Black Caribs to rise against the Anglophil Reds, and the island was torn asunder by a bloody civil war, in which the Blacks were ultimately defeated, and their chieftain, Samboler, slain. English troops completed the suppression of the rebellion in 1796, receiving the surrender of 5000 Black Caribs and 1000 French. The French were deported to S. Lucia and Martinique, while the Blacks were shipped *en masse* to the islands of Rattan and Bonacca and the Mosquito Coast, where they settled down and multiplied, and became that important part of the Mosquito kingdom of which we read so much in Mr. Young's narrative. One of the most loyal and respected leaders of the Caribs on the coast in Mr. Young's day was 'Colonel' Samboler, son of the Carib chieftain slain in the battle of 1795.

These Caribs were not always content to settle where they first landed. Although at first darkly suspected of cannibalism, treachery, and incorrigible savagery, and for that reason held at arm's length by their neighbours, they soon proved their usefulness as energetic, intelligent workmen, and became eagerly sought after as labourers, whether on the Spanish plantations of the interior, or the mahogany cuttings in Belize and British Honduras. Many of them were shipped with government assistance to Belize, and many more managed to find their way to the Toledo coast and the neighbourhood of Stann Creek, where they survive in large numbers to this day. In Mr. Young's time they are described as an exceedingly friendly, reliable, and honest people, addicted to polygamy and obeah superstitions, but ever ready to welcome a Christian missionary when one is available, and particularly eager to receive the benefits of education. Their gift for languages is specially mentioned, many of them being able to speak English, Spanish, French, and Mosquito. Every Carib town acknowledged the authority of its own mayor or 'Captain' and gave allegiance to the Mosquito King. There was very little serious crime or violence, and all ill-feeling against the British had long been forgotten, although the Spanish, especially the Spanish nearer to the coast, were still bitterly hated.

Such were the diverse races and cultures which made up the Kingdom of Mosquitia, stretching perhaps somewhat vaguely and without explicit international recognition along the narrow coastline from the Rio San Juan in southern Nicaragua up to Cape Gracias à Dios and then westward to Roman River and the frontiers of Truxillo in Spanish Honduras. It is clear from Mr. Young's account that the abandonment of political rights under the Treaty of 1786 had not prevented the development of promising trade relations between England and the Coast. Among the exports mentioned are sugar, tobacco, mahogany, logwood, hides, sarsaparilla, cochineal, indigo, copper, silver, coconuts, mules and cattle. Among the 'British goods most suitable for exchange' are enumerated liquor, muskets, cutlasses, knives, and ammunition as the most eagerly sought after—a somewhat sinister priority, alas! But clothing and cotton goods come a good second: checks, ginghams, Osnaburg cloth, shawls with 'large showy patterns', reels of cotton, threads, and 'trowser' buttons. 'All the dry goods ought to be well packed, as they go out to Belize for the Spanish market in ware cloth and wrapper bales.' He advises settlers to take only English money, but chiefly 'shillings, sixpences, and threepenny pieces', as these will pass for currency anywhere. It is clear that every year which passes has cemented more firmly the ancient though unwritten Treaty of Amity and Commerce between Great Britain and the King of the Mosquitos.

During the early thirties the adjoining Spanish republics, now more securely established and sensitive to their territorial rights, ventured to express their resentment at the continuance of this independent Anglophil monarchy on their threshold. Matters came to a head in 1837, when Nicaragua was reported to be preparing an armed offensive against the Mosquitos, and the Indians accordingly appealed to England for protection. Lord Palmerston, then Prime Minister, was not the man to refuse an invitation like that. Promptly he dispatched a man-of-war, H.M.S. *Nimrod*, to demonstrate off the Mosquito Shore. Up and down the coast she sailed with bristling cannon and fluttering pennant, from Castillo Point and Cape Cameron to Bragman's Bluff, Bluefields, Monkey Point, and down to San Juan del Norte. The British garrison of Rattan Island was strengthened, too, and for the moment Nicaragua felt it wiser to hold her hand. In the following year, however, she plucked up courage enough to seize the Mosquito capital at San Juan del Norte (where the projected canal was expected to debouch into the bay). The Indian King managed to effect his escape by sea, taking refuge in Belize. Superintendent Macdonald heard his story, personally escorted him back on a gunboat to San Juan, and ejected the Spanish officials with a stern warning against the repetition of their conduct. When the matter was taken up at a higher level, the British Consul at San Salvador unequivocally repudiated Nicaraguan pretensions to ownership of the Shore.

Nicaragua was not the only offender to have her knuckles rapped. In 1839 the Superintendent of Belize had to rebuke the Republic of Spanish Honduras for inciting the Commandant of Truxillo to threaten the British settlers who had occupied Rattan. Here again local action was promptly followed by support from England, Lord Palmerston dispatching H.M.S. *Rover* to the island 'for the purpose of hauling down any foreign flag which may be hoisted upon it'.[1] At the southernmost end of the Mosquito Shore the authorities of Costa Rica were likewise warned against interference with Indian territory. 'The Mosquito Coast,' they were informed, 'is within the territory of the King of the Mosquitos, an ally of the British nation.' Superintendent Macdonald at the same time sent a schooner to occupy the bay islands of Utila, Guanaja, Elena, Barbareta, and Mosat. The Spanish seized a party of British subjects by way of reprisal, but released them at once on protest by our consul.[2]

In the midst of these alarums and excursions it is pleasant to read of more personal gestures of friendship towards the Mosquitos. In 1843 the Colonial Secretary commissioned a Mr. George Brown to visit the Shore, taking with him presents for the widow of the late King Robert Frederick, as well as £100 for the maintenance of Prince George and Princess Agnes. We learn also that Prince Clarence was sent by Superintendent Macdonald to England for his education, in the personal charge of Mrs. Macdonald. The kindly Superintendent had obtained a grant of £100 from public funds for the purpose, 'and if any more is needed,' he promised, 'I will pay it myself'.[3]

Palmerston's retirement from the Foreign Office in 1841 did not result in any change of policy towards the Mosquitos, nor did the resignation of Superintendent Macdonald make any

---

[1] Burdon, ii, 407.   [2] *Ibid.*, iii, 49.   [3] *Ibid.*, iii, 64.

difference. The new Superintendent of Belize, Charles S. John Fancourt, was instructed by the Governor of Jamaica in 1843 on the line he was to follow. While taking a benevolent and protective interest in the Indians, the British Government had no wish to interfere in their affairs. They must be allowed, for example, to elect their own King from the family of the late monarch. As to the rest, 'His Majesty's Government recognized the independence of the Mosquito Indians, and would not regard with indifference any encroachment on their territory or rights'.[1] At the same time it was felt expedient to station a permanent British Resident on the Shore, with special attention to the now considerable settlements on the islands of Rattan and Bonacca. Shortly afterwards the new King was elected, as advised, and again it was Belize which had the honour of witnessing his coronation. On May 7, 1845, King George Augustus Frederick was crowned by the Bishop of Jamaica in S. John's Church.

It will be understood, of course, that all this was very distasteful to the Spanish republics. As in the old days Mexico had looked upon Belize as integrally part of Yucatan, and had continually attempted to enforce her territorial rights over the British settlers, so now the republics adjoining the Shore protested hotly against what they regarded as a further attempt at encroachment by Great Britain upon immemorial Spanish rights. Nicaragua, Spanish Honduras, and Costa Rica were the republics most nearly affected, but the rest of Spanish America supported their point of view, and was continually attempting to secure the adhesion of the United States to their cause. The British Government at this time, however, had made up its mind to the policy of the Strong Hand. Its treatment of the British settlers in the Bay Islands and of British allies on the Shore was now very different from the indolent vacillation with which it had once watched the struggle for survival of the logwood-cutters in Belize. But now of course there were far greater commercial interests at stake.

To continue, King Frederick sailed for the Shore immediately after his coronation, with a newly appointed consul, Mr. Patrick Walker, in his retinue. One of the King's first decrees was to annul all concessions of timber-cutting granted to non-British subjects—which did not please the Americans. At the same time Consul Walker proclaimed that San Juan del Norte, the traditional

[1] Burdon, iii, 67.

capital of Mosquitia, was definitely within the realm of King Frederick, and a Mr. Hodgson was appointed as the city's Governor.[1] There followed a great increase in British activities in those parts. A flood of immigrants poured from Belize into Bluefields, Pearl Lagoon, and San Juan. In the Bay Islands the Rev. N. Newport, with every practical support from the Superintendent of Belize, spread the Anglican Faith and built churches. The Mosquito King expanded his standing army and acquired an embryo navy. In 1847 the *Archives* speak of a Commander Watson, Master of 'His Mosquitian Majesty's Cutter *Sun*'. On May 17 he reported to Belize that the Commandant of Truxillo had insulted the flag. The gallant Commander offered to 'take Truxillo with the cutter's crew and other assistance, and to chastise the Commandant'. On receiving permission, he 'landed at Roman River, captured all the guns and ammunition found in the fort, and drove away the troops of Spanish Honduras'.[2] On the matter being referred to the higher authorities, the Governor of Jamaica protested against the Spanish pretensions. 'The Mosquito Coast,' he reiterated, 'is a distinct Territory and Realm under the Protection of the British Crown.'[3] Warnings to the same effect were sent also to Nicaragua and Guatemala. The Governor of Jamaica sent a man-of-war to Belize to inform the Superintendent there of the the firm line that was being taken by the Foreign Office: 'The Consul-General at Guatemala and the Chargé d'Affaires at Bogota have been instructed that any attempt to encroach upon the rights or territory of the King of Mosquito, who is under the protection of the British Crown, will not be viewed with indifference.' Nothing could be clearer. British policy had been 'feeling its way' to this position for many years, and now at last the Mosquito Shore was explicitly embraced within our West Indian Empire as a British Protectorate. In the following year (1848) the name of San Juan del Norte was officially changed to Greytown, and so remains on English maps to this day, commemorating the highwater-mark of our Imperial ambitions on the Spanish Main.

For many years previously, however, the United States had been growing more and more suspicious of our intentions in Central America. It looked as though British foreign policy was aiming, especially under Palmerston, to secure a controlling

---

[1] Villacorta, p. 213, states that he was a mulatto.
[2] Burdon, iii, 92.   [3] *Ibid.*, iii, 97.

interest in the country through which the trans-Isthmian canal would most probably have to pass, or at least to establish bases in the vicinity of the canal from which the British Navy would be able to blockade it in time of trouble. In this connection British Honduras would be useful, which was one reason why Belize had recently been accorded a place in the Imperial sun. But the Mosquito Shore and the Bay Islands would be still more advantageous, as both the Spanish republics and the United States were quick to see. Palmerston at the height of his power might have stuck to his guns, but by now his influence over the Queen and the Cabinet was waning. The consequence was a sudden collapse of his Central American policy just before his final dismissal. In 1849 negotiations on the subject were entered into with the United States, which resulted in the celebrated Clayton-Bulwer Treaty of 1850.

In this Treaty both England and America, with their eyes on the future of the canal, promised not to fortify any places in Nicaragua or 'in any other part of Central America'. The canal, when completed, should belong to no individual state, but should provide a right of way across the Isthmus for all shipping on equal terms. According to the letter of the Treaty, the British occupation of Belize might seem to have been outlawed, but it was clearly understood by both the contracting parties that this was not so. Bulwer put it in black and white at the time that 'His Majesty does not understand the engagements of the Convention to apply to His Majesty's Settlement at Honduras or to its dependencies'. Clayton explicitly concurred. Yet there were voices in the Senate which clamoured for a British evacuation of all her territorial holdings on the Main and in the Bay Islands without exception, voices which were naturally echoed by the Spanish powers. With regard to the Mosquito Shore, at any rate, the implications of the Treaty were clear: any further territorial nibblings on the coast of the bay would have to cease. The United States would 'not view with indifference' any European attempt at annexation, British or otherwise, on the mainland of Central America.

Yet all was not lost. The terms of the Clayton-Bulwer Treaty did not in so many words prohibit a British *protectorate* over the Indians, nor a close offensive and defensive alliance with them. Nor did it in so many words, while checkmating territorial ambitions on the mainland, make it certain that the islands off the shore were also included. Disraeli accordingly made up his mind to risk one final adventure on the Spanish Main, and to salvage what he could of the ship of Empire so recently stranded on the Clayton-Bulwer shoals.

The sudden proclamation of a new British 'Colony of the Bay Islands' in 1852, only two years after the aforementioned agreement with America, startled the whole world. It looked as though Disraeli's little finger was going to be thicker than his predecessor's loins. A commission under His Majesty's Great Seal blandly ignored the heated discussions which had flickered around our territorial claims in the bay ever since the days of the buccaneers, and announced that we had decided (unilaterally) to annex the Bay Islands to our West Indian Empire. The document enumerated the islands of Rattan, Bonacca, Utila, Helena, Barbareta, and Mosat as comprising the new Colony, and appointed Superintendent Wodehouse of Belize as its first Lieutenant-Governor.[1] Needless to say, the United States and the Republic of Spanish Honduras (whose territory was chiefly affected) protested warmly, invoking both the Monroe Doctrine and the Clayton-Bulwer Treaty. The atmosphere became explosive.

The Mosquito King, our ally and protégé, was overjoyed at this demonstration of British energy and spirit in what he doubtless regarded as the best buccaneering tradition. He at once repudiated some American concessions at Punta Arenas near Greytown which had been granted, without his consent, by the Nicaraguan Government. The United States, their protests having been summarily rejected, sent a cruiser, the *Cyane*, to the spot. Marines were landed, but were opposed by armed Indians, and forced back to their ship. Whereupon the *Cyane* actually bombarded Greytown from the sea, playing havoc with the harbour and civic buildings. The King appealed to England. At New Orleans the Americans began fitting out privateer schooners for an expedition against the Shore. The Superintendent of Belize urged the British Government to send a fleet of 'steam-propelled vessels' (a novelty in those days) to counter this move.

Rarely were the vials of wrath so full without over-spilling. But the Crimean War just ended had sickened people of strife, and the new Government (1856) desired nothing so much as a

[1] Burdon, iii, 157.

breathing space for recovery. The last it desired was a rupture with the now rich and powerful United States. Moreover, the 'Walker Affair' was demonstrating to all men of goodwill the vital necessity for stability in Central America.

William Walker of Tennessee, blazing with indignation at the emancipationism of *Uncle Tom's Cabin* and its admirers, had conceived the wild idea of setting up a slave-holding republic, with himself as President, somewhere beyond the reach of the Stars and Stripes. His first adventure (1855) took him to Nicaragua, where, after helping to suppress a rebellion, he seized the Presidency of Granada, assassinated all rivals, confiscated their property, and invited American slave-holders to sell him their slaves at a low price before emancipation should reduce their value to nothing. Despite American prohibitions, many like-minded recruits flocked to his standard. He thus assembled a considerable army, with which, seizing the river-steamers of the gold-mining Transit Company, he defeated successively the troops of Costa Rica, Guatemala, and Salvador. In 1856 he elected himself President of Nicaragua, in which office, strange to say, he was 'recognized' by the United States. To counter his designs, the British Government sent a cruiser, H.M.S. *Cossack*, to the Mosquito Shore. All Central America was in an uproar.

Walker's exploits thus brought to a head the uneasiness of all sensible men, and especially of all business men, over the chaotic conditions in the Isthmus. It was idle to think of starting a canal, or opening new markets, while this sort of thing was going on. The British policy of the Strong Hand had proved more trouble than it was worth. Apart from the danger of embroiling England and America in war, it was bad for trade.

Suddenly the British Government made up its mind to 'pull out'. By the Dallas-Clarendon Treaty of 1856 she abandoned once and for all her carefully built-up position on the Mosquito Shore. At one blow, the old alliance with the Indians was broken off, the Protectorate renounced, and support for the Indian claim of independence from Spanish suzerainty withdrawn. Bluefields, Greytown, and the rest were to remain British henceforward only in name and memory. She also liquidated her short-lived Colony of the Bay Islands. By a Treaty with Spanish Honduras, the islands of Rattan, Bonacca, and the others were ceded to the Republic. No more would the national flag fly on the islands where it had flown, with intervals, for over three centuries. The new Colony had lasted less than four years—1852–1856!

To many, and especially to the bewildered Mosquitos, it seemed a shameless surrender. There was indeed a proviso in the terms of cession, that any Mosquitos who desired to remain under the British flag must be permitted to emigrate to Belize, and it was hoped that their King might be allowed to retain his kingdom as a semi-autonomous reservation within Nicaraguan territory. But in effect our ancient allies were abandoned to their traditional foes. For a generation or more after the Great Betrayal they refused to realize what had happened. The old ties of sentiment and religion persisted. Many Church of England congregations still, in fact, survive to this day on the Mosquito Shore, oases of Anglicanism in a Catholic world. As late as 1946 there were Church of England congregations, schools, and churches at Greytown, Bluefields, Pearl Lagoon, Ritapura, Kakabilla, Square Point, Orinocco, and Tasbapauri. In 1947 they were handed over to the spiritual jurisdiction of the American Protestant Episcopal Church along with the other southern states of what had been the Anglican Diocese of British Honduras. When things went wrong, for years the Indians turned to England for help. As late as 1903 they were asking us to defend them against Nicaraguan persecution. The Kingship, after dwindling to a mere shadow of reality, was brutally ended in 1905. As a last shamefaced gesture to a bygone attachment, a British gunboat rescued the last King of the Mosquitos, Robert Henry Clarence, and took him to Jamaica, where the Government pensioned him off to the end of his days. It was the least we could do.

The whole edifice of British influence in this part of the world thus fell to pieces like a pack of cards. Yet there was, of course, a valuable *quid pro quo*. In return for our surrender, we obtained one supremely important concession. The United States agreed to confirm, and even to extend, our territorial holding in British Honduras, the southern boundary being now fixed at the Sarstoon River, instead of at the Sibun River, thus doubling the area of the Colony, as we shall show in more detail in a later chapter.

As to William Walker, whom we left as President of Nicaragua in 1856, the briefest summary of his subsequent exploits must suffice. Badly beaten by a Spanish federation in 1857, his stolen fleet recaptured, his 'American Phalanx' of Big Shots dispersed, he was rescued from Spanish fury by an American gunboat, and taken back to New Orleans. Here he found himself *fêted* as a national hero, and acquitted after trial of legal offence. Indeed he received so many gifts from admirers that he was able to fit out a second expedition. With this he sailed again to the Mosquito Shore, eluded an American patrol boat, and seized a Nicaraguan fortress near Greytown. American marines, however, chased him up the San Juan River, arrested him, and took him home again on the *Susquehanna*. For the second time tried and acquitted, he wrote an account of his adventures which brought him enough money to furnish yet another vessel with guns, ammunition, and a crew of desperadoes. Hearing that Rattan had been handed over by the British to Spanish Honduras, he occupied it in approved buccaneer style as a base for raids upon Truxillo. This time the British Navy made itself responsible for him. Sailing promptly from Belize, H.M.S. *Icarus* overpowered his crew, and handed Walker to the Honduranian authorities. They shot him at dawn on September 12, 1860. Thus came to his inevitable end a picaresque but gallant adventurer born a great many years too late.

The way had thus been prepared by treaty and by suppression of disorder for the inception of the long-mooted trans-Isthmian canal. After planning a cutting through Nicaragua, the United States decided after all to purchase Lesseps' bankrupt Panama Canal Company in 1895. In 1901 the Clayton-Bulwer Treaty was modified by the Pauncefort-Hay Pact, soon afterwards to be itself extended by the Hay-Bunau-Vasilla Treaty of 1903, which enabled the United States to carve out a broad avenue of territory—the American Panama Canal Zone—stretching from the Pacific to the Caribbean along the line of the projected cutting. Work was then renewed on the deserted site, American efficiency (particularly in sanitation) succeeded where the French had failed, and the first ocean steamer passed through it on August 3, 1914—just in time for the First World War.

Chapter X

*

BELIZE BECOMES A COLONY

RETURNING to the Belize settlement itself, and to the opening years of the nineteenth century, we will now see how it made use of the new freedom and security won in the Battle of S. George's Cay. It is a remarkable record, and in many ways unique. The victory of 1798 was only the beginning of a still more exacting struggle on the part of the settlers to reap the full fruits of victory and to make it worth England's while to gather them into the Imperial fold—to promote the settlement, in fact, to the status of a fully integrated Colony within the British Commonwealth. Belize had been on probation, as it were, far too long; it was time the matter was settled one way or the other. The story of the nineteenth century, therefore, is one of hard work, enterprise, optimism, courage, and steadfast loyalty with this end in view. It is also a story with a happy ending, for the settlement got what it wanted and deserved.

Politically, the line taken from the beginning was that Belize had already achieved colonial status in fact if not in theory. The Superintendent, the Governor of Jamaica, and normally even the Home Government acted on this tacit supposition. Everything was done that could be done, short of actual Proclamation, to emphasize the British character of the settlement, to wipe out all memory of Spanish pretensions, and to encourage exclusively the British way of life.

One of the first outward and visible signs of a British Colony in those days was the establishment of the National Church. We have seen already that the buccaneers and their logwood-cutting descendants were probably, so far as they had any clear-cut religion at all, of the English Protestant faith. But the formal introduction of the Church of England seems to have been effected from the Mosquito Shore. As early as 1776 it is recorded in the *Archives* that 'At the request of the principal gentlemen in Belize, the Rev. R. Shaw (a missionary lately sent by the Society for the Propagation of the Gospel to Mosquito-land) preached among them, and after two or three Sundays they met and drew up a handsome Call to him, declaring that they had no other motive than a desire of having the Gospel preached in the Settlement'.[1] Shortly afterwards (1791) we read that 'Three Magistrates were appointed Trustees for the purpose of raising funds and making arrangements for building a public Place of Worship'.[2] The Napoleonic War intervened, however, and postponed the project for the time being.

At the time of the Battle of S. George's Cay we hear much of a Chaplain of the settlement, a Rev. William Stanford, who also came from the Mosquitos, and seems himself to have possessed somewhat of a sting. Just before the battle he had to be reprimanded for challenging the Superintendent to a duel![3] After the victory, however (November 11, 1799), we find him publicly thanked for his 'great exertions', so he must have had his good points too.[4] The following year nevertheless he was threatened with a court martial for 'insolence'.[5] Yet in 1803 he succeeded in organizing a public 'Memorial in favour of a Religious Establishment, and for the payment of £200 from Public Funds to the Officiating Clergyman for Divine Service in addition to Private Subscriptions.'[6] After retiring in 1807 to a house on the riverside called 'Isle of Erin' (was he Irish?), he was soon dug out again to serve as 'Rector of Honduras' and Police Magistrate, in virtue of which office he issued orders for the closing of all shops on Sundays and decent behaviour in the streets.[7] In Stanford's last appearance in the *Archives* (1809) we find him fiercely denouncing the Superintendent for wanting to live at Haulover, which in the Rector's opinion was 'too far away' from Belize.[8]

On his final retirement (1810), we read of a committee appointed by the Magistrates 'to enquire into the best method of obtaining a clergyman from England, and of building a church'.[9] As a result, the Rev. John Armstrong arrived in Belize in 1812, to find that work on the church, to be dedicated to S. John the Baptist, had already started.[10] Part of it was ready for use in 1815, when the first churchwardens were appointed, together with a clerk-schoolmaster.[11] The churchwardens soon made their presence

[1] *S.P.G. History*, 238. [2] Burdon, i, 194. [3] *Ibid.*, i, 240.
[4] *Ibid.*, i, 275. [5] *Ibid.*, i, 283. [6] *Ibid.*, ii, 62.
[7] *Ibid.*, ii, 121. [8] *Ibid.*, ii, 130. [9] *Ibid.*, ii, 144.
[10] *Ibid.*, ii, 154. [11] *Ibid.*, ii, 181.

felt, issuing an edict in 1816 that 'the pews on the East End of the church shall be solely appropriated to white and married persons, and no kept mistress shall be entitled to sit in any pew at that end of the church'.[1] That such a regulation was necessary seems to be confirmed by a perhaps unconsciously revealing epitaph in the public cemetery at Yarborough opened about this time: 'In Reverend Memory of George Hume, Mahogany Cutter and Bayman, but God-fearing.' In 1820 a steeple was erected on the church, but afterwards removed as too heavy for the structure.[2]

A certain Erastianism is evident in these early days of the Establishment, but the clergy do not seem to have truckled overmuch to the civil authorities. From about 1820 a Rev. William Gerrard, Rector of Belize, was criticized by the 'Quality' for taking more interest in ministering to the 'Lower Orders' than in conciliating his superiors. The Superintendent, Colonel Arthur, however, had the grace to appreciate the Rector's point of view, commending him to his successor in the Superintendency, General Pye, thus: 'The religious instruction of the slaves as well as of the adults of the lower class generally has been almost systematically opposed, but the moral effects which under the blessing of Divine Providence must eventually flow from the measures now in operation are so evident that I entreat your particular countenance to the support and maintenance of them. The Rev. Chaplain is by the express orders of the Earl of Bathurst placed under the Superintendent's protection, and of his zeal to enlighten the minds of the poorer class I cannot speak too highly.'[3] General Pye, however, seems to have formed a less favourable impression. Scarcely had he assumed office than he called a Public Meeting of the principal inhabitants in Belize at which the Rector was severely reprimanded, apparently for his 'enthusiastic' or evangelistic leanings, for it was resolved that henceforward 'the forms of Public Worship of the Established Church be strictly adhered to, and the Psalter of David be used in lieu of the Hymns hitherto adopted. Also that the former arrangement of the interior of the Church be restored'. The turbulent priest, however—how Stanford must have chuckled in his grave!—defiantly asserted his right to decide such matters for himself, and 'spoke slightingly of the Public Meeting'.[4] The correspondence between him and the Superintendent was submitted to the Bishop of London. The

[1] Burdon, ii, 184.   [2] Ibid., ii, 223.   [3] Ibid., ii, 258.   [4] Ibid., ii, 263.

Home Authorities, however, supported the Rector. On this and other accounts General Pye was recalled (1823), and the new Superintendent, General Codd, began his work by an appeal for a better temper all round, referring to 'past ebullitions of passion on the part of men in high stations who ought to have set example of moderation'.[1] Mr. Gerrard, however, resigned in the same year over a dispute about hymn tunes. It can be very hot in Belize![2]

The new Rector, the Rev. Nathan Newport, commenced duty in 1824, in which year Belize, hitherto under the Bishop of London, was formally annexed to the Diocese of Jamaica. The Church of S. John the Baptist, which had already been in use for some years, was consecrated by the Bishop of Jamaica on April 13, 1826.[3] His Lordship's visit to Belize on a subsequent occasion (April 16, 1830) was marred by an untoward incident. Some seamen had to be sentenced to five days in prison on bread and water, with an hour daily in the stocks, for 'bathing naked in the River as the Bishop of Jamaica and the Superintendent with their ladies were passing by'.[4]

The work of the Church went on apace from this time, being highly commended by the superintendents from time to time especially for its attention to the Negroes and emancipated slaves. In 1845 subscriptions were started for building a second church, S. Mary's over the River. This led to protests by the Presbyterians that the Church of England was receiving too large a share of State favour, and a Bill in Council was passed for the erection also of a Prebyterian Church, to be endowed out of public funds. The incomes of the various ministers of religion were fixed (1854) as follows: the Rector of S. John's, £600; the Rector of S. Mary's, £300; the Presbyterian Minister, £300—generous salaries for those days.

From about the middle of the century the position of the Church of England began to deteriorate, for two main reasons. The beneficial effects of the Establishment were now less noticeable than its interferences. Various superintendents claimed, as representatives of the King, to be Supreme Head of the Church in the Colony, with a decisive voice in clerical appointments, parochial boundaries, ministerial fees and salaries, clerical discipline, church building, and so forth—even to laying down the law on the question of High or Low Church, which by that time

[1] Burdon, ii, 271. [2] *Ibid.*, ii, 273. [3] *Ibid.*, ii, 291. [4] *Ibid.*, ii, 321.

had begun to agitate Anglicans all over the world. In 1855, for instance, the Superintendent pronounced that 'The predelictions of the people are decidedly evangelistic; an High Churchman as a Minister cannot be recommended'.[1] In 1857 he demanded that all incumbents of S. John's and S. Mary's must have obtained the Degree of M.A.[2] To this sort of thing the clerical climate of the day was distinctly antipathetic, and it became obvious that the Establishment had outlived its usefulness in Belize. Parallel with this was the rising tide of Dissent. Baptists, Methodists, Roman Catholics and others resented bitterly the Superintendent's refusal to recognize dissenting marriages; there was trouble about burials, places of worship, and so forth. In 1866 a committee appointed by the Superintendent reported on Public Expenditure on the Services of the Church of England and the Presbyterian Church thus: 'The members of those churches form but a fractional part of the community, and being richer than those who belong to the Roman Catholic, Methodist, and Baptist Churches (who not only sustain their own services but are forced by taxation to pay for the support of their richer brethren) there should be no hesitation to relieve the Public of this expenditure of $8600 p.a.'[3]

The Anglican and Presbyterian churches were accordingly disendowed (May 1, 1866) and finally disestablished in 1872.[4] In the latter year there was only one clergyman of the Church of England in the settlement, so Disestablishment could not have done it much harm. From this time, in fact, the Anglican ebb began to turn. The Colony became an accepted part of the missionary field, being supported particularly by the S.P.G. At length, in 1880, British Honduras was important enough in this respect to be made into a separate Diocese, the celebrated Bishop Tozer of Zanzibar being its first Bishop. This was towards the end of his arduous life, however, and ill-health compelled his resignation in the following year. No further episcopal appointment was made until 1891, when Bishop Holme was shipwrecked on the way to his See, and died of the effects. He was followed by Bishop Ormsby in 1893, since when the sequence has been unbroken, the record for long service being held by Bishop Arthur Dunn (1917 to 1943), who became Archbishop of the West Indian Province.

Mention has been made of the Negroes and Negro slaves in

[1] Burdon, iii, 183. [2] *Ibid.*, iii, 197. [3] *Ibid.*, iii, 268. [4] *Ibid.*, iii, 268, 325.

the settlement. Early in the nineteenth century the colour question began to be raised in the West Indies as an inevitable consequence of the liberal ideas of the French Revolution. In San Domingo (Hayti) events took a terrible turn with the ferocious Negro uprising of Toussaint l'Ouverture (1800), the first island in the New World to be colonized by Europeans being stained for a generation by nameless cruelties. The West Indies in general reacted to this by adopting a policy of oppression and even inhumanity towards the Negroes in their power. But British Honduras was an honourable exception. We have already noticed the traditional good-comradeship obtaining between the logwood-cutters and their slaves from the earliest days of the settlement. This attitude of mutual esteem, loyalty, and even affection had been greatly enhanced by the magnificent behaviour of the Negroes at S. George's Cay. It is pleasant to read Colonel Arthur's Report to the Foreign Office on this subject in 1816. He sets forth 'the kindness, liberality, and indulgent care of the wood cutters towards their Negroes, so that Slavery can hardly be said to exist in the Settlement, were it not for the very different attitude of a few unprincipled adventurers in Belize. The men work for their masters five days a week, Sunday being entirely their own and any labour on Saturday being paid $\frac{1}{2}$ dollar for, first by usage, latterly by law. The women are employed only for domestic purposes, and are exempt from work if they have young children. He had in no part of the world seen the labouring class of people possessing anything like the comforts of the Slave Population of Honduras'.[1] The *Archives* are full of such entries—commending the slaves, recognizing their rights, defending them against injustice. No crime was more severely punished than cruelty on the part of the whites against the slaves under their hand.

The 'Colour Bar' was never countenanced. A Report on the position in British Honduras in 1827 states that 'Two-thirds of the property in Honduras in land, slaves, and personalty belong to the Free Coloured Class, who enjoy privileges unknown to their brethren in other colonies. All classes white and brown mix in society, whereas in Jamaica the brown races are wholly excluded. The prejudice on account of Colour is at Honduras comparatively very small. The Coloured Class who preponderate both in number and wealth would never adopt any measures

[1] Burdon, ii, 187.

injurious to the interests of the Settlement. There should be no discrimination on account of Colour only.'[1] In 1831 an Act was passed formally 'equalizing the rights and privileges of all His Majesty's Coloured Subjects of Free Condition in the Settlement and their issue with British Subjects born of white parents'.[2] This has been the prevailing attitude on the Colour Question ever since.

This act of common sense and justice towards the Free Negroes preceded by only a few years the total emancipation of all slaves. It was followed in the meantime by a flat prohibition under any circumstances of the flogging of female slaves, as 'a punishment universally and justly held in abhorrence',[3] and by many similarly enlightened pronouncements preparing the way for emancipation. The Abolition of Slavery Act was put into force in Belize on August 1, 1834, with the happiest results. The Superintendent was able to report a year later that 'Since Abolition the Negroes perform their labour better and more cheerfully than ever before, and Emancipation has fulfilled the utmost hopes of its most sanguine supporters.'[4] The final instalment of Emancipation came four years later (1838) with the Abolition of 'Apprenticed' Labour. Negroes sat up all night, often alongside their masters, to watch the dawn of Liberty rise. When it came, it was 'celebrated by Divine Service and a Public Holiday. Immense crowds of apprentices met at the Court House and proceeded with banners to the Church, where an impressive Service was held. Yet all were back at work, after a day of festivity and rejoicing, the following morning'.[5] British Honduras has little to be ashamed of in her treatment of slaves or her attitude towards the Colour Bar.

Nor can the Colony be accused of other kinds of racial discrimination. There must be few countries of the West Indies which have shown themselves more hospitable to strangers than British Honduras. The Maya Indians may be mentioned first. Although presumably indigenous they had abandoned the Belize district long before the seventeenth century. Afterwards, however, hearing of the mild rule of the logwood-cutters as contrasted with Spanish arrogance and cruelty, they percolated over the frontiers from Mexico and Guatemala, in such large numbers that

[1] Burdon, ii, 300. [2] *Ibid.*, ii, 330. [3] *Ibid.*, ii, 327.
[4] *Ibid.*, ii, 377. [5] *Ibid.*, ii, 401.

to-day these Indians compose more than one-sixth of the total population, with a culture, industrial life, and a Reservation of their own. Next in numerical importance were the Carib Indians, the aboriginal inhabitants of the Windward Islands after whom the Caribbean Sea was named. At one time a ferocious race of cannibals, many of them were expelled from S. Vincent and Grenada at the beginning of the nineteenth century, and received, though with some hesitation on account of their known proclivities, into the settlement. 'The first group of 150, who settled in Stann Creek, proved to be so industrious and well-behaved that others were subsequently admitted' (1948 Report), and they now form a valued element in the population some 4000 strong. In 1814 all restraint on the admission of Jews to the settlement was withdrawn.[1] In the north of the Colony, especially around Corozal and Orange Walk, a large number of Spaniards took refuge after the Yucatan Indian raids in the middle of the century (of which more hereafter), and their descendants still predominate in those parts.

After the suppression of the Indian Mutiny (in India), Parliament transported 1000 Sepoy mutineers with their wives and families to the Colony (1858), where many hundreds of their descendants still remain.[2] The 500 Chinese indentured labourers who were brought over in 1865 were less fortunate, for 'most of them died of disease or overwork, or were seized by the wild Indians, or fled'.[3] Three years later, some Americans from the Southern States, refugees from the Yankee invasion of their homes, were allowed to settle in the Toledo district. At the end of hostilities, however, all but 500 of them returned to the States.[4] In the same year a number of Italians, fleeing from Guatemalan persecution, were allotted locations at Manattee. The racial medley includes even a body of 120 Syrians. There was also of course a steady flow of immigration from the over-populated islands of the West Indies, white and black. All these were welcomed with open arms by our warm-hearted Colony, and rapidly assimilated. They now compose its motley yet harmonious population of 60,000 souls.[5]

Such were some of the predominant aspects of the religious,

---

[1] Burdon, ii, 166. [2] *Ibid.*, iii, 201. [3] *Ibid.*, iii, 313, 315. [4] *Ibid.*, iii, 303.
[5] The recommendations of the Royal Commission of 1948 for a large-scale disposal of 'displaced persons' in British Honduras will at least have the backing of precedent!

social, and racial background of the growing settlement in the nineteenth century. We will now turn to the more material side of its development.

Shortly after the Treaty of Amiens, in 1802, war with Spain was renewed. But by this time the Spanish provinces in Central America were losing touch with their mother-country, and hostilities hardly spread to the Spanish Main. After the Battle of Trafalgar had established the supremacy of the British Navy in 1805 there could be no more danger by sea to our possessions in the West Indies. The War with America which suddenly broke out in 1812 did cause, however, a certain amount of apprehension in the settlement. Belize and its approaches were hastily fortified, a boom flung across the river, and look-outs placed among the cays. For a year or two the coast was infested by American privateers, quite after the old style, who interfered with shipping and occasionally landed raiding parties ashore. But the capture of the principal American man-of-war, the *Chesapeake*, by H.M.S. *Shannon* in 1814 put an effectual end to this nuisance. Enemy action between the two great English-speaking nations had never been taken very seriously, and shortly afterwards this wasteful and unnecessary war was concluded by the Treaty of Ghent.

In the meantime, it had become evident that the days of the Spanish Empire in Central America were numbered. After Hidalgo's abortive but infectious declaration of Mexican independence in 1810, Yucatan was too busy with her own affairs to interfere any more in those of Belize. Spanish raids, which by river, sea, and land had disturbed the peace of the Colony for over a hundred years, now ceased, greatly to the advantage of British trade and progress. The Colony benefited, too, by the added prestige accruing to all things British after the victory of Waterloo (1815), and by the deterioration in Spanish-American morale resulting from the failure of the Mexican Emperor Iturbide (1821–23) to unite the jarring states. Internecine strife among the new Republics—Mexico, Guatemala, El Salvador, Spanish Honduras, Nicaragua, Costa Rica, Panama—engrossed their attention and dissipated their strength, but seldom overlapped into Belize, secure under the ægis of her British nationality, and seeking her markets not inland but overseas. On the frontiers a certain amount of trouble with excited slaves was fomented by the Spanish, amounting at times to mutiny or even concerted revolt, but these were mere pin-pricks, and easily dealt with.

More irritating and damaging were the exploits of many amateur privateers or pirates who seized the opportunity of Central American chaos to harry the Spanish coasts, and who were not over-particular about interfering with British shipping. The buccaneering tradition died hard in this part of the world. In 1822, for example, the Belize Magistrates had to equip and send out a couple of armed vessels to deal with a pirate who had eluded a man-of-war off Glover's Reef, and had started to plunder the settlements on Calabash Cay. In the following year the notorious pirate Laffite wrought a great deal of havoc among small ships in the bay, and, when pursued, succeeded in decoying H.M.S. *Revenge* on to a sunken reef. The cays and bush-hidden inlets on the coast made irresistible lairs for such highwaymen of the sea in days when the Colony's territory was more than half unexplored. As late as 1826 the *Archives* record the 'smoking-out' of a nest of freebooters on Sapodilla Cay, almost on the doorstep of Belize. The settlers themselves, however, had lost all taste for buccaneering by this time, and scarcely remembered their own somewhat similar exploits in the far-off seventeenth century. A determined effort was made to police the shores, and the episode of 1826 recorded above seems to have been the last of its kind.

By 1823, with the creation of a Spanish Federation of Republics, some sort of a pattern in Central American politics began to emerge, and the territorial status of the British colony once more to be questioned, especially as the United States now showed a personal interest in the matter. The American Monroe Doctrine of that year (warning all European Powers to keep out of the Americas) had explicitly excluded the Belize settlement from its scope, but Mexico was not so accommodating. Negotiations between the now democratic Mexican and the British Governments led in 1826 to an Anglo-Mexican Treaty in which Great Britain 'recognized' the independence of the young Republic in exchange for Mexico's recognition of the ancient settlement's territorial rights. A more detailed account of the situation will be given in Chapter XIV. Here it will suffice to say that Guatemala, whose frontier adjoined that of Belize on the west, denied the validity of the Mexican pact. The old annoyance of Spanish pin-pricking was renewed. Negro slaves were decoyed into El Peten by promises of emancipation and lucrative employment. Guatemala even threatened war, menacing the British settlements on the River Sibun by a gunboat in 1827. The Baymen were encouraged by the Home Government to resist such aggression 'by force if necessary', and Jamaica sent immediate military and naval assistance.[1] Guatemala's pretensions to ownership of the Colony seemed too ridiculous for argument. The days had gone by when British diplomacy was ready to concede any Spanish territorial rights in Belize, least of all those of Guatemala. When about this time the republic impudently allotted land in the Sibun River area to a commercial concern, the British Government bluntly denounced it as 'a deliberate and insidious encroachment on British sovereignty', and the scheme was quickly scotched.[2]

By this time the Home Government was beginning to look upon the thriving settlement with new eyes, not only for its commercial, but also for its possibly strategic importance in the western Caribbean. It was deemed opportune to promote it. Accordingly in 1840 Her Majesty approved the appointment of an Executive Council to assist the Superintendent in the administration of its affairs, and a few months later issued a Royal Proclamation ordaining that 'the law of England is and shall be the Law of this Settlement or Colony of British Honduras'.[3] This was the first time the title of Colony or of British Honduras had been officially used, and it became clear that full colonial status was only a matter of time.

At this juncture the United States, with the project of a trans-Isthmian canal solidifying, intervened in Central American politics with her insistence on the Clayton-Bulwer Treaty of 1850, applying (in effect) the Monroe Doctrine to Central America. Great Britain was careful, however, to ensure that Belize was not included in the restrictions, as we have seen, and America, appreciating the antiquity of the settlement and our determination to hold it, acquiesced. At this time, it will be remembered, the question of our holding in Belize was closely interlocked with that of the Mosquito Shore and our newly created Bay Island Colony. Finding that we were prepared to surrender our claims in the two latter respects, in the Dallas-Clarendon Treaty of 1856 America agreed to confirm, and even to extend, our territorial

[1] Burdon, ii, 297. [2] Ibid., ii, 366. [3] Ibid., ii, 411.

boundaries in British Honduras. She now conceded that the southern limit of the Colony should be fixed at the River Sarstoon, instead of as hitherto at the Sibun, it being assumed that the Spanish-American Republics for their part would raise no objection, in view of the considerable moral and financial support they had received from the States in their controversies with Great Britain.

By this agreement the area of British Honduras was almost doubled, being now 8600 square miles, or about equal to that of Wales or Palestine, and twice that of Jamaica, the largest island in the British West Indies. Thus it came to pass that the logwood settlement, which had commenced with the Belize River banks in 1640, had afterwards extended to the New River, and then in 1786 to the Rio Hondo on the north and the Sibun River on the south, now (1856) reached its furthest southern frontier on the obviously natural dividing line between Guatemala and the Toledo district, namely the River Sarstoon, where it has remained ever since. To the west the boundary was more indeterminate, stretching roughly in a vertical north-south line from Garbutt's Falls just west of Benque Viejo to the Gracias à Dios Rapids on the upper Sarstoon.

A few years later, in 1859, the Republic of Guatemala confirmed this agreement in the Anglo-Guatemalan Treaty of 1859, which still governs the diplomatic situation, for a subsequent convention drawn up in 1863 was never ratified.

Shortly after this settlement with Guatemala, the long-deferred hope and ambition of the inhabitants was at last fulfilled. In 1862 the territory was officially gazetted as a British Colony *de jure* as well as *de facto*, with the title of British Honduras—to contrast it with the Republic of Honduras, sometimes called Spanish Honduras, further south. By this measure Sir Frederick Seymour was to be addressed no longer merely as Superintendent of the settlement of Belize, but as Governor of the Colony. A further honour awaited it: in 1871 Her Majesty Queen Victoria accorded it the status of a full Crown Colony of the Empire. In 1884 the final maturity of the Colony was proclaimed by Letters Patent conferring the title of Excellency, Governor, and Commander-in-Chief upon the Crown's representative in Belize, and so freeing it completely from the last traces of dependence upon Jamaica. The Governor ruled in accordance with a Constitution bestowed upon the Colony in 1871, when a Legislative Council of five official and four unofficial nominated members was established. In 1892, after a dispute with the Governor, the Constitution was modified. The Council then consisted of three ex-officio and five nominated members, still with the Governor as President. The alteration was intended as a response to the insistent demand, so characteristic of the settlers from the earliest times, for a democratic 'say' in the government of their Colony. For the time being it satisfied popular opinion, and the Constitution remained thus established up to the end of the century, although, as we shall see, in the following century the Constitution would again become a matter of complaint and discussion, and go through still further modifications.

All this political activity—the legal creation of the Colony, its elevation to a Crown Colony, and its ultimate recognized independence with a Governor and Legislature of its own—was extremely interesting and gratifying to the authorities and the 'governing classes' in Belize. But it was far above the heads of the man-in-the-street, in the dorey, or on the river 'banks', who had long taken it for granted that he was a Colonial by rights, if not by right.

There were other developments, however, also of a semi-political nature, which had more immediate repercussions on the life and commerce of the Colony. Since the break-up of the Spanish Empire and the relaxation of control by Madrid, Central America had become a boiling cauldron of revolutions, internecine strife, and personal vendettas. For the most part, the tides of bloodshed and burnings had swept past the British settlement without affecting it. The *Archives* of the Colony in the first half of the century barely allude to these eruptions of the Spanish world around. But long-suppressed nationalistic ambitions and resentments had been revived, and in 1848 the Colony suddenly heard the tocsin of war from an entirely unexpected quarter. A large force of some 10,000 'Wild Indians' from Santa Cruz, in Southern Yucatan, descendants of the Mayas, rose in revolt against their Mexican masters, with the object of wresting the Land of their Fathers from the oppressive clutch of Spain. Armed chiefly with bows and arrows they took Bacalar by storm, and burnt it to the ground. Upon this, the Superintendent of Belize—heaping coals of fire on his traditional enemy's head—sent H.M.S. *Vixen* with a number of British troops to the assistance of the Governor of Yucatan, and imposed a truce for negotiations.[1] All might have ended happily had not the Spanish soldiers broken the truce, and so renewed a 'war' that was to last for over twenty years, involving much loss of life and property, as well as interference with the economic development of the Colony. At this time the new town of Corozal was founded, just south of the Rio Hondo in British territory, largely by refugees from the massacre of Bacalar, bringing with them the sugar industry, which was soon to prove so valuable a product in the Colony.

After sporadic raids of a minor nature, Indian disaffection came to a head once more in 1857—the Yucatan Indian Mutiny thus coinciding almost exactly with the Indian Mutiny at Cawnpore. In that year a force of Chinchenha Indians massacred 1800 Spaniards at Tekax, as well as 16 British subjects south of the Rio Hondo. Bacalar was seized again, its streets being littered with dead. President Carrera of Guatemala, himself a full-blooded Indian, feared a general uprising of the Mayas throughout Central America. Thousands of bloodthirsty braves crossed the Rio Hondo into British Honduras, menacing Corozal, Orange Walk, and the New River settlements as far south as Spanish Creek and Young Gal. British envoys sent to negotiate were grossly maltreated at the Temple of the Speaking Cross. Year after year went by without a decision, the Indians being easily able to hide away in the bush when pursued. In 1864 the town of Corozal was raided, 3 British being killed out of hand and 24 kidnapped. The Indian Chief Canul, anticipating the methods of the Chicago gangsters in our own day, extorted heavy payments in return for 'protection', as well as a ransom of $12,000 for his captives. In 1866 a British force was ambushed and put to flight, with the loss of its equipment. Canul was defeated in the following year by a stronger force, rocket-tubes being in action for the first time, but was able very soon to renew his surprise attacks on the settlers up and down the New River district.[2] Corozal, where a new church had recently been erected by the S.P.G., and a strong British trading centre established, suffered worst and most frequently, despite almost continuous appeals for a garrison and frontier guards. In 1870 the town was again captured, and held to ransom by a mob of Ycaiche Indians under Canul. An assault

[1] Burdon, iii, 107. [2] *Ibid.*, iii, 283.

on Belize itself seemed imminent. Only on the dispatch of H.M.S. *Lapwing* from Nassau with a strong detachment of troops did the Indians melt away—but undefeated.[1]

Canul soon returned to the offensive. The raids and burnings continued until commercial and industrial progress in the north of the Colony came virtually to a standstill, and every settlement had to stand perpetually under arms. In 1872 the Indians again crossed the Rio Hondo for a determined attack upon Orange Walk, August Pine Ridge and Water Bank.[2] At Orange Walk the small British garrison of 38 men was driven to take shelter within its log-cabin barracks. The Indians set fire to it, but a desperate sally by the troops, despite the collapse of their officer severely wounded, drove them off, and by good fortune killed the dangerous Canul himself. By this small but decisive action the so-called 'War of Colours' came to an end, after lasting spasmodically from 1848 to 1872. The next we hear of Indians crossing over into British Honduras is in 1874, when they are reported as unarmed, starving, and begging only for bread.[3]

In the meantime, despite all these excursions and alarms, the economic prosperity of the settlement had increased by leaps and bounds. In those days there were no elaborate Royal Commissions, nor grants-in-aid of colonial development, at any rate as far as British Honduras was concerned, no Lend-Lease, or other loans. We have seen already that even military assistance had often to be paid for by the inhabitants, nor had they been able always to rely on diplomatic support. All through the nineteenth century there were no roads in the Colony beyond rough tracks liable to seasonal flooding, no bridges except in Belize itself, no canals (the invaluable Burdon Canal came later), no railways of course, and no deep-water harbours. All transport of merchandise had to be effected by mule or human pack-carriers, or by man-propelled boats, pit-pans (flat-bottomed barges) and doreys (hollowed-out canoes), making use of the innumerable rivers and creeks—the former barely navigable owing to rapids and 'top-gallant' floods, the latter frequently blocked by solid masses of water-weeds. As to the harbourage, to this day everything at Belize has to be shipped at the quayside into shallow pit-pans, for there is no draught of water for ocean-going ships nearer

[1] Burdon, iii, 320. [2] *Ibid.*, iii, 327. [3] *Ibid.*, iii, 334.

than a mile off shore.[1] In addition to this there were all the discomforts of tropical life, then little mitigated by science or sanitation. Yellow fever, island fever, blackwater fever and malaria were a persistent scourge, as any one who scrutinizes the monuments in Belize Cathedral will realize. Under such circumstances it is amazing that the Colony was able to do business at all.

Yet exports of logwood rose from 700 tons at the beginning of the century to a maximum of 35,000 tons in 1896. Exports of mahogany increased from 2000 feet in 1800 to 14,000 in the middle of the century, partly owing to the railway boom in England at that period. Chicle, which is the sap of the sapodilla-tree used in chewing-gum, started late, but by the beginning of the twentieth century had become an important export of 2,000,000 tons per annum. Another late-comer was the banana, of which over 400,000 stems were exported at the end of our period. There were also valuable exports of sugar, rum, coconut, oranges, tobacco, cassava, cohune oil, cedar, rosewood, tortoise-shell, shark-leather, and the celebrated sponges of Turneffe. At the beginning of the century the population had been estimated as less than 4000: at the end of it there were 40,000 inhabitants, 12,000 of them in the now considerable city of Belize. Thus the Colony had more than justified its existence by the end of the century, and that with little more material assistance than the provision of British shipping facilities and markets for the disposal of its produce, followed later by similar encouragement on the part of the United States.

Such was the varied, colourful, and often tumultuous background of the Colony's progress during the nineteenth century. At the beginning of it nothing but her stubborn foot on the threshold had prevented the door from being slammed for ever in her face. The possibility of her being engulfed in the rising tide of Spanish Americanism had been very real. But by the end of it she had butted her way through all the opposition of her enemies and the indifference of her friends to the proved position of a valued outpost of Empire, a Colony in her own right, well populated, twice her original size, commercially prosperous, proudly confident in her destiny, and passionately loyal.

There is no accounting for loyalty in these affairs. Sometimes the children on whom has been lavished the most unstinted care

[1] The more southerly jetties and piers, however, are rather better placed.

have turned against the Motherland for no apparent cause. It must be confessed that England, or at any rate British officialdom, had deserved little of this tiny slice of Empire in the far west of the world. Yet the Bayman of Belize, 'in spite of all temptations to belong to other nations had remained an Englishman', and when at long last Queen Victoria brought new hope to the Colony, stretching out to it a helping and appreciative hand, she soon found that she had no more loyal subjects in her realm than the citizens of British Honduras. The official Report on the Colony presented by the Colonial Secretary of Belize in 1901 undoubtedly reflects the general attitude of his people to the Crown at the end of the century: 'The death of Queen Victoria was as much felt here as in any of Her Majesty's other Colonial possessions. It is probable that no ruler has ever hitherto succeeded in casting so strong a spell on her subjects dwelling thousands of miles beyond the seas. Confidence in her justice and beneficence was so great that it had become an implicit and unreasoning article of faith that nothing could emanate from her but what was good, wise, and kindly. The accession of King Edward was celebrated here with becoming ceremony, and His Majesty succeeded to a throne held in reverence and profound respect and love by all classes of his colonial subjects.'

Chapter XI

*

FROM HEYDAY TO HARD TIMES

THE dawn of the twentieth century flooded the white verandas of the Belize waterfront with a rosy glow of confidence in the achievements of the past and hope for still better things in store. The Colony was now undeniably thriving. All the world, or at any rate the English-speaking part of it, was bathed in the same sunshine. Apart from a few minor clashes of arms, romantic, picturesque, and pleasantly exciting, but confined chiefly to professionals, the onward surge of civilization had been retarded by no important war for nearly a generation—indeed, if we are to judge by modern standards in such affairs, for nearly a century. Peace had become a habit, plenty was only just round the corner, optimism the order of the day. History, philosophy, science, religion all agreed on the inevitability of progress. It was a law of Nature, proved every day before men's eyes by the spread of the British Empire, and the growing prosperity of every country which opened its markets to British trade.

It was proved in particular by the trade returns of British Honduras. The progress which had been so marked under the beneficent rule of the great Queen had more than retained its impetus under her energetic successor. The annual Colonial Office Reports of the Edwardian period are enough to make the heart of any lover of Honduras burn within him, and to puff the breasts of all who still remember those halcyon days (only forty years ago!) with nostalgic sighs. The prevalent note in these old Reports, straight from the mouth of the Colony's Secretary in Belize, is one of almost lyrical content: 'Abnormal increase in the output of the woodcutting industry . . . a year of great prosperity . . . the tide of prosperity which commenced last year continued unabated . . . the Government revenues increased, and the substantial surplus of $125,464 remained at the end of the year' (1903). 'It may safely be predicted that in the course of time, when exploited by capital, the Colony will hold its own as a rich possession of His Majesty' (1904). 'Another prosperous year, with a great demand for labour, and wages high' (1910). 'The year has been one of increased prosperity. The export of bananas and coconuts was higher than it had ever been before' (1912). And so on, up to the very eve of the First World War, when the Report states that 'At the beginning of the year everything pointed to an exceptionally good trade year, and this is borne out by the actual figures. For the first seven months of the year these were better (for exports) by 54 per cent. than the corresponding period of the preceding year' (1914). The year before the War, in fact, made an all high record for the Colony's commercial prosperity.

The invasion of Belgium put an end to all that, of course, as it did to a good many other pleasant things. But in the case of British Honduras the clock was set back, as we shall see, only for a time, and the truly tropical resilience of the Colony under its many blows was once more to be abundantly proved. In the meanwhile, however, let us quote the actual figures of those wonderful years 'before the War'. We have no intention of allowing this chapter to degenerate into a dull catena of statistics, but there are occasions when figures speak louder than words. Here they are:

TRADE FIGURES BEFORE 1914
(In multiples of 10,000 dollars)

	EXPORTS	IMPORTS
1899.	127	103
1900.	130	119
1901.	138	122
1902.	136	122
1903.	185	177
1904.	186	175
1905.	183	187
1906.	201	220 (doubled)
1907.	221	241
1908.	220	267
1909.	220	270
1910.	234	281
1911.	265 (doubled)	288
1912.	285	349 (trebled)
1913.	312	318

It will be seen at a glance that in eleven years, 1899 to 1911, the value of the Colony's exports more than doubled at a time when prices were fairly stable throughout the world. After 1911 it continued to increase even more steeply right up to the War. It will be noted that in the first six years of this period the exports greatly exceeded the imports, showing that the Colony was saving more than it spent, so far as foreign trade was concerned. Yet it was no unhealthy sign when the value of the imports began in 1905 to exceed that of the exports, for it implied that outside capital was beginning to flow into the country, and that the standard of life was rising, in either case greatly to the advantage of the Colonial Exchequer. It must also be noted that many of these imports were in transport through the country on their way to re-exportation abroad. The chief articles of import at this period were manufactured goods like furniture, haberdashery, millinery, hardware, hats, machinery, oil, liquors, clothing; but even in those days there was a large amount of food (including tinned milk) imported into the Colony, somewhat to the discontent of far-sighted observers, who felt that so fertile a country should be self-supporting in this respect. However, most able-bodied workers were too busy reaping the natural harvests of timber, bananas, and so forth to spare time for agriculture—an employment which had always been somewhat despised as servile or unmanly, compared with wielding an axe.

Of the products in which the Colony did such a roaring trade with the United States, Great Britain, Europe, and Central America, the most important was still the timber from her almost inexhaustible forests, as it had been through the centuries.

Logwood, the oldest of them all, may be mentioned first. Although it had long ceased to be of prime importance, the market for this wood had by no means completely closed. In most countries dyeworkers were now relying more and more on the new aniline dyes, but some of them—France and Russia in particular—still clung to logwood, so that in 1899 British Honduras was able to sell as much as 24,000 tons of it, to the value of 550 thousand dollars—no mean sum for these days. The trade, however, dwindled steadily thereafter, until in 1913 only 3600 tons were exported. It was evidently not on its original *raison d'être* that Belize could depend to make its fortune.

As to mahogany, at the beginning of the century there was

much anxiety about its future. The colossal sales of this tough and beautiful wood in the palmy days of wooden ships, railway coaches, and Victorian furniture had tempted too much capital into the business and too reckless a felling of the trees. This had resulted in the deforestation of the main river banks, which in turn caused a steep rise in the cost of haulage from cuttings at a distance from the stream: the demand for more and more skilled labour meant higher wages and a relaxation of discipline: huge stocks of logs accumulated: to darken the scene still further, West Africa had now entered the European market as a competitor: prices dropped catastrophically, and three large mahogany companies went bankrupt in a single year. In terms of figures, the decline in mahogany exports in two successive years, 1902 and 1903, had amounted to nearly two million feet each year, and only the very finest woods had any chance of sale at all.

Suddenly all this was changed. The unforeseen entry of the United States into the market, a *nouveau riche* country with too many dollars chasing too few goods, made all the difference, especially since their mahogany concessions in Mexico were on the point of expiring. Almost overnight, the slump was converted into a boom. Every log which could be floated down to the barcadero in Belize was sure of a place in American holds. The quantity of export soared from the six million feet of 1899 to over sixteen million feet in 1914, with prices continually on the upgrade.

The chief difficulty was now the transportation of the heavy logs. It was bad enough dragging them down by rough mahogany wagons drawn by mule or bullock to the river-side, but it became quite impossible when long-lasting droughts reduced the flow of water in the shallows between El Cayo and Belize. To improve the river in this respect became essential, and persistent efforts were made during these early years of the century to clear the bed of rocks and other obstructions. In 1905, for example, a mass of granite was blown up at Little Falls, and downstream the river was greatly widened at the Narrows near Haulover. In the following year the Belize River was so transformed that for the first time it became possible for a loaded power-launch to proceed from El Cayo to the sea without check, and a journey which used to take ten to thirty days (for a hundred miles!) could now be performed under favourable circumstances in twenty-seven hours. Nothing could be done to prevent the droughts, of course, but an up-to-date steam-dredger deepened the bed of the river, and in 1910 a long overdue improvement was made in the water approaches to Belize by the dredging of the silted bed above the harbour, 'so that we no longer have the sight of a dozen lighters at a time stuck on the bar'.

In the following year the same dredger was employed to reclaim the swampy ground where historic Fort George had once stood, a number of acres of firm building land being thus added to the growing city. Communications were greatly facilitated by the installation in 1910 of a telephone, primitive but effective, connecting Belize via various river-side villages to El Cayo. Anyone who has waited on the bank of a tropical stream for the arrival of an untimed, unscheduled, utterly problematical boat without being able to communicate in any way with any possible port of call, up or down the river, will appreciate what this telephone meant to the mahogany and other workers in the interior.[1]

Mahogany was not the only valuable timber exported in these years. The cedar of British Honduras is of a particularly fine quality, and was soon discovered to be so by the many cigar-making firms in Havana and the southern States. Enterprising Americans saved a great deal of time and money by installing steam-sawmills in the Colony, buying the untrimmed cedar logs from the cutters, and themselves preparing them for transport. During the years before the War, the export of cedar mounted from 350 thousand feet to two and three-quarter million feet (1913), chiefly for the American market. There were also small experimental sales of banak (for cigar-boxes), as well as of pine, rosewood, and other timbers.

But by this time there were other important industries in the Colony besides forestry. Coconut palms grow easily along the coast and on the cays, and are unusually fruitful. In the years before the War, the coconut and copra trade steadily grew. Between 1899 and 1913, to give the figures, the export of coconuts increased from two and three-quarter million nuts to over six and a half million.

At the beginning of the century bananas were almost unknown

---

[1] The first telephone, however, had already been laid on locally in Belize, and from Belize to Punta Gorda in 1903.

in England, and very few of them seem to have reached that country from British Honduras before the War. Exports of this fruit to the United States, however, jumped up quickly in these years from 273 thousand stems (bunches) in 1899 to 470 thousand in 1913. The chief banana-growing district was around Stann Creek, and such were the prospects of the trade (now listed among the Colony's 'principal exports') that in 1906 it was decided to build a railway—the first and only railway in British Honduras —from the banana station of Middlesex twenty-five miles inland to Stann Creek on the Caribbean and the jetty at Commerce Bight. As this was too costly and important a work to be left to private enterprise, the Belize Government advanced the capital, confident of recouping it through freight duties on the railway and higher land taxes on the plantations adjoining the track. Expert labourers were imported from Jamaica, incipient strikes and violence quickly suppressed by the newly recruited Volunteer Force of the Colony, sanitary measures taken against malaria and yellow fever, and at last, on October 17, 1908, the new railway (the first fifteen miles of it being completed) was opened in state, together with a new pier of reinforced concrete at Commerce Bight. The steamship *City of Belize*, bedecked with bunting, moored safely at the quayside, forty of the Colony's leading citizens stepped on to the waiting cars, enjoyed the thrill of a journey up and down the line, and returned to the city the same evening.

Among those present on this auspicious occasion was the new Bishop of Belize, the Righ Rev. Dr. Bury, who forthwith wrote an enthusiastic description of the Diocese entitled *A Bishop among the Bananas* (1909), which was actually (we think) the first popular book on the Colony ever published.[1]

The work of extending and improving the cultivation of bananas was taken over by the celebrated United Fruit Company (Elder & Fyffe) of America, than which no more capable or experienced company of banana experts could be found. The White Fleet of 5000-ton specially equipped banana boats began to call at Stann Creek on the way from Bocas del Toro to New Orleans from 1908 onwards. With the consumption of bananas

[1] The first *Handbook on British Honduras* was that of W. A. Morris, published in 1883, but it was soon completely out of date, and had no successor till that of Metzgen and Cain appeared in 1925. Sir John Burdon greatly improved on this in his *Brief Sketch of British Honduras* (1927) and this in turn has been finally revised and brought up to date by A. H. Anderson's really excellent *Handbook* of 1949.

FROM HEYDAY TO HARD TIMES 143

increasing everywhere, the prospects of the Colony's 'Green Gold' bringing great prosperity to the Treasury seemed bright indeed. And so, up to the outbreak of the War, it proved. Year by year the export of bananas showed a 'gratifying increase', until by 1914 it had mounted to 673 thousand stems as compared with the 273 thousand of ten years earlier. This involved not only a satisfactory flow of dues and taxes into the Colonial Exchequer, but a great increase in the amenities of the district; for the United Fruit Company never stints its employees in the provision, as fas as possible, of an environment which makes for social intercourse and content.

The export of plantains, a coarser, hardier variety of the banana, very popular in the New World as a vegetable, enjoyed an even more spectacular increase—from a million and a half plantains in 1900 to nearly three and a half million in 1912. Being easier to grow and to transport, it even became a rival in some places to its more delicate sister.

Another product which showed an enormous increase in these years was chicle. Much of this was gathered, or 'bled', in the forests of Peten across the Guatemalan border beyond Benque Viejo, being shipped downstream from El Cayo to Belize for re-export, so that the whole credit for the increase in chicle exports cannot be claimed by British Honduras. Yet transport duties brought increased profits to the Exchequer, and aided in the remarkable progress which was now being made in every direction. The number of pounds weight of chicle exported from Belize rose from 260 thousand in 1899 to nearly three and a half million in 1914, the bulk of it going at this time, of course, to the United States.

Sugar-cane at the beginning of the century was grown on a very small scale for local consumption only, although a little of it was available for export in the form of rum. From 1905, however, the export of sugar and rum began to increase, several modern cane-crushing factories and distilleries being erected, especially in the Corozal and Orange Walk districts. By 1913 the Colony was exporting 15 thousand gallons of rum, and 123 thousand pounds weight of raw sugar.

Similar encouraging increases were reported in all the other traditional industries of the Colony, with the exception (already noted) of logwood. Cacao, cassava, sarsaparilla, rubber, sponges, tortoise-shell, shark-skin, alligator-hide each made their contribution. Satisfactory progress was made in the experimental planting of oranges, limes, and the new grapefruit, now a popular feature on American breakfast-tables. The harvesting of cohune nuts (for their oil) had already begun on a small scale, and a cracking mill had been set up.

Everything was going steadily up—exports, imports, profits, wages, and revenue. Labour was in short supply, but not extortionate in its demands: employers could afford to be generous, but not to presume on necessity: unemployment was unknown, except of course among those who preferred that state of life. The standard of education, of housing, and of medical facilities was low, it is true, but it was nobody's fault, and there were few complaints. Moreover, the Government was visibly trying to cope with the more pressing problems of the day. Vital statistics showed steady improvement, epidemics had become increasingly less frequent and more quickly controlled. Five hospitals were equipped up and down the Colony, not counting the Mental Asylum and the Poor House Sanatorium, and many schools were set up by the various religious bodies, on whose initiation in education the Government still preferred to rely.

As to the revenue, this had naturally increased *pari passu* with trade. In 1900 it had amounted to a 'Grand Total' of 325 thousand dollars: by 1913 this had almost doubled—to 643 thousand. At the end of the financial year (April) in 1912 the surplus on the general revenue account was actually larger than the whole of that original Grand Total of 1900—it was 342 thousand dollars. All this had accrued through various excise duties, import duties, profits on Government enterprises, local taxes, and a very low land tax. There was no income tax before the War. Expenditure of course, had correspondingly increased. In 1900 it had been no more than 246 thousand dollars: by 1913 it had grown to 659 thousand, which was somewhat in excess of income for that year. But in this case the over-expenditure was a sign of vitality, being devoted largely to capital development which could be relied upon (except in unforeseen circumstances) to pay handsome dividends. Thus out of that 659 thousand dollars expenditure in 1913, nearly 200 thousand dollars went to the Stann Creek Railway and other public works. The only debts of the Colony were local loans, chiefly for the improvement of the city of

Belize, provision for their repayment being amply made by the investment of sinking funds.

Such facts and figures show that the buoyant optimism of those early years of the century was no romantic chimera, but the reasoned calculation of hard-working, hard-headed business men, who saw in British Honduras a little Eldorado waiting to be more thoroughly explored. They were no fools. Even in the heyday of easy success, those responsible for administering the Colony were alert to certain danger signs, and full of plans to meet them. Few of the bright suggestions made by various official commissions of our own day but were anticipated by those early Edwardians. The importance of making the Colony agriculturally self-supporting—the need for more and better-quality live stock, poultry, farm and garden produce—the necessity, if such developments were to be made, of more and better roads and harbour facilities, all this was understood. The excessive imports of foodstuffs were regretted—the increasing tendency of trade to shift from Great Britain to the United States—the poor standards of education and of housing—the moral and economic peril involved in the traditional pursuit of seasonal trades—the inadequacy of the water supply—the primitive arrangements for sanitation—the disease-carrying propensities of mosquitoes and land crabs—these and many other points were as acutely realized and recorded in the official reports of British Honduras from 1900 to 1914 as they are in those of the nineteen-forties. In one respect, it must be admitted, the authorities in Belize were a little old-fashioned: they omitted to ask for financial help from the Mother Country, over-confident, perhaps, that they could compass all difficulties by their own unaided efforts. Thus when for the first time a Colonial Office Commission paid them a visit for the purpose of 'discussing the development of the Colony', and subsequently issued the first Colonial Office Report on British Honduras (in 1904), they were not disappointed when nothing further came of it. And, judging by the progress already made, there is little doubt that the Colony would have gone from strength to strength under its own steam, working out its own salvation in its own way, had it not been for the War.

Two great enemies of progress they made special efforts to control—Fever and Fire. Once upon a time British Honduras had been known as one of the 'White Man's Graves' of the tropical world. Anyone visiting Belize Cathedral and reading the pathetic memorial tablets plastering its walls will realize how short in the nineteenth century must have been the expectation of life for Europeans. Malaria was a great scourge, but the most fatal of all was yellow fever. Almost the first tablet one sees on entering the Cathedral is a memorial to the daughter of the then Governor, Sweet-Escott: she died of yellow fever at the age of seventeen in 1905. In that year a terrible epidemic swept the Colony, and forced the authorities to take drastic measures to prevent its repetition. Various new methods of dealing with the plague-carrying mosquitoes had been learnt from the experience of the new Panama Canal workings, and these were put into operation in Belize. From that year the Vital Statistics show a steady improvement.

As to the danger of fire, it can readily be appreciated how serious this may be in a tropical town with mostly wooden buildings. Two destructive fires in 1909 and 1910, involving loss of life, led to the formation of trained fire brigades with modern steam fire-engines, which at once minimized and localized, though they could not entirely check, future outbreaks.

On the political side, a great improvement in the administration of the capital, and one which suited well the traditionally democratic leanings of the Colony, was the inauguration in 1912 of the Belize Town Board—the equivalent of a Borough Council. The day of the first election of members, November 22, was celebrated by a public holiday, 'observed by all with great enthusiasm and healthy interest'. In the same year the mercantile community felt that a great deal of prestige had been added to their business dealings when the Royal Bank of Canada opened a branch in the capital.

During all these happy and prosperous years, despite increasing dependence on commerce with the United States, the loyalty of the Colony to the British Crown, so feelingly expressed at the death of Queen Victoria, continued unabated. The inhabitants, white and coloured, were proud to call themselves British subjects: conversely, British traders, officials, clergy, teachers, and the like were proud to serve in British Honduras. The census of 1911 revealed that, notwithstanding the great influx of nationals from other countries, 'the personnel of the Colony was more British than ever. During the decade our own people have not left us, and although the rush of labour to the Panama Canal has retarded progress, it has not set the Colony back'.[1] In that year a detachment of the Honduras Volunteers was dispatched at the Colony's charges to attend the Coronation of King George V, amid great enthusiasm at the quayside.

Alas! on that happy note the song of peace and progress was suddenly dashed from the Colony's lips by the 'Kaiser's War', never again to be taken up with quite the same verve and confidence. For nearly a decade, from August 1914 onwards, British Honduras along with the rest of the Empire had the mortification of seeing her painfully accumulated treasure frittered away on destruction, her energies diverted from building up to tearing down. There is no need to go into statistical detail. The products of the Colony were not such as could claim priority in the War Effort. In any case, the lack of shipping made it impossible to move them. Trade, which in the first half of 1914 had been 54 per cent. better than in the corresponding period of the previous year, quickly declined to zero. Since the inhabitants had long formed the habit of importing most of their food from abroad, they now found themselves threatened with real privation, and the price of such food as could be grown within the country naturally rocketed, just at a time when unemployment and wage reductions became the order of the day. The Government did its best by loans for public works and grants in relief of destitution to minimize the sufferings of the people, but the distress was great. Casting a further shadow over their spirits, one of the most respected members of the Legislative Council, the Hon. Alan Dredge, was drowned, along with his wife, in the sinking of the *Lusitania* in 1915.

Nevertheless the Colony did not lose heart. For so small a place, her contribution to the War Effort was noteworthy. Over six hundred volunteers joined up as a contingent of the West Indian Regiment, and saw active service in Mesopotamia, being specially complimented in Lord Allenby's dispatches. Hundreds more were mobilized for Home Defence within the Colony, prepared to defend it against German raiders and others. In 1916, for instance, they were called upon to repulse a raid by Guatemalan troops upon the frontier at Benque Viejo. 'Patriotic feeling ran high', observes the Report. The religious bodies worked hard

[1] (1911 Report). The total population was then 40,458.

for the alleviation of distress and the upkeep of morale. It says much for the generosity of the impoverished people of those days that they subscribed liberally to the Prince of Wales' Fund, the Belgian Relief Fund, and the Red Cross.

Towards the end of the War, the Anglican Church was particularly fortunate in her new Bishop, Dr. E. A. Dunn. Arriving from Canada in the dark days of 1917, he immediately brought fresh life and confidence to the clergy and people of a diocese whose spiritual jurisdiction over Anglicans extended from the cathedral city of Belize to the Panama Canal Zone. For the next twenty-six years (a record in the West Indian episcopacy) Bishop Dunn defied all difficulties—shortage of staff, shortage of money, hurricanes, tidal wave, and two catastrophic World Wars—to prise him from his post. In 1936 he was elected Archbishop of the West Indian Province, an office which he held (in addition to his Bishopric of Honduras) until 1943, when advancing age at length compelled his retirement. Even then, he continued to reside in the Colony, and to take an active part in its church life.

The long and bitter years of War came to an end at last in November 1918, but their effects continued long after the Armistice. The dislocation of trade had been too great, lost markets were not soon regained, shipping was still in short supply—in fact, it was a different world. When the new Governor of the Colony, Sir Eyre Hutson, reached Belize in 1919 it was a desolate and depressing spectacle that met his eye. On his way to Government House he had to pass the smoke-blackened ruins of the Government Offices recently destroyed by a terrible conflagration which had engulfed the Colonial Office and all its irreplaceable records. The once trim and prosperous city bore also many marks of damage caused, not by the late enemy, but alas! by the citizens of the capital themselves, not without support from the demobilized soldiers just returned from Mesopotamia, rioting in protest against unemployment, homelessness, and high prices.

As if that were not enough, the new Governor had to hear of the virtual ruin of the once lucrative banana plantations at Stann Creek, infected with the dreaded Panama disease, which not only kills the crops but poisons the ground for years. This had involved the abandonment of many of its plantations by the United Fruit Company, the cessation of the regular visits of the White Fleet, and a disastrous loss of revenue to the Colony through the disuse of the Stann Creek Railway, which had been completed in its full and costly extent of twenty-five miles and fifty-two bridges only just before the War.

For about four years after the cessation of hostilities the general trade depression continued, with no lifting of the clouds. Hundreds of the best labourers emigrated to Guatemala or Spanish Honduras: many of those who had worked on the Panama Canal during the War refused to return. The mahogany forests, recklessly exploited in the boom years and not systematically replanted, were stacked with unsaleable logs rotting in jungle growth. Over the rusty machinery of once bright and busy sugar-mills the tropical octopus had climbed, devouring roofs and walls. The production of chicle dropped to less than half its pre-War mark. Logwood was but a memory. Tortoise-shell had been superseded, apparently for ever, by synthetic imitations sold in every dime store. As for sponges, not only had they now to compete with substitutes of indiarubber, but some deadly disease had played havoc with the carefully tended beds at Turneffe Cay. Droughts and forest fires had been more troublesome than normal. As if to show that fickle Fortune had finally turned her back upon the devoted Colony, a large motor-launch, the *E M L*, sank with all her passengers and crew off Corozal in 1923, among the many drowned being the Right Rev. F. C. Hopkins, Roman Catholic Bishop of Athribis and Vicar Apostolic of Belize.

To anyone who did not know the Colony from the inside, or was ignorant of its long and successful struggle with the vicissitudes of Fate, the outlook might well have seemed hopeless. The official prophecy made so confidently only twenty years earlier, that British Honduras 'would become in the course of time one of His Majesty's richest possessions in the West Indies', must have seemed wildly off the mark. But those who remembered how often during the past two centuries Belize had been written off as lost, took courage from the remark of the Governor of Jamaica in 1775, when Belize had been laid waste by the Spaniards and every Englishman expelled, that 'he had no doubt the logwood-cutters would soon repossess themselves again, according to their usual custom'. And so they did.

Chapter XII

*

BETWEEN THE WARS

SUDDENLY, mysteriously, about four years after the Armistice the tide of adversity began to turn, as it had so often turned before. After a brief period of erratic oscillation, the graph of the Colony's trade returns began to climb steadily upward. It was incredible that, after wellnigh a decade of growing depression, recovery should be so swift. Yet it was no illusion: the plain figures stared one in the face, as year by year the official statistics were carefully compiled, presented, audited and found correct. Here they are, from the Colonial Office Reports of those years:

	EXPORTS	IMPORTS
(In multiples of 10,000 dollars)		
1922.	281	329
1923.	319	403
1924.	333	389
1925.	357	449
1926.	392	416
1927.	454	453
1928.	404	448
1929.	487	505

It will be seen from these remarkable figures that by 1923 the value of the exports of British Honduras had actually exceeded that of the pre-War peak year (1913). The comparison is not altogether just, of course, for prices had risen considerably during the intervening ten years. But this rise in prices does not affect the fact, proved by the above statistics, that the relative increase in exports year by year from 1923 onwards was even steeper than that of the ten years before the War. Once again the extraordinary resilience of the Colony, its indomitable refusal to admit defeat, its eager determination to take advantage of any chance of fighting back, was proved by hard facts.

There was no sudden windfall to account for the improved

trading position, no new discovery, no buried treasure unearthed. The articles for export remained much the same as they had been before the War. It was the markets and prices that had risen, together with a corresponding increase in production. Thus the decline in chicle was arrested, the sales jumping in eight years from two million to four million pounds weight. Copra (from coconuts) shot up from 58 thousand pounds weight in 1920 to over two million in 1927. Mahogany soared from nine million square feet to nearly twenty-five million. Rum decanted over 15,000 gallons. Grapefruit, no longer in its experimental stage, but now figuring among the staple exports of the Colony, sent out more cases every year, until in 1929 they amounted to nearly 4000. By this time Stann Creek grapefruit was reckoned among the best in the world for sweetness, size, and shape, having won both the Gold and the Silver Medals for grapefruit at the 1928 Imperial Fruit Exhibition in England. Various kinds of timber not much exported before the War now began to appear among the articles listed in the reports, such as rosewood, banak, Santa Maria, tamarind, yemeri, and pine, both dressed and in logs, much of it finding a ready sale in Central America. Bananas and plantains unfortunately still showed diminishing returns, but against this could be set increased production of such agricultural products as cacao, oranges, sugar, cassava, tobacco, sarsaparilla, beans, and so forth. Sponges were not doing well, but there seemed to be good prospects for the new rock-lobster (crayfish) canning industry established near Stann Creek. So, in one way and another, the volume of exports steadily grew, and along with it, of course, employment, wages, profits, revenue, and general wellbeing.

At first the even steeper upward gradient of imports into the Colony excited uneasiness, especially as they included a larger proportion than ever of essential foodstuffs. By 1926, however, a healthier tendency had appeared, imports from now onwards being more proportionate to exports, and more food being grown within the Colony itself.

Thus for six or seven happy hopeful years trade in the Colony boomed. From Belize to Benque Viejo, from Punta Gorda to Corozal, the country throbbed with pride at having got upon its feet again, and with excitement at the thought of further victories ahead. Once again traders and prospectors of many nations flocked into the harbours, sailed up the rivers, trekked through the bush.

The streets of the capital were filled with jostling crowds, the waterfront with doreys, lighters, pit-pans, launches, schooners. Among the latter were certain rather sinister-looking craft reminiscent of the old pirates, whose shades must surely have rubbed their hands with glee at the sight of the bootleggers and highjackers loading up their illicit kegs for the Land of Prohibition, and bringing, it must be admitted, no little grist of dollars to the shops (or 'stores', as they call them) of Belize.

The Colony quickly became a hive of industry and progress in every department of its life. In 1923 a long-felt want was supplied by the establishment of a Forestry Department with a staff of European experts and research workers. It was, in point of fact, the pioneer of such departments in Central America. Within the next few years communications at sea were improved by additions and improvements to the lighthouses on the cays, by fixing new buoys in the shallows, and by the construction of a new concrete pier at Stann Creek. Ashore, transport was enormously expedited by the making of new roads, and by the erection of a swing-bridge across the river which cuts the city of Belize in two. Better and bigger Public Offices were built to replace those burnt down in 1918, and a determined attempt made to improve the housing situation by the draining and clearing of the low-lying mangrove swamps south of the city. Scores of wooden-pile houses were erected on the site, chiefly for the use of the troops who had returned from overseas, the new suburb being named Mesopotamia accordingly—for it was in far-off Babylonia that the men had chiefly fought. At the famous Wembley Exhibition of 1924 a special pavilion for British Honduras displayed the products of the Colony, claiming its mahogany as the finest in the world, and introducing to the British Public the luscious Stann Creek grapefruit, for which a similar claim might have been made.

Among the exhibits at this pavilion was a piece of sapodilla wood, a moulding taken from a Maya Indian temple near El Cayo. Despite its age-long exposure to the elements—for over 1200 years —it was still in a remarkable state of preservation, showing the extreme durability of Honduranian timber. For most of the British public this Imperial Exhibition was the first time they had ever heard of Belize, but henceforth British Honduras was definitely 'on the map'. The Maya relic just mentioned added much prestige to the Colony by proving the great antiquity of its cultural history.

Unlike many of the better-known outposts of Empire—Africa, Australia, Canada, Newfoundland—British Honduras had a Past: she could hang ancestors on her walls. The man-in-the-street now heard for the first time of the great Maya Civilization which had recently been discovered under the jungle growth of centuries in various places in Central America, and the fact that this civilization had once established itself within the frontiers of British Honduras stirred the interest of students and explorers, introducing the Colony to the British Museum itself. The new Governor, Sir John Burdon, was just the man to encourage this new approach to his beloved charge. He was highly delighted, shortly after his arrival in Belize on April 14, 1925, to hear that the well-known archæologist-explorers Dr. T. Gann and Mitchell-Hedges had recently visited the ancient Maya district around San Pedro de Colombia, in the Toledo region, and had uncovered in the jungle some exceptionally interesting ruins of the Indian civilization. From that time forward this enclave of Maya temples, tombs, obelisks, and the like became known as Lubaantun, 'The Place of Fallen Stones', and it is so marked on the maps to this day. Year by year it was revisited, cleared of jungle growth, reconstructed as far as possible, and described in detail both in many learned archæological journals and in Gann's more popular books, such as *Mystery Cities*. The British Museum sent its own expert, Captain T. A. Joyce, O.B.E., in 1926 and in subsequent years to Lubaantun, and to the Maya ruins at Xunantunich, near El Cayo. New ruins were discovered at Xumucha, east of the River Moho. For the first time in history the name of British Honduras was blazoned in the headlines of the world's Press, and the Visitors' Book in Government House began to scintillate with famous signatures—for Sir John Burdon was very particular in requiring that every visitor to the Colony should immediately report himself at headquarters. Among such visitors was the celebrated airman, Lindbergh, who in 1927 flew from Guatemala to Belize in his historic monoplane, the *Spirit of S. Louis*. It was the first time an aeroplane had landed in the Colony.

More important and fruitful, as it happened, was the visit of Baron Edward Bliss of Buckinghamshire in 1926. It is an extraordinary story, unique in Colonial annals. Baron Bliss had one great passion in life: he was an ardent fisherman, especially of the larger and more savage varieties of sea-fish. Always on the look-out for fresh fishing grounds and keener sport, he had heard in the summer of 1925 of the huge tarpon, black snapper, whale shark, jewfish, and other outsize monsters of the deep to be hooked in almost limitless quantities around the cays of British Honduras. He became interested. He received a letter from an official in the Colony saying that the writer, though an inexpert fisherman, had caught twelve huge tarpon in the Belize River in the course of a single afternoon. It was Holbein's Anne of Cleves to Henry VIII: Baron Bliss fell in love with British Honduras forthwith. In the following year (1926) he sailed his luxurious steam-yacht the *Sea King* to Jamaica and thence to Belize. Unfortunately, for himself, he was taken seriously ill within sight of the shore, and, never having actually landed, died suddenly in his cabin on March 9.

Before dying, however, he managed to get a lawyer on board and make a hurried will. The contents of this bequest must rank among the most curious in testamentary history, but they were extremely advantageous to British Honduras. For although Baron Bliss had never set foot on its soil, had scarcely even heard of it until the year before his death, had no previous connections with it or any of its inhabitants, and knew no more than that it was reputed to be a paradise of deep-sea fishermen, he decided there and then to bequeath all his considerable fortune to the Colony. The full benefits of the will would take a little time to mature, for there were certain small life annuities to various legatees, and an annuity of £5000 a year to his widow, but it was a great windfall for the Colony just at a time when it needed help, and must have brought great joy to the heart of the Governor.

As a result of this bequest, the Baron Bliss Trust was formed, and still exists. In fact it exists more than ever, for the death of Baroness Bliss has now released her marriage settlement, and all but about £300 a year of the annuities have expired. The full effects of these annuities having fallen in have only quite recently been felt, for there was much delay in settling the amount of Income Tax and Surtax, Death Duties, Legacy Duties, and other Government charges on the bequest. It was unfortunate for the Colony that Baron Bliss died at sea, thus enabling the Imperial Government to claim its full pound of flesh from his estate, and to delay its full fruition until the devaluation of the Honduras dollar in 1950 still further reduced the value of the benefaction.

Nevertheless, a considerable capital sum remains. It is believed that the annual income when all is settled will amount to about £10,000. In the administration of this money neither the British nor the Belize Government, as such, can interfere. Under the Trust it is to be expended at the sole discretion of the three Trustees—the Governor, the Colonial Secretary of Belize, and the Attorney-General of the Colony—subject to certain restrictions. It may be expended, for example, only on capital (structural) improvements in the Colony. Even here there is one very lamentable proviso—none of the money must be spent on building schools,[1] of which the Colony is in crying need, and which must still rely almost entirely on the voluntary funds of the religious bodies. In any case difficulties are bound to arise. It is all very well building libraries, museums, institutes, public offices and the like for the benefit of the Colony, but such things require maintenance and repair. 'Sooner or later,' remarks Sir Alan Burns in his *Colonial Civil Servant*, 'the Courts will have to be asked to vary the Trust, for there must be a limit to the amount of capital expenditure which can be reasonably invested, with due regard of the community to maintain the amenities provided.'

However, since the creation of the Trust, large sums of money have been spent on the amenities and public utilities of the Colony. The very useful Belize to Cayo road, and many other roads which have lately been constructed, owe much to grants from the Baron Bliss Trust. Typical of the kind of work which can be helped by the Trust are the Industrial School for Boys at Stann Creek (1926), the celebrated Burdon Canal (1929) connecting Belize with the River Sibun, the new market-place at Stann Creek (1947), improvements to the supply of drinking water and the water-tanks in Belize, the construction of a public promenade on the south foreshore, the installation of an institute for the scientific survey of soils, and the erection of a magnificently planned combined museum, art gallery, and cultural centre to be known as the Baron Bliss Institute. Work on some of these projects has been held up since 1939 by the shortage of necessary materials, but there is a large balance in the Trust earmarked and awaiting better times.

One exception to the rule against using the Trust money for current expenditure was made by the will in favour of an annual

---

[1] Except purely vocational training centres.

official regatta, or rather two regattas, one in the harbour, the other on the river. The first of these was held in 1927, and they are still held every year, to the great delight of the Colony, at a very small cost (about 500 dollars) to the funds.

In our account of the Baron Bliss Trust we have rather anticipated our story. We must now return to the period between the Wars. Those were great days for British Honduras. The years that the locust had eaten were almost forgotten. Peace, plenty, and progress had settled into their stride. The resilience and vitality of the people were something to marvel at. To take the signs of the times at random—a cricket ground and golf course were drained and laid out on the north side of the city: the first popular handbooks on British Honduras, as noted above, introduced the Colony to travellers, business men, and historians: a modern cinema was opened in Belize: rivalling in public interest the regattas already mentioned, an annual Marathon Bicycle Race from the capital along the new road to El Cayo was inaugurated (1928): Lindbergh and his wife visited the Colony a second time (1929): Sir John Burdon started his enthusiastic committee for the collection of the Colony's archives: the Anglican Church of S. Mary, Belize, was thoroughly restored, beautified, and fitted with electric fans [1]: great enterprise was shown in the development of the Colony's natural resources outside the capital, for example in the scientific propagation of sponges at Turneffe Cay, additions to the very successful lobster-canning industry near Stann Creek, the experimental planting of tobacco and other crops, the exportation for the first time (1925) of pine planks, the organized prevention and control of forest fires, and a civic campaign for the extermination of land-crabs: the consecration of an Anglican Mission Boat, the *Mary Christina* (1926), and a great improvement in the mails, shipping facilities, and other communications with the outside world. All the religious denominations were playing their part (a very large one in British Honduras) in the abounding life of the Colony, and in every way the wind seemed determined to set fair for Belize in this world and the next.

But—at least as far as this world is concerned—it was not to

[1] It had been built by the devoted efforts of its first rector, Archdeacon Murray, in 1889. Archdeacon Murray is one of the saints and heroes of the Diocese, in which he served for thirty-seven years, and where he died, at the age of eighty, on June 28, 1925.

be. Quite unexpectedly two great disasters, the first world-wide, the second only local but not less disastrous, crashed down upon the Colony's rising prosperity and hammered it to the dust.

The first was the World Trade Depression of 1929, that economic earthquake which shook to its foundations the painfully built-up commercial edifice of four hundred years on both sides of the Atlantic, and inevitably involved British Honduras in the catastrophic 'slump'. Scarcely had she begun to make real progress after the depression of the First World War, when an even greater depression overtook her; and just as she was beginning to get the better of that depression, a terrible hurricane, such as the Colony had never experienced before, laid waste the land. Thus it was that—to express the disaster in figures—her exports toppled down in three years from nearly five million dollars in value to only just over one million—to the very figure, in fact, from which she had been gallantly striving upwards since 1899, namely, $1,030,000. In the same period imports dropped like a stone from over five million dollars to just over a million and a half, which, remembering that most of these imports were food and clothing, speaks volumes for the distress and misery of the population. Once again, as so often before, everything seemed lost, and the future to hold no hope of recovery.

The hurricane of 1931 was an entirely unforeseen visitation. Not for over a hundred and fifty years had Belize experienced anything more destructive than a strong gale. It was taken for granted that she lay far outside the Hurricane Belt, so that there were no concrete houses, window-shutters, reinforced roofs, windbreaks, or any of the anti-hurricane devices so well known in the Bahamas or other places in the Belt. When the first wireless warning of the storm's approach was received, on September 10, it was not taken very seriously, especially as the whole city was on holiday, the streets crowded with children and happy faces, celebrating the glorious Victory of S. George's Cay in the traditional way. Suddenly at 2 P.M. a terrific gale came screaming from NNW. with instantly increasing force, until at 160 miles per hour it broke the wind-vane on the Court House. Everyone rushed indoors, most of the children fleeing to the churches and schoolrooms where their festal teas had been laid. But it was questionable whether it were safer indoors or out. The streets were soon blocked with fallen houses, or houses lifted bodily from their foundations, crashing trees and telegraph posts, live electric wires, and flying sheets of corrugated iron from the roofs which beheaded one or two unlucky passers-by like a guillotine, and wounded many others. Indoors the windows fell in, the walls collapsed, furniture slid across weirdly canting floors, ceiling rafters fell and pinned beneath them those who had taken shelter. Fortunately the cooking stoves and lamps which were overturned were unlighted, or fire would have added its horror to the scene.

However, as quickly as it had arisen, the first blast of the hurricane ceased at 3 P.M. Everyone, too excited and curious to be panic-stricken, poured out of doors to view the wreckage. Most of the houses were severely damaged, many of them had collapsed in a heap of planks and beams. The churches, schools, and public buildings had suffered equally. S. Mary's Church, beautified and restored only a few years earlier, had disappeared, along with its adjoining rectory. The big Diocesan Secondary School had gone. In some cases, by a strange freak of the storm, the lower storey had disappeared while the upper storey had dropped down into its place. The Cathedral, unroofed and windowless, was an empty shell. On the sea-front an incredible spectacle met the eyes—the sea had vanished! It had just been blown out of the shallow bay and piled up on the distant cays. It was learnt afterwards that S. George's Cay had been practically submerged, with great loss of life.

But there was little time to spend in wondering at the view. The cries and groans of many hundreds of people pinned beneath the fallen houses roused everyone to the rescue. It was then that the worst blow fell. For before the victims could be extricated, the doomed city was caught in the returning vortex of the gale, roaring up now from the opposite direction (SSE.) with unabated force, and driving in front of it the livid, foaming mass of sea-water which had at first been blown out of the bay. In a few minutes this fresh blast of wind not only completed the destruction caused by the first, but buried the ruins and those that were pinned under them in a swirling tide of water to the depth in many places of fifteen or twenty feet. Corvetting giddily on this tide came the vessels which had lain at anchor in the harbour, crashing against what was left of the houses, tearing their path through the walls, getting smashed themselves in the process. After the waters had gone down, boats and big ships were found deep in debris and slime half a mile or more inland. The heavy dredger was discovered perched on the Court House roof. But what was far more serious, over a thousand bodies were found, drowned as they struggled helplessly to wrench themselves free from the imprisonment of fallen girders.

Little could be done to save them, even when their plight was known. There was no rising ground in the city whither one could take refuge, and to descend from one's precarious foothold in the branches of some tree, or the upper storey of some not quite demolished house, into the flotsam-laden maelstrom below was to invite certain death. To make things worse, the storm had brought with it a sudden utter darkness like the dead of night, a darkness that seemed to have the solidity of a London fog. It was impossible to do anything for anyone while this lasted. And it lasted till 6 P.M., at which time the wind gave one last triumphant sigh of content, and died: the awful clamour, which had made it difficult to hear even a voice at one's ear, suddenly fell to a death-like silence, almost as terrifying by contrast: the waters which had been sucking at one's feet and ankles began to sink. But by then the sun had set, and the only light was the light of the stars.

The following morning rose over the bay as brightly and cheerfully as though nothing at all had happened, but it shone on such a scene of misery and desolation as Belize had never seen before, for never before in the most evil days had it offered so wide a front to the shafts and arrows of misfortune. Little by little, as the sun dried up the slime and lit up the unrecognizable streets, the full extent of the damage began to be realized. Ninety-five per cent. of the buildings great and small had been struck, perhaps half of them being rendered uninhabitable. In terms of money the loss was estimated at over a million dollars. But worse than that was the loss of life. The Official Report (1931) says: 'The actual number of lives lost will never be known, because, to protect the health of the survivors, great funeral pyres had to be raised in certain areas where the death-roll was heaviest, and the task of removing the dead from the labyrinth of destruction was rendered almost impossible. The deaths are estimated to have been over a thousand, and the injured nearly as many.' Nor was it only in Belize that the hurricane had struck. All along the Old River it had spread death and ruin. Great trees lay about the ground or blocked the stream like cut flowers: houses, schools, churches, and, worst of all, the gardens and crops of the poor people had been scattered far and wide. Their livelihood was gone, and all their stores.

It was fortunate for the Colony that a man like Sir John Burdon was in charge at such a time. Although he himself, as already related (p. 12), had nearly lost his life in the tidal wave, and his own home, Government House, had been half unroofed, Sir John did everything a man could do to minimize the effects of the disaster. One of his first cares was to see that his people had something to eat and drink. There was no food in the city save the scattered and battered stocks of canned goods from the splinters which had once been shops; and there was hardly any drinking water, for the leggy cisterns and tanks upon which the populace depended had been laid low by the storm. Sir John, however, had the broken radio station quickly repaired, and flashed his SOS to the outside world. As a result, within twenty-four hours the sky was full of aeroplanes and the sea of ships rushing to the rescue. The United States, Mexico, Guatemala, the islands of the Caribbean rivalled each other in sending supplies of food, water, and medicines. The crews of the visiting ships took off their coats and helped in clearing up the mess. Relief funds were started everywhere. In Belize the authorities welcomed the assistance of the religious bodies in organizing the distribution of necessities, and the provision of shelter for the homeless. Last but not least, the Imperial Government came forward with its first substantial offer of practical aid to the Colony, a loan of £325,000 under the British Honduras Loans Act of 1932, thus inaugurating a new era in the financial relations of the Colony with the Motherland.

The hurricane and tidal wave of 1931 are described in the Official Report as 'the most awful calamity in the Colony's history', and, coming on top of the trade depression of the previous years, it seemed to many that at last the end had come. There were not wanting wiseacres to prophesy that this time British Honduras would have to throw up the sponge: it should be handed over to Guatemala, or Quintana Roo of Mexico, or Spanish Honduras, all of whom had cast covetous eyes on the territory for years: or it might be offered for sale to the United States, like the Louisiana Purchase or the Panama Canal Zone: at the very least, Belize should be written off as a total loss, and the capital of the Colony transferred to Corozal or Stann Creek. And so forth.

Never for a moment, however, did the colonists themselves dream of such a thing; nor did Sir John Burdon, of course, who knew the history of the Colony's ups and downs better than any man. One seems to hear the echo of his characteristic voice in the conclusion of the Official Report of December 1932: 'The motto on the Arms of the Colony is "*sub umbra floreo*",[1] and the population of the Colony is showing itself worthy of its motto by its spirit in rising triumphant over its disasters.' And this, be it noted, was penned after yet another disaster had struck the city, in the shape of a destructive fire (April 1932) which devoured three business blocks and fifty-two of the houses which had survived the hurricane.

Blows which would have knocked most other people out of the ring merely spurred British Honduranians to greater energy and determination. Large numbers of temporary 'barracks' for the homeless sprang up like mushrooms. Hundreds of barrels of all sizes were collected for holding drinking water, and either 'screened' with fine-mesh wire-netting or supplied with 'poolsies' —tiny fishes which devoured the larvæ of disease-carrying mosquitoes. All stagnant pools were carefully oiled. Quinine was distributed free of cost to the necessitous. Much labour was spent on scavenging and drainage, and to everyone's surprised relief one peril at any rate was averted, the peril of an epidemic. To ease the unemployment situation, extensive public works were put in hand, such as improvements to the Cayo-Belize road, towards which useful sums were contributed by the Baron Bliss Trust.

The courage of the stricken Colony stirred everyone's admiration. For the first time in history, British Honduras featured in the cinema News Reels of the world: people could see, as well as read, what it was like. Its problems could no longer be overlooked. In one respect at least the disaster did the Colony a good turn: it induced the Colonial Office at home to send out a Commission of Enquiry into its financial difficulties, opportunities, and prospects. For the first time the natural resources of the country were scientifically surveyed and enumerated, its revenue

---

[1] Latin: a free translation would be: 'When things are at their blackest, I am at my best.'

and expenditure analysed, its features and areas elaborately mapped. The final result was published as a Blue book available for any member of the public who might be interested, entitled *British Honduras, Financial and Economic Position* (the Cunliffe-Lister Report of March 1934). Those who sympathized with the extreme penury into which the Colony had fallen at that time were rather struck by a small footnote appearing in the Report to the effect that the expenses of this Commission (£1144, 17s. 11d.) were to be borne by the funds of the Colony.

In 1934, with this Royal Commission Report still in its mind, the Colonial Office dispatched Mr. (afterwards Sir) Alan Burns as the new Governor of the Colony. Sir Alan must have been an exceptional man to be chosen for, and a brave man to accept, so responsible a post at such a crisis in its affairs. He could have expected nothing but hard work among a dejected people, whom nothing short of a miracle could restore to solvency. As it happened, however, Sir Alan's arrival coincided with, if it did not accelerate, a turn in the tide. By the end of the year the figures in the Official Reports show that the nadir of the Colony's fortunes had been passed. For the first time in five years the value of the exports and imports showed a marked upward trend. It was no flash in the pan. Surprisingly, under the inspiring leadership of the administration, the figures continued to climb. They ascended with a rapidity which took one's breath away, a rapidity which actually exceeded that of any past records, as will be seen from a comparison of the following figures with those already given:

	EXPORTS	IMPORTS
(In multiples of 10,000 dollars)		
1933.	104	168
1934.	152	191
1935.	168	267
1936.	241	327
1937.	260	398
1938.	326	400

The above columns show that in five brilliant years the Colony actually trebled its exports. Once again the old optimistic note crept into the Official Reports: 'There was a considerable revival of trade during the year under review . . . the market for mahogany is reviving, and there has been a large increase in the export of sawn mahogany to the United Kingdom . . . the citrus industry seems definitely on its feet . . . the production of fresh vegetables continues to show improvement . . . the rice industry is making headway'—and so forth. Although Panama disease still affected the plantations around Stann Creek, bananas were now being successfully grown in the north of the Colony, between El Cayo and Corozal, and the export of stems doubled in a single year (1934). Similar favourable figures were reported for the export of cedar, rosewood, Santa Maria, and banak wood. Sawn pine timber offered a promising future. The export of coconuts increased, and oranges and tangerines began to make quite a show on the trade returns. A small amount of logwood and cohune nuts was still sold. Alligator-skins (enumerated among 'forest products') were much sought after for ladies' handbags, bringing combined sport and profit to the hunter who, paddling his dorey up the creeks by night with an electric torch fastened to his forehead, shot the inquisitive reptiles between their shining eyes. There was a revival of interest in the tortoise-shell for which the Colony had always been celebrated, as well as in shark-skin, that toughest of all leather. The lobster-canning factory at Stann Creek was now working at full pressure, and attempts on modern scientific lines were again being made to stimulate the cultivation of sponges on the sea-beds at Turneffe Cay, under the enthusiastic supervision of Captain F. Milton. Particularly gratifying was the reported increase of production in the farms and gardens up-river. Agriculture was gaining in prestige, largely through Government encouragement and the setting up of various experimental stations, research laboratories, and grants. Rice, maize, beans, and vegetables were now produced in considerably larger (though still far too small) quantities, and even in live stock—cattle, pigs, and poultry—there was an improvement. The main trade of the Colony was still, however, predominantly in her forest products, these accounting (in 1938) for over 80 per cent. of the total exports. Thus during the five or six years before the outbreak of the Second World War, in 1939, British Honduras was once more a hive of happy industry and enterprise, the ground lost by the depression and hurricane had in a fair way been regained, and the future was bright with promise.

With this no one was more pleased than the Colonial Office far away in Downing Street. Since the hurricane, relations between

British Honduras and the Mother Country had become more cordial than ever in its history. The Report of the Royal Commission of 1934 had both evinced and stirred a new interest in what had often been known as 'A forgotten Colony', 'A Cinderella of the Empire', or even (very rudely and with gross exaggeration) 'An Imperial Slum'. The published *Archives* of Sir John Burdon had brought to light the romance of the Colony's long and lonely pilgrimage on the road to Imperial recognition, and this was reflected in the Colonial Office's new attitude. Above all, the Royal Commission had produced some practical results. Many of the enterprises described above had been assisted by the advice and help of the Home Government. In addition to generous loans from the National Exchequer at a low rate of interest, many grants were made from the new Colonial Development Fund. In 1934, for instance, the Colony received both a loan of £20,000 and a grant of £3000 from these sources respectively: in 1936 a fine concrete bridge 334 feet long was built at Haulover at the cost of the Treasury: in 1938 a new road was constructed from Punta Gorda to San Antonio by the same agency. And there were many other instances of such 'gracious and ready help' in that time of need—indeed to the present day. The Colony was grateful, for in these days nothing can be done without capital, and this prototype of 'Marshall Aid', so to speak, from Great Britain to our Central American dependency greatly speeded up the development of its resources. Thus the revenue of British Honduras increased almost *pari passu* with the financial aid it received. By the end of 1938 it had mounted to over a million and a quarter dollars, *exclusive* of nearly half a million dollars from the Colonial Development and Loan Funds.

Not that this new feature in the Colony's financial affairs was entirely without its own problems. Gratitude has been defined as 'a lively expectation of more to come', and a certain somewhat unfamiliar readiness to adopt an Oliver Twist attitude to the Home Government began to appear. There were complaints of too many words, too few deeds. More unreasonable was the resentment occasionally voiced by the Legislative Council, or rather by a few of its members, at the audit of colonial expenditure required by the British Treasury in order to discover how its loans had been spent. It was certainly irritating at times to have to wait for Treasury sanction before some urgent work could be put in hand, and no doubt a hard-pressed, understaffed Colonial Office sometimes seemed a little slow in the uptake. But these were unavoidable flies in the ointment, harmful only when magnified to the size of gadflies by irresponsible demagogues. More worrying, of course, was the constantly increasing burden of the Colony's Public Debt. By 1938 this had grown to nearly three and a half million dollars, and the charges upon it had become a menace to solvency. No doubt all would have been well, however, had it not been for the Second World War: but the problem still remains.

Lest it be thought that finance and trade were the only interests of the Colony, let it be recorded that in every department of its varied colourful life progress went on apace. Within five or six years of the hurricane, the whole dreadful episode seemed to have been forgotten, and it would certainly have been difficult to find any traces of it in the bright new city of Belize which had risen phœnix-like from the debris. The disaster had done for the capital of the Colony what the Great Fire did for London. Belize had become out of all remembrance a trim, well-built, dignified little place of which the inhabitants were rightly proud, despite the outlying suburbs of dingy or dilapidated shanties which still remained to be dealt with, but which hardly anyone ever saw. In 1935 a fine Carnegie Library and Museum, the latter specializing in Maya relics, was opened in Belize; and a large area of swampland, drained and ballasted for the building of houses, became the new 'estate' of Freetown. In the following year an enormous improvement was made to the city's water supply by the installation of six huge tanks of pressed steel, a present from the Colonial Development Fund. In 1936 the religious world was greatly flattered by the holding for the first time in the Colony of a Provincial Synod of the West Indies, at which the new Anglican Bishop of the Windward Islands, the Rt. Rev. H. N. V. Tonks, was consecrated by the Bishops of British Honduras, Trinidad, Gambia, and Jamaica. Vast congregations gaped to see the chancel of the Cathedral crowded with copes and mitres.

There was some political excitement too. President Ubico of the Republic of Guatemala had identified himself with the revival of his country's almost forgotten claim to British Honduras. Among many pin-pricks had been the closing of the Peten border to transport, and the consequent serious curtailment of the trade in chicle via Belize. In 1938 the Guatemalan Government published a voluminous White book in Spanish and English (of sorts) which was rousing sleeping dogs in North and South America. But more immediately interesting were political developments within the Colony itself. In 1936 and the following years certain elements in the capital pressed for and secured a modification in a democratic direction of the local Legislature. A new constitution was granted to the Colony by the Crown, embodied in the British Honduras Constitution Ordinance and its amendments of 1936–38. Henceforward the Legislative Council was to consist of the Governor as President (it was Sir Alan Burns at the time) with a Casting Vote and Reserve Powers giving him a positive and negative initiative in legislation, together with five Official and eight Unofficial members. Of the latter, two were to be nominated by His Excellency, and six to be elected by secret ballot of the Colony's registered voters. And so it stands to-day.

The Government departments in these years were full of energy. Particular attention was paid to Health, a qualified Sanitary Inspector being appointed for the first time, through whose efforts the drainage and scavenging arrangements were greatly improved. Six hospitals up and down the country were now in good working order, but blue-prints were in existence for the building of a really modern and well-equipped infirmary in Belize. Vocational training centres and agricultural experiments were started everywhere, including twenty school gardens. With the help of the Colonial Development Fund and the Baron Bliss Trust many miles of new all-weather roads were constructed every year. A telegraph line now stretched from Belize to Chetumal across the Rio Hondo and so to Mexico City and the States. A powerful wireless station in Belize was in daily communication with Jamaica, Guatemala, and New Orleans. There were small aerodromes at Stann Creek, Punta Gorda, and Corozal, as well as the large one at Belize. The railway at Stann Creek still operated, the Burdon Canal and the river were full of doreys with paddles, doreys with sails, doreys with outboard motors, pit-pans, and tunnel-boats laden to the gunwale with cargo. Owing to the extension of the roads, the number of motor-cars and motor-trucks was growing year by year. Business enterprise was encouraged by the light taxation that prevailed. There was no import duty on industrial machinery, land tax remained (except on the Stann Creek Railway route) at 1½ cents an acre. Income tax (first introduced in 1921) was very low, the charge on incomes up to $30,000 being only 7 per cent. Everyone was very happy, not overworked, not over-organized, not over-anxious about wages or profits, but steadily moving onwards and upwards to the blessed bourne of being 'comfortably off'. Munich, Berchtesgarten, and all those places seemed very far away: gale warnings were not much regarded. It was good to be alive.

Then came the Second World War. From 1939 to 1945 the whole world seemed to have gone mad with the lust of destruction, or production only to destroy. The Colony's trade returns jumped meaninglessly up and down like a seismographic needle in an earthquake. Hundreds of her best woodmen sailed for the forests of Scotland, hundreds more were engaged at rates beyond the dreams of avarice for work on the Panama Canal, hundreds enlisted in the Forces. Belize became unrecognizable, a city of strangers, rumours, spy-mania, nervous tension. German submarines nosed about the cays. Nature herself seemed to have gone crazy: droughts, floods, the whiplash of several hurricanes, and an unprecedented plague of locusts added to the general dislocation. When the Blackout ended, and the lights went up, the world found itself perched precariously on the edge of a bottomless pit.

Chapter XIII

*

BRITISH HONDURAS TO-DAY —AND TO-MORROW

BELIZE is not very difficult to reach from England, and nowadays there are many routes. The most obvious and cheapest is still the old sea-rovers' way by boat from Bristol Westward Ho! across the Atlantic, touching at the Azores, then over to Turk's Island in the Caicos, through the straits between Tortuga and Santiago de Cuba into the Caribbean Sea and so past the ruins of Port Royal into the splendid harbour of Kingston, Jamaica. Changing here into a smaller vessel, one reaches Belize after a voyage of about three weeks in all, having covered just over 4700 miles, and gained six precious hours of time by westering. The journey can be shortened to less than a fortnight, if everything fits in, by sailing to New York, taking the train thence to New Orleans, and so by boat or air to Belize. Quicker still, of course, but beyond the means of ordinary mortals, are the numerous airways connecting North and South America.

To a newcomer the first view of Belize from the upper deck may be a little disappointing. The famous buccaneers' capital is certainly no Rio de Janeiro! Leaning over the taffrail and waiting for the harbour officials and the squat grey lighters to come out from the quayside half a mile away—for the water is too shallow for ocean-going liners to approach any nearer—one observes with some disillusionment the waveless, yellowish, oily-looking surface of the bay, the long low land beyond it like a canal bank only a foot or two above sea-level, the monotonous line of buildings in the background with no edifice of striking design or outstanding height to focus the attention, and, as far as the eye can see, not a rise in the ground, still less a hill or a peak of any sort to vary the flat circle of the horizon. Comparing this with the graceful coconut palms waving over the silver beaches of S. George's Cay, and the white foam breaking over the coral reefs as we threaded our way through the barrier which once made Belize so desirable a refuge for freebooters, we are disappointed with the coastline for the very reason which first caused it to be chosen as a landing-place. One can scarcely tell where the land begins and the sea ends, nor where the dull-green tangle of mangrove bushes creeping down into the tideless waters may be seen, on a closer view, to part asunder here and there at the mouth of a river or a creek. No spray of breakers marks the shore, no shimmer of shelving beach discloses the secret careening ground; along the whole mangrove-cluttered stretch of 170 odd miles of coastline from north to south there is scarcely one distinguishing natural feature to help a strange mariner get his bearings. Belize has been called 'a badly placed capital' by one of the recent Royal Commissions. They could not have known much about its history. Actually it was ideally placed by old Wallace, its founder, and even to-day it would be difficult to suggest a better geographical situation,[1] for the city is central and accessible, not only from the sea, but from the interior.

British Honduras is rather like Palestine in size, and shape, and contour—except, of course, that it faces east instead of west towards the sea. Its exact area is 8900 square miles, a fact which incidentally makes it larger than all the British West Indian Islands put together, and alone entitles it to special consideration in all plans for colonial development. Roughly, like Palestine, it is about 170 miles long, from north to south, and 90 wide, with a maritime plain varying from 5 to 25 miles in breadth, rising in the hinterland to a shephelah and to mountainous heights of 3000 feet or more. But the Jordan (so to speak) of British Honduras runs west to east instead of north to south, and it was as the mouth of this great river, the Belize or Old River as it it called, that the capital of the Colony was deliberately and cunningly placed. For the Belize River was, and remains to this day, despite recent roadmaking achievements, the main highway from the interior to the sea. There are said to be as many rivers in the Colony as there are days in the year, and many of them branch off, with little offshooting creeks of their own, from the hundred-and-fifty-mile-long river, which is navigable nearly all its length.

---

[1] The chief disadvantages of Belize as a building site are (1) its low elevation, making drainage difficult, and (2) its swampy foundations, which have to be made firm by vast quantities of coral (pipeshank) dredged up from the sea, and bedded in.

Thus Belize is connected by sea and by inland waterways, which cost little or nothing in maintenance, with all the chief inhabited towns and villages in the Colony. By river from the city one can travel in motor-boat, pit-pan (barge), yacht, or the ubiquitous 'dorey' (canoe) almost anywhere—to Boom, where the great mahogany rafts are chained, to Flowers Lime Walk, Never Delay, Banana Bank, Happy Home, Mount Hope, Spanish Lookout, and Duck Run, up to the considerable chicle depot of El Cayo at the terminus.

Note the old logwood-cutters' names still clinging to these 'banks', as the river-side villages are called, and picture them crowded with happy black people running down to the water's edge to wave as the rare vessel passes by. From the main stream one may branch off by Black Creek and then by Spanish Creek to the village of Limonal, so reaching the vast mahogany camps round Hill Bank, and the long lagoon which leads to Orange Walk and Corozal in the far north of the Colony. Or southwards one may paddle through the Burdon Canal [1] into the Sibun River, and so to Gracie Rock and Churchyard. A perfect network of small streams, flooded savannahs, and lagoons link the clearings and little market-gardens with their mother-city, not at all 'badly placed', especially when it comes to floating the huge mahogany logs down to the 'barky dear' (barcadero) for shipment to the world. It is a very picturesque and interesting way of travelling, too, gliding between green avenues of flowering trees and towering palms, or under overhanging limes and grapefruit, with butterflies as big as plates and of all colours fluttering around, bright-plumaged birds [2] among the branches overhead, big green iguanas peeping through the bush, the scuttle of wild pigs, a loglike alligator sluggishly sliding from its bed of mud, gleaming tarpons jumping for a humming-bird, turtles swimming, and lovely white water-lilies bobbing in the wake of the motor-boat.

By sea, too, Belize is most conveniently placed for communication with the maritime plain, where many of the most important places are situated. From the harbour one may sail south (perhaps on the good old s.s. *Heron*) to Mullins River, Stann Creek, where

---

[1] Named after its originator, Sir John Burdon, Governor of the Colony.

[2] *E.g.* parrots, macaws, toucans, perhaps even the brilliant quetzal, Guatemala's Bird of Freedom.

grow the best grapefruit in the West Indies; All Pines and Monkey River, where they ship bananas; Placentia, where the retired Archbishop made his home and built a lovely new church, and so to Punta Gorda and the Sarstoon River, which separates the Colony from Guatemala. Or northwards (maybe in the s.s. *Romulus*) one may sail to Ambergris Cay and on to the largish town of Corozal, once the centre of a thriving sugar industry. Or out to sea, of course, to the pretty holiday island of S. George's Cay, or the sponge fisheries of Turneffe Island, or to Puerto Barrios, the port of Guatemala, or even to Jamaica, 600 miles away. From the airman's point of view, Belize offers a pretty good landing-ground at Stanley Field, wide, flat, and with 'good visibility' for miles. In fact it would be hard to think of a better site for the capital, when all is said and done. The only other location would be Stann Creek, but the better harbour facilities, with deep water inshore, would scarcely compensate for its lack of river communications, and its distance from the main 'industrial' areas of the north.

Stann Creek, it may be stated, marks the great divide between the northern and the southern half of British Honduras, the characteristics of each region being very different. Draw a line due west from Stann Creek to Benque Viejo, and all to the north of it you will find flat riverine logwood and mahogany country, 'mostly drowned', as the old geographer puts it; while all to the south of that line is a vast area, nearly half of the whole Colony, consisting of thickly forested mountains (except for the seaboard strip of plain) still almost uninhabited and unexplored. It is a land of mystery, not only in the sense of the 'Mystery Cities' of the ancient Maya civilization about which so little is known even to this day, but in the geological sense. What minerals, what unsuspected source of wealth lies beneath that terrific mountain mass of sandstone, slate, and quartzite which even the scientists have as yet been unable to probe? The lofty chain of the Maya Mountains stretches from Middlesex in the Stann Creek District down to Dolores on the Temash River in the far south, and over into Guatemala. It rises in the east centre to the towering peak of the Cockscomb Mountain, so called because of its striking resemblance to a cock's dentated comb, famous of old as a landmark for sailors far out at sea, soaring like a volcano (which it is not) to over 3700 feet.

At the southern end of the Maya Mountains, in what is known as the Toledo District, the cataracts of the Rio Grande (a tiny version of its more famous namesake) rush precipitously to the sea at a point near Punta Gorda, with many streamlets branching from it. In this well watered region many relics of the ancient Maya civilization have been found, including the famous ruins of Lubaantun, with its remarkable carved temple pyramids, mural wall-paintings, and remains of terraced cultivation.[1] It is only by a coincidence, however, that some 2000 Maya Indians are living in this neighbourhood to-day, in an Indian 'Reservation' allotted them by the Government, and especially in the totally Mayan town of San Antonio, founded 1883. For the original Mayas had migrated northwards from Lubaantun about a thousand years before the first British settlers arrived, and it is re-immigration in comparatively modern times which has brought these 'aboriginals' back to British Honduras, refugees for the most part from Spanish maltreatment and exploitation. They keep themselves very much to themselves. A man may cover the ordinary trade routes in the Colony for years without meeting a Maya Indian, and would be surprised to learn that out of a total population in the Colony of about 60,000, these people number over 10,000, usually living in somewhat primitive villages under the loose jurisdiction of a not too highly respected *alcalde* (mayor) appointed by the Government.

So far it cannot be said that the Colony has really succeeded in assimilating these Indians. They support themselves self-sufficiently by cultivating their *milpas* (cornfields) by the prehistoric method of 'squatting', that is burning the bush, exhausting the soil, and then moving on. They seem to live entirely on home-grown maize, rice, and black beans, and although the more enterprising of them go in for poultry, turkeys, and pigs as a side-line, it is usually to sell them to the outer world for alcohol. Most of them are illiterate, while half of them speak no language but their own local Maya dialect,[2] and the other half have as their second language not English (the language spoken universally elsewhere in the Colony), but pidgin-Spanish. Their

---

[1] The most accessible Maya ruins to-day are to be seen near Benque Viego, on the Guatemalan border.

[2] Language is sometimes a problem in Maya schools. 'I have heard German nuns trying to teach Maya children out of an English text-book which they had to explain in Spanish,' writes Sir Alan Burns.

religion is one of their secrets: it is said that some of the ancient rites of the old fertility gods are still practised under a thin veneer of Roman Catholicism. Economically they are of small importance to the Colony, contributing little beyond the one pound per annum which they pay as rent for as much Crown Land as they are able to cultivate. Yet where they have been given a real chance in life, in open grassland clear of the depressing rain-forests of the Toledo District, with sanitary conditions to improve their miserable health, and in places accessible to enlightened influences —for example in the sugar-growing district around Corozal— their villages are often spaciously laid out, clean, tidy, and with bright and happy children in the schools. It would seem that much more might be made of this very considerable Maya element both to their own and to the Colony's advantage.

To an exile with nostalgic memories of 'England's green and pleasant land', the most attractive scenery and surroundings in British Honduras will be found in the so-called Pine Ridge District, on the north-west of the Maya Mountains as they slope gently down to the Guatemalan border beyond Benque Viejo. The view at a little distance is one of rolling grassy uplands, windswept, wide, and suddenly free from the dank entanglement of the airless bush, while scattered singly or in graceful spinneys are the pines which give the ridge its name, pines like those out of which they cut planks and pit-props at home. The effect is not unlike parts of Derbyshire, with here and there even outcrops of limestone to give it greater similitude. The area is not a large one —perhaps fifteen by twenty-five miles—and it is deplorably inaccessible at present, but its possibilities are obvious. Here, as everywhere else, the main problem of the Colony is transport and all-weather roads linking such places with Belize. This is where financial help from the home Treasury is absolutely essential, as every Royal Commission has recognized, for it is difficult country for road-making—innumerable rivers or rivulets to be bridged, flooded savannahs to be drained, jungle growth to be cleared, and everywhere (at any rate in the populated northern half of the country) a depressing dearth of the raw materials out of which metalled roads are made. But it would be an excellent investment for Imperial capital.

Given reliable and swift communications, the Pine Ridge, already supporting thousands of rather scraggy and udderless cows,[1] could be made the centre of a great dairy-farming enterprise. True, the green grass on a closer view is seen to be somewhat thinly spread upon the sandy soil, but it is well within the wit of man to-day so to fertilize the soil and breed new grasses that where one blade grows to-day, two would sprout up to-morrow. As to cows, the modern stockbreeder could soon provide the kind best adapted to the Colony's environment. It would not be long before we should see the up-river farmers sending refrigerator trucks full of milk, butter, and cheese down to the capital and every village along the route. That this is no idle dream may be perceived by anyone who takes the trouble to read the sober, expertly reasoned, yet confidently proposed plans for colonial development put forward by the recent (1948) Evans Report on British Honduras—from which most of the statistical figures of this chapter are taken.[2]

If the Pine Ridge and similar districts could be used for dairy-farming, it is likewise only the absence of good communications which prevents the 'banks' (villages) along the Belize and other rivers from becoming prosperous farms, market-gardens, and luscious orchards. The soil along the river banks is composed of rich fertile marl, the tiny allotments at present cultivated being amazingly productive despite inferior seeds, methods, and tools. There is almost nothing that British Honduras could not grow, and grow well. All that is needed is the incentive of being able to sell the surplus of one's produce to the outer world for cash, and, of course, being able to spend the cash on something useful or attractive when it has been earned.

Both these things—the marketing of produce and the local supply of 'consumer goods'—depend again on roads. The rivers are too slow, exhausting, and unreliable for brisk commercial transport. Even on the most navigable of them, the Belize River, there are floods, rapids, and tossing logs from the mahogany camps, and though it is comparatively easy to get down to the coast, it is terrible work paddling back again upstream. The Open Sesame to prosperity in British Honduras is roads. Actually,

---

[1] The 1947 *Colonial Annual Report* figures are 16,650 cows, 11,300 pigs, 1330 sheep, 450 goats, and 68,700 chickens, turkeys, and ducks for the whole Colony—already a vast increase on former figures. But in 1948 these figures show a considerable drop—cattle 10,600, pigs 10,000, sheep and goats 500, poultry 45,000.

[2] *Report of the British Guiana and British Honduras Settlement Commission.* Colonial Office. 1948.

during the last ten years or so this has been not only recognized but acted upon. With assistance from Colonial Development and Welfare funds, excellent roads, metalled, and with bridges, have been opened up with a combined stretch of over 300 miles, this being about 295 miles more than were in existence twenty years ago. In those days the journey from Belize to El Cayo took two or three days by boat; to-day one can do it in a car within three hours. There is now also a good wide road from Belize to Corozal, and many others, while the Commission recommends expenditure to the tune of half a million pounds on further roadmaking, in the certain hope that this improvement in communications would at least make the Colony self-supporting.[1]

Surely it is one of the biggest economic puzzles in the Empire that a Colony so rich in agricultural resources and advantages as British Honduras should up to the present be importing so much of her food from abroad, to the annual value of over $2,160,000 for a population of only 60,00 in a country where even the telegraph poles take root and grow! To say nothing of tobacco. Imagine importing $54,000 worth of tobacco to a Colony where the buccaneers grew more tobacco than they could smoke by merely planting their dottles, so to speak! No wonder the Commission speaks hotly (for a Royal Commission) about the 'abnormal neglect of agriculture' in the Colony, and its many wasted opportunities.

Agriculture, fruit-growing, and forestry of various kinds is the obvious *métier* of this place. It was intended by Nature for that very purpose. It is true that the mineral possibilities of the mountainous southern half of the Colony have not been explored. The traces of gold, silver, and tin which have been found there may or may not be indications of rich veins or pockets of precious metal, hidden beneath the roots of the gigantic trees which bar the slopes to any but the most toilsome access. The copious oil-bearing substratum of southern Mexico may or may not be continuous under the mountain massif which connects it with the Toledo District. But what of it? The crying need of the world to-day is food. This is the 'Green Gold' of the tropics, and the scientists warn us it may be still more precious the day after to-morrow. Here is the true treasure-trove of our Colony, and

[1] It would also, of course, make it a better customer for British motor-vehicles and the like.

more worth digging for than any of the 'Buried Treasure' of the pirates, old or new.

Here is a list of the exports from Belize from the figures (for 1946) given in the Evans Report. What a pitiable picture of neglect or decay most of them present! Bananas, ravaged by preventable disease and soil erosion, have dropped to a mere 84,000 stems. Coconuts (copra) have sunk from a peak of over 9 millions to just over 2½ millions. Mahogany, which touched the 25 million mark in square feet twenty years ago, has dropped to 6 million. Cedar with 250,000 square feet is barely one-tenth of what it used to be in the palmy days of the trade. Even chicle (chewing-gum) has declined from 3 million pounds to an unsteady 800,000. Some of the old 'staple industries' of the Colony—sugar, tortoise-shell, sponges, logwood—are too unimportant for mention in the statistics of 'Principal Exports'. Only two items show notable increases: citrus fruits and (strangely enough) crayfish or 'rock-lobsters' for canning.

The Royal Commission lays great stress on the development of this Green Gold in all its many forms. Some of them have already been tried with success: some have been tried and found wanting, but not with modern methods or scientific knowledge: many have never been tried at all. Under the heading of 'Forestry', the Commission take for granted, of course, the continuance of the traditional trade in mahogany, sapodilla gum (chicle), cedar, and pine. But others could be started or revived. Sugar has a long chapter all to itself, the total cost of growing, crushing, transporting, and marketing being carefully worked out to the last cent, with promising results—not forgetting its by-products, especially rum. Cocoa has another closely knit chapter to itself. Experience has already shown that the soil and climate are peculiarly adapted to this plant, and trees set more than fifty years ago are still bearing fruit without any attention at all. It is a long-term policy, for cocoa crops take five years to mature, but the Commission is enthusiastic about its future, especially as most of the other cocoa-producing areas of the world seem more or less worked out. As for citrus fruits, there can be no question that the Colony offers a veritable gold-mine for this Green Gold —oranges, lemons, limes, and the Gold Medal grapefruit already mentioned. To say nothing of coconuts, mangoes, pineapples, custard-apples, yams, paw-paws, sweet potatoes, plantains, melons, and all the other fruit or vegetable dainties for which the West Indies are famous, including cassava, rice, and (despite previous failure through disease) the now resistant type of banana, yellow or pink. There are many other vegetable growths which should certainly, according to the Commission, be given a trial, such as sea-island cotton (grown successfully two hundred years ago by the freebooters on the cays); abaca for the manufacture of hempen ropes, most of which at present comes from the Philippines, and has to be paid for in dollars; and the floss of the native polak-tree, which is superior to kapok. Groundnuts, despite the disastrous experience in Africa, are already being tried out. The outlook for sisal is good. Nutmegs flourish wherever cocoa grows, and so on with a score of minor crops.

While on the subject of natural products, mention should be made of the hitherto almost unplumbed resources of fishery. The old settlers knew all about the wonderful fishing around Belize and the cays: it has a clause all to itself in many of the old treaties with Spain: and to-day (quoting the Commission) this area 'appears to be among the most fertile fishing grounds in the Caribbean', both for sport and food. All that is needed to raise it to a staple industry are canning factories and cold-storage ships. Sonnets have been dedicated to the tasty land-crabs of Belize, and the reefs off shore suggest an ideal planting ground for oysters—perhaps for pearls. All this is in the nature of Green Gold or its concomitant alloys, so to speak.

Yet up to the present the rich soil of this bounteous country has been scarcely scratched. Members of the Evans Commission were palpably shocked by the neglect of what might so easily become one of the most fertile and lucrative gardens of the Empire. They point out that 'British Honduras is a compact area which presents no major physical obstacles to development', and 'are confident that it offers opportunities for considerable development in agriculture', and so forth. They came to the Colony to see if it were a suitable place for the settlement of immigrants (especially Displaced Persons) from Europe and the overcrowded islands of the West Indies, and ended by enthusiastically recommending it for the purpose.[1] The population density in Barbados is 1200 to the square mile: in British Honduras, a country the size of Palestine but incomparably more

[1] 100,000 immigrants in ten years is the figure suggested.

productive, the density is 7 to the square mile. What could not Israel have done with a land like this!

The Commissioners, prepared for the worst by the miserable hotel accommodation awaiting them in Belize (they mention it at least thrice in accents almost human in their anguish), were nevertheless astonished to find this Cinderella of the Empire quite so poverty-stricken, in the midst of plenty. They could hardly believe the official trading figures, even hinting at 'distortion'. It is certainly puzzling to find that the exports of home-grown produce in this fertile land are only $3,500,000 including everything, while the retained imports exceed that amount by nearly $1,561,000: stranger still to discover that this adverse trade balance is much more than accounted for by imports into the Colony of *food*, to the value of $2,160,000—not delicacies, mind you, but ordinary milk, butter, cheese, meat, grain, potatoes, vegetables, cocoa, and the like, including $112,186 worth of *sugar*, $22,299 of *canned* vegetables, and $7,770 of *canned* fish! Coals to Newcastle is nothing to this! It would be more tolerable if the trade of the Colony were preponderantly with the Mother Country, but this is not so. Three-quarters of the exports of all kinds (75 per cent.) go to the States and Canada, only 16 per cent. to Great Britain; while of all that our Colony buys from abroad, the tradesmen of the States or Canada supply 73 per cent., various other countries 18 per cent., and Great Britain less than one-tenth (9 per cent.).[1]

As regards the Home Country the financial position is even worse with regard to British Honduras than the trading figures would suggest, for the British Treasury has to lend or give her considerable monetary aid as well. Under the recent Colonial Development Act alone an allocation of £600,000 was made to Belize, while the interest on her Colonial Debt amounts to nearly $164,000 a year, or 5.6 per cent. of her total revenue of just over $2,206,000. Not that England grudges the money: she knows it is an excellent investment, and one that is already bearing fruit (in more senses than one). As the Commission point out, 'very great benefit has already accrued from the facilities afforded by

---

[1] The figures in this chapter are given in Honduranian Dollars. Up to 1950 the dollar was worth 4.03 to the pound sterling, *i.e.* 5*s.*: in 1951 it was raised to 2.80 to the pound, *i.e.* 7*s*. in value. To translate dollars roughly into English money, divide by three. The figures quoted here are from 1946 and 1947 returns, before the devaluation was made.

these moneys for the improvement of communications'. More and better roads have aided enterprise and raised the spirits of the Colony generally, especially the great highways which now connect Belize with El Cayo and Corozal—and indeed, via the latter, with Santa Helena and Mexico itself. In the last year for which figures were available at the time of writing (1947); the total revenue had already increased by $300,000, income tax (without changing its incidence) by $86,000, customs by $300,000, total exports by over $900,000, and (perhaps most significant of all) the Government Savings Bank in Belize, which stood at $410,000 before the War, now shows popular savings of $1,736,000. Things are looking up, and the Treasury grants are already justified. They ought to be much larger: indeed, that is what the Commission recommends, to the tune of a further £10,000,000. With this blood transfusion and the requisite human energy, skill, good will, and man-power to make use of it, there can be no doubt that British Honduras would very soon be in a position to repay the Mother Country a worthy *quid pro quo* in dollars, food, timber, and—last but not least—prestige. For it does England little good in the eyes of North or Central America to have a 'possession' so fecklessly neglected, a waif at the window of the wealthiest and most industrially progressive nation in the world.

We have spoken of man-power, without which, of course, nothing can be done even in this labour-saving machine age. Obviously the present population of 60,000 (over 20,000 of them in Belize itself) is far too small to cope with the plans of development outlined by the Royal Commission. It is assumed that there will be a steady flow of controlled immigration at the rate of perhaps 40,000 a year into 'prepared positions' with housing accommodation, amenities and jobs all ready to receive them. But the present 60,000 inhabitants will form the nucleus. They are quite a medley of races, as explained in earlier chapters, but the bulk of them (about 42,000) are coloured folk of African origin, that is to say Creoles, or descendants of the original settlers, mostly diluted with European blood, varying from ebony-black negroid types to dusky white. English (the official language of the Colony) has been their mother and only tongue for centuries, which explains their vexation when people in England during the War congratulated them on their fluency in the language!

They are a fine, upstanding, muscular, cheerful and self-assured people, with strong patriotic feelings, so far but little contaminated by the political and racial bitterness which affects much of the coloured world to-day—and little wonder! It must be remembered that there is here no history of past oppression under slavery, or of an excessive Colour Bar, nor is there any serious quarrel with the Government of the Colony, which, as they well know, is doing its best in the interests of the whole community under very difficult economic conditions. In addition to these coloured Hondurans (as they like to be called) and the 10,000 Maya Indians already mentioned, there are about 4000 sturdy and intelligent Carib Indians, originally (1797) transported from the Windward Islands as auxiliary labour,[1] about 1300 East Indians, 120 Syrians, 50 Chinese, and 150 other races who have found their way to the Colony for one reason or another. The number of whites, chiefly British officials and American or European business men, technical experts, clergy, schoolmasters, and traders, is normally just over 2000.

A labour force drawn from so small a population is obviously entirely inadequate for anything like the overall development of a country the size of Palestine or Wales, but whether it is inadequate in morale as well as in numbers is a matter of opinion. It has been said that 'West Indian labour in relation to its output is the most expensive in the world', in other words, that the coloured man in these parts is lazy, inefficient, and unambitious. Probably the first two counts in this indictment are dependent on the third, for if circumstances over which he has no control bar every possible outlet for ambition, what incentive has any man—black or white—to exert himself unduly? That the Honduran is naturally neither lazy nor inefficient at a job he has been properly trained to perform the present writer can vouch from experience: that he lacks the white man's eagerness to improve his fortune and get on in the world may be true. Indeed, it is almost inevitable under present circumstances. When the average Honduran has earned enough money to feed and clothe himself withal, there is so very little more upon which to spend his surplus earnings, except gambling, drink, and vice. Next to roads,

---

[1] The Caribs are almost unique in having two native languages, one for the men and another for the women of the tribe. They are rather looked down upon by the Negroes as an inferior race.

the crying need in British Honduras is for houses, especially in the towns. In the poorer quarters of Belize the housing conditions are definitely bad—overcrowded, insanitary, and not even picturesque, being mostly rough unpainted clinker-built pinewood huts with corrugated-iron roofs, raised on piles above swamps, and dependent on the sluggish river or canal for drainage. Yet alas! the latest Annual Report confesses that 'No improvement has been effected in the housing situation in Belize.' Till that is remedied, it is fatuous to talk of incentives or the black man's lack of healthy ambition.

It is a difficult problem in any case. By time-honoured tradition British Honduras is a forest-worker's country,[1] and forestry is necessarily a seasonal trade. A few months each year mahogany-cutting or chicle 'bleeding' fills a man's pockets without giving him much opportunity of spending, so that he saves his cash perforce (almost) until his annual 'retirement' to the gay streets and lighted taverns of the city for one long whoopee. Approaching the problem from another angle, the clever coloured boy with white-coated ambitions, fresh from his secondary school examination successes, has little to look forward to but a minor clerking job in an office, or a place behind the counter in a 'store'—unless, indeed, he become a schoolmaster or a minister of religion, which are the least remunerative (financially) of all.

When the projected flood of immigrants arrives, if not before, the whole system of education will have to be overhauled. In Belize itself the schools, both primary and secondary, are surprisingly good considering their handicaps, but elsewhere the standards both of attainment and attendance leave much to be desired. School attendance is supposed to be compulsory, but the present method of scholastic organization is obviously out of date, and quite incapable of meeting any increased demands upon it. It is that which prevailed in England about eighty years ago —every school has to be initiated, built, furnished, and maintained by one or other of the religious denominations out of their voluntary funds, though afterwards (if it proves a success) it may be aided by Government grants. The surprising thing is that the schools are as good as they are, and that they have been able to attract so many really devoted teachers, many of whom are lay

[1] Agriculture was regarded as a job for the stay-at-home weakling, and is still somewhat under a cloud for this old prejudice.

preachers or catechists as well, so that they work a seven-day week for a mere pittance. But there are less than 80 schools in the Colony, and this paucity is aggravated by the lack of transport facilities to collect children living at a distance—roads again!—so that only 45 per cent. of the children can attend at all, and there is much illiteracy. Yet the eagerness for schooling is attested by the fact that of those that are on the registers the average attendance is over 80 per cent., which is by far the highest in the West Indies. Of these about half are Roman Catholic, while the other half is divided between Church of England and Nonconformist. Most of the teachers outside Belize are coloured, either Carib, or Honduran, or (most usually perhaps) from Jamaica. A great need in the Colony is for a Teachers' Training College.

The Medical and Health Services are excellent in quality but deficient in quantity. There is a fine, well-staffed hospital in Belize, and six others up and down the country, with an average of twenty-five beds (including maternity) in all. The health of the Colony, however, is not bad, despite the shortage of doctors, nurses, clinics, and the usual incidence of tropical diseases. Many years ago Belize may have been almost a 'White Man's Grave', like Jamaica and Panama, but those days are long past. As the latest Annual Report observes, 'The climate of the Colony, which in the cooler months is particularly delightful, is quite suitable for people used to temperate zones and little, if any, impairment to health is suffered from prolonged residence.' Only once in the last fifty years has there been any serious epidemic. Cholera and yellow fever are rarely or never heard of. Malaria accounts for most of the certified deaths through disease, but the figures are low. In fact British Honduras—quoting this time the Evans Commission—'has always been famous for the salubrity of its climate and the healthiness of the woodcutters and their labourers'.

The climate of the Colony is, in fact, far from unpleasant for Europeans, especially in the northern half of the country. The Cunliffe-Lister Report (1934) went so far as to say that 'during our journey over the Pine Ridge, the climate would be considered delightful in any country'. In the south the hot humidity of the long rainy season can be trying, but elsewhere the dry season lasts nearly half the year, and from October to January with their prevalent 'norther' winds it can be distinctly cool. The heat in Belize and other places on the coast is always modified, especially towards sunset, by invigorating trade winds from the sea. At the worst, the temperature rarely rises beyond 90 degrees, and frequently falls to 50. Dr. Hunter (1890) summed the matter up in these words: 'For the black man no better country exists, and as a temporary residence for Europeans it equals any and surpasses many of the West Indian colonies.' As to the earthquakes and volcanoes which so trouble the rest of Central America, there are none in British Honduras. Until 1931 there were no hurricanes either, but of late the hurricane belt seems to have become unbuckled a little, as related in a foregoing chapter. The Evans Commission reports that by and large the country is eminently suitable for immigration both by West Indians and by Europeans, despite the usual tropical insects and creepy-crawlies which infest the bush, but may with a little ingenuity be denied admission to dwelling-places. Screened windows, nets, 'Flit' guns, and modern insecticides have made life miserable for mosquitoes, and their old-time whining 'ping' at the drum of one's ear as one tried to sleep is far less often heard.

Dangerous wild animals there are none, except the snakes already mentioned, which are only to be feared in out-of-the-way places. As one tracks through the bush towards evening an occasional 'tiger' (Honduranian jaguar) or a long-nosed tapir may be glimpsed through the trees running for dear life from the smell of a human, a herd of wild pigs (peccaries) may crash through the undergrowth, a sleepy-eyed alligator may flop into the water at the sound of one's motor-boat, or monkeys may roar like lions all through the night. But it is possible to live and work in the Colony for a lifetime without meeting any of these creatures face to face, and one soon gets used to the night noises. In fact, one grows to like them. Near Crooked Tree among the flooded savannahs of Black Creek there is a species of frog chorus which sings *Home, sweet Home* quite movingly.

For those who prefer more sophisticated entertainment the Colony provides various forms of sport and pleasure. Game-shooting in the forests or on the Pine Ridge offers, besides the quarry already named, deer, gibnut, warree, ocelots, armadillo, and 'lions' (Honduranian pumas), also quail, pigeons, wild turkey, partridge, duck, teal, snipe, and so forth. 'There is wonderful sea-fishing all along the coast and round the Cays,' says Sir John Burdon. 'Tarpon are numerous, and other species of interest abound in great numbers.' Tropical sea-water bathing is, of course, one of the major joys of life, especially when protected by a 'kraal' from the attentions of shark or barracuda. In Belize there are tennis courts and a golf course—'with more than 100 holes, all but nine of them made by land-crabs' (says Sir Alan Burns, Governor 1934-39). Polo and football are played in the winter, cricket in the summer. The Belize Jockey Club provides very sporting race meetings at Christmas and the New Year, and the new roads have encouraged the Belisians' favourite sport of Bicycle Marathons. Baron Bliss made special provision in his will for a Yacht Club and two annual regattas —one at sea, for which the harbour and cays around the capital are superbly adapted, the other on the river at Christmastide. The city, which of course is electrically lighted, with ice-boxes, air-conditioning, cinemas, wireless, telephones and the rest, possesses several social and recreation clubs. Indeed the Evans Commission sees no reason why, with suitable hotel and 'country club' accommodation, Belize should not become a popular holiday resort for rich Americans etc. On the more serious side, there are opportunities for archæological research, a museum, a public library, two newspapers, and a useful bookshop. Church life is strong, all the usual denominations being represented,[1] as well as some unusual. In fact a man may have a very good time, in every sense of the word, in Belize, and if his work should compel him to live in some more remote spot, well he cannot be more than seventy miles distant from the city whichever way he goes, and transport is improving every day.

The administration is that of an Imperial Crown Colony. His Excellency the Governor of British Honduras receives his appointment from the King, kisses hands, and within his Colony is the single and supreme authority responsible to and representative of His Majesty. The Governor presides over an Executive Council of three ex-officio members, *e.g.* the Colonial Secretary (of Belize), the Attorney-General, and the Financial Secretary, and such other members as the Royal Instructions empower him to appoint. He

---

[1] Statistics for 1947 as given in *British Survey: British Honduras* were: Roman Catholic, 35,000; Church of England, 12,500; Wesleyan, 8500; Baptist, 1000; Seventh Day Adventists, 900. The Anglican Cathedral in Belize is the oldest non-Roman church in Central America.

presides also over a Legislative Council of three ex-officio members and ten unofficial members. Of these ten, four are nominated by the Governor and six are elected by the votes of the citizens, all questions being decided by a majority of the Council, with certain reserve powers, both negative and positive, retained in the Governor's hands. The administration of justice lies with a Chief Justice and a Magistrate in the capital, with District Commissioners at various stations in the Colony. There is, of course, no Colour Bar, several of the high offices in the State having been held by native-born Hondurans, with conspicuous (it may be added) success. The laws are those of England.

As to the suffrage, every man (or woman), without distinction of race, colour, or creed, who has attained the age of twenty-one is entitled to a vote on certain conditions. (1) He must be under no legal disability; (2) must be a British subject; (3) is not an undischarged bankrupt; (4) has resided in the Colony for at least twelve months prior to registration; (5) has a certain financial standing or stake in the country, viz. he must either draw an income of at least $300 a year (a labourer's wage), or own real property in the Colony to the value of an unencumbered $500, or pay a rent in respect of such property of at least $96 a year; (6) must not have been in receipt of public relief for at least twelve months; (7) nor have been convicted of serious crime. Finally (8) he must be able personally to fill in the date and his signature on the form of application. All this sounds a little cumbersome in these days, but the intention is obvious: the voter must have a real sense of responsibility for the welfare of the Colony, and must be sufficiently well educated to know what he is voting about, and whom he is voting for.[1]

Needless to say, there are agitators who would stir up the people to clamour for unqualified Universal Suffrage in the name of 'Democracy'. At the present time, however, small as is the proportion of registered voters to the total adult population, the proportion of qualified persons who take the trouble to use their vote is smaller still. The percentage of illiteracy is very high, not through lack of intelligence, but by reason of the lack of opportunity for many children to attend school, or to keep up their reading after they have left it. Outside of Belize and the other

[1] This paragraph is summarized from A. H. Anderson's *Brief Sketch of British Honduras* (1948).

towns, there are few facilities for people to keep in touch with national or even local politics, and it is generally considered that to give votes indiscriminately all round would be merely to throw tempting lambs to the many political wolves who would climb to prominence upon their credulity. Even in a comparatively well-informed place like Belize, there is enough of that already, as anyone who has listened to the wild orations on the 'Battlefield', the Hyde Park Corner of Belize, will agree. Nor is the 'value of restraint and moderation' recommended by the West India Commission of 1938 for 'those responsible for the conduct and tone of the Press' always appreciated. Scurrilous abuse of one's betters is always a good way of boosting circulation—and not only in Belize.

Sir Alan Burns has a good story to tell in this connection.[1] The Chairman of the Belize Town Board came to him in great distress one day to say that some Battlefield agitators were getting up a petition to Whitehall for his removal from office as Governor of the Colony. Instead of being terribly hurt or alarmed, as had been expected, Sir Alan announced that he would be only too happy to forward the said petition to the Secretary of State with his own strong recommendation. Furthermore, he would be much obliged for a copy of the document, for he was sure his wife would be glad to append her signature. The message was duly delivered to the agitators. Whether they suspected some sinister trick, or whether they burst out into roars of laughter (which, knowing them, I think is more likely) no more was heard of that particular petition. When Sir Alan relinquished his post in 1939, after almost exactly five happy and productive years of office, he was able to say at his farewell party in Belize: 'No Governor could have wished for a pleasanter people to deal with, and no Governor could have hoped for a more generous appreciation of his efforts than I have received from the people of this Colony.' And he adds in his book: 'I meant what I said.'

The Revenue of the Colony is raised in the usual colonial way. The heaviest item is Import Duties ($1,042,000), which naturally make the cost of living rather high. Against this, there is no import duty on machinery or equipment introduced into the country for the purpose of agricultural or industrial development, which it is desired by all means to assist. Nor is there any tax

[1] *Colonial Civil Servant*, 139.

levied upon the Colony by or on behalf of the British Treasury —a rather unnecessary remark, were it not for the old-standing misconception that in some way our overseas 'possessions' are exploited and mulcted for the benefit of the Mother Country, whereas the very opposite is usually the case. The only payment due from British Honduras to the United Kingdom is interest (at a low rate) on past Government loans. The large sums given to the Colony through the Colonial Development and Welfare funds are of course free of any charge at all. Internal taxation in the Colony is anything but exorbitant. Land tax remains still at the pre-War level of $1\frac{1}{2}$ cents per acre, while income tax for private individuals, though naturally increased of recent years, seems almost too good to be true by English standards. For example, a married man without any children on an income of £1000 a year has only £37 to pay in income tax. Upon which Utopian note it seems fitting to bring this chapter to an end.

Chapter XIV

*

THE CONTROVERSY WITH GUATEMALA

WE must now trace in more detail the legal process by which the settlement in and around Belize became a British Colony in the nineteenth century, not only in her own eyes, but by official recognition as such in Parliament and in the eyes of International Law.

In earlier chapters we brought the diplomatic story down to the LONDON CONVENTION of 1786. According to this, it will be remembered, we agreed to evacuate the Mosquito Coast, and in return secured certain concessions from the Spanish Government. Briefly, the British settlers were granted the right to cut logwood and mahogany for commercial purposes within an area bounded by the Rio Hondo on the north and the Sibun River on the south. Neither by implication nor by argument did we contest the Spanish title to territorial sovereignty over the country at that time. In fact, it was stated in so many words that 'the lands in question are indubitably acknowledged to belong of right to the Crown of Spain'. In order to emphasize this, it was laid down that no fortifications should be erected, nor any system of government, whether civil or military, set up in rivalry to the Government of Spain.

As it happened, this was the last Treaty to be made with Imperial Spain. It was never modified, still less abrogated by that Power, nor denounced—at least for many years—by the British. In practice of course the Victory of S. George's Cay made all the difference to our relations with Old Spain, but the claim to possession by Right of Conquest made at that time (1798) by the local settlers was never officially put forward in any international court, nor officially endorsed by the British Parliament. Even if this claim had been officially made and agreed, it would presumably have been set aside by the TREATY OF AMIENS in 1802 (confirmed by the *Treaty of Madrid* in 1814), whereby all conquests made by England in the war just ended (with the sole exception of Trinidad) were to be restored to Spain. In the strict letter of diplomatic law, therefore, the London Convention was still theoretically in force at the time of the break-up of the Spanish Empire at the beginning of the nineteenth century, and the proclamation of the independence of the Central American Federation on September 15, 1821.[1] The basic standpoint of the London Convention on the subject of Spanish territorial rights in Belize was accepted by the House of Commons for at least twenty years after the Victory of S. George's Cay. As late as 1819, for example, the British settlement was described officially as 'not within the territory or dominion of His Majesty, but merely a settlement for certain purposes in the possession and under the protection of His Majesty'. How it could be 'in possession of' His Majesty and at the same time 'not within the territory of' His Majesty was one of those ambiguities only too typical of early Foreign Office statements about Belize. Vaguely, perhaps unconsciously, one feels that the phrase reveals a growing realization that something would have to be done about the settlement in view both of the failing clutch of Imperial Spain and the increasing prosperity and independent spirit of the settlers.

The break-up of the Spanish Empire in Central America marked a kind of watershed in the political status of Belize: naturally it created a completely new situation. The questions were soon raised: How far were the new republics legitimate heirs to the old Spanish patrimony? How far were they bound by the pre-Liberation treaties? Were they entitled to renew those treaties or repudiate them at will?—and so forth. The problem was still further complicated by the question: how far could these Republics claim to exist at all as political entities, until they should obtain 'recognition' from the Great Powers? And this again was complicated by the desire of the Great Powers to use their grant of recognition as a bargaining counter for trade concessions.

Great Britain's policy since the Victory of S. George's Cay had been to put a blind eye to the telescope as far as Belize was concerned. While paying lip-service in diplomatic quarters to the

[1] In scrupulous accuracy one might argue that the London Convention remained law until 1863, when at last the Spanish Crown was persuaded to recognize that its territorial rights in Guatemala had passed to the new Republic!

theoretical sovereignty of Spain as asserted in the London Convention, she quietly allowed the settlement itself to work out its own salvation on colonial lines, no questions asked and none answered. There was no attempt, for instance, to check the growth of various kinds of plantations for commercial use, nor of fortifications, nor of the local legislative and executive assemblies, all of which strictly speaking were in contravention of the Convention. So that Belize, as we have seen, quickly became a Colony of the Empire in all but name. At the same time, Great Britain secretly encouraged Mexico's exertions to throw off the Spanish yoke, and was by no means antagonistic to the ambitions of the Emperor Iturbide. For it was with Mexico (as she thought) that she would have to deal if any question should arise as to the independence of Belize, and the recognition of the one could be made contingent on the recognition of the other.

It was Iturbide's success in establishing the independence of Central America in 1821, and himself later on as Emperor of the whole, which called forth the first non-Spanish attempt to clarify the new situation. Anxious to forestall a possible scramble for the sweets of empire on the part of any European Power, the United States proclaimed in 1823 the celebrated MONROE DOCTRINE, by which it was made clear that any attempt by a European Power to seize, purchase, or gain in any way a territorial foothold on the Central American mainland would be regarded as a hostile act, and if the fledgeling republics were not strong enough to resist it, the whole force of the United States would be used to do so.

The occasion of the formulation of this 'doctrine' by James Monroe was the rumour that the Holy Alliance intended to help Spain to recover her lost overseas Empire, but doubtless the new cry 'America for the Americans' had other possibilities in mind of a more commercial and less romantic type. However, on Great Britain's inquiry for more information, it was made clear that the Doctrine was aimed only at fresh aggression and certainly not at the expulsion of any Europeans who had already established a recognized footing on the Main. The settlement in Belize, in short, was explicitly neither menaced nor questioned by the United States in the Monroe Doctrine.

The newly liberated Spanish republics, however, sat up at once and took notice that a powerful neighbour was at hand to defend their interests. Mexico, whose Emperor Iturbide had by now been deposed and taken refuge in London, was the first, not unnaturally, to raise the question of the English occupation of Belize. As heir, so she claimed, to the old Spanish inheritance in that part of the world, she graciously offered to renew or confirm in her new status of a free Central American Republic the old Spanish Convention of London, proposing to allow the English settlers to continue in occupation on the lines of 1783 and 1786.

This was Great Britain's opportunity to declare her intentions and define her position in Belize. She was at this time by far the strongest Power in the world, and her word, when she chose to utter it, was practically law in the council of the nations. She might so easily have taken a decisive course. She might have declared that the British settlement, now established for two hundred years, was as much entitled to liberation as any other state in Central America. She might have demanded that Mexico, or Guatemala, or any other adjacent Spanish state, should either show its title-deeds to Belize or else hereafter for ever hold its peace. She might at least have contended that the end of the Spanish Empire had automatically cancelled the London Convention, and that the whole question must be negotiated *ab initio*. Or she might have simply annexed the settlement on the grounds of long use and custom, or on those of possession by Right of Conquest. Unfortunately she did none of these things. She merely looked lazily into her Belize pigeon-hole, took out the latest document bearing on the subject, namely, the dusty old London Convention of 1786 (then nearly forty years old), and made this the basis of her discussions with Mexico. With almost incredible unrealism, she asked Mexico to renew or ratify this Convention —as though the Victory of S. George's Cay had never taken place, as though the then flourishing Colony in Belize was still 'a settlement for certain purposes' on sufferance on Spanish territory, and as though the 1786 limits (the Rio Hondo to the Sibun River) could still contain the Colony's growing power and prospects! On this basis accordingly an ANGLO-MEXICAN TREATY was signed in 1826, in return for England's recognition of the Mexican Republic, and the expenditure of much English money on its liberation and establishment.

But it was worse than that. The sand had scarcely been sifted from the parchment of this fatuous Treaty before the neighbouring Republic of Guatemala protested that it was *ultra vires*. Mexico, she declared, had no territorial rights in Belize at all. The area of the English settlement had never really been included in Yucatan, a province of Mexico, but in El Peten, which had always belonged to Guatemala. It was to Guatemala, therefore, not to Mexico that England should have applied. Against this novel view of the matter, both Mexico and England protested strongly. Belize, they claimed, had always been reckoned part of Yucatan. Whenever Old Spain had wished to intervene in the settlement, which had been very often, it had fallen to the Governor of Yucatan or the Commandant of Bacalar (in Yucatan) to do so. To this Guatemala replied that the Mexican province of Yucatan had always ended at the Rio Hondo, and that if the authorities of Yucatan had taken action in the Belize area, it had simply been out of a desire to be of service to the Land of the Quetzal. Mexico for her part, having secured her recognition, and being not averse to a sly dig at Great Britain, suddenly changed her ground, admitted her mistake, apologized to Guatemala, and tore up the invalid scrap of paper. The Anglo-Mexican Treaty was null and void. Thus all that had happened was a return to the diplomatic *status quo* of 1786. In theory and in strict law Belize was back again where she had been in the declining days of the Spanish Empire, still cutting logwood and mahogany in an area bounded by the Sibun River, by kind permission of a Madrid which had long since almost forgotten the very name of Belize. Not that the settlement worried overmuch, prospering exceedingly on timber, sugar, rum, tobacco, and the rest, and spreading far and wide from the Rio Hondo to the Peten forests and towards the River Sarstoon in the far south.

After this fiasco Great Britain was in no hurry to negotiate any more treaties with an unstable Central America. She would wait until the storm-tossed republics came safely to an agreed harbour where their frontiers and claims should be finally charted. In the meantime, the view that had long been maintained in the settlement, that Belize now belonged to Great Britain by Right of Conquest, as well as by long use and custom, began to take shape in Parliament itself. In 1828, for example, the King's Advocate gave it as his opinion that 'The government were justified in retaining possession of the country (of Belize), which was acquired in the War of 1798. . . . Although the Treaties with Spain disclaimed the acquisition of any territorial rights, he considered that a possessory right had been acquired over the land.'[1] Thus the Home Government was being forced by circumstances to adopt a realistic view of the situation, and once again a new colony was nosing its way into the Imperial family in that unplanned, untidy, indeed almost unwanted way which had become so typical of the Empire. For over two hundred years the foundling had been crying on the doorstep, and now reluctantly a hand from within was beginning to fumble with the latch. But the door had not yet opened. There was still nothing to show in black and white, no deed of adoption, no legal formalities confirming her right to adoption.

Nor did the young Spanish Republics find much time to spare for Belize, preoccupied with their interminable civil wars, assassinations, revolutions, and the mere business of keeping alive. Not until President Carrera, bloodthirsty but efficient, had established once and for all the independence of Guatemala towards the middle of the century, and brought something like stabilization to the other Central American Republics—El Salvador, Nicaragua, Costa Rica, Spanish Honduras, and Panama—was it considered worth while reopening the question of the status of Belize. The opportunity came in 1847, when a Mr. Chatfield was sent from London to act as British emissary in Guatemala, with a view to negotiating a Treaty of Recognition. Chatfield did attempt to obtain Guatemala's acceptance of the British rights in Belize, but met with unexpected resistance, and did not press the matter. The TREATY OF PEACE, AMITY, COMMERCE, AND NAVIGATION which Great Britain signed with Guatemala in 1849 omitted all mention of the Settlement, although Chatfield's covering memorandum explained that the terms of the Treaty deliberately left open the question of defining *boundaries* to a later date. His use of the word "boundaries" is significant. It indicates that already the British Government had made up its mind that the Belize settlement was an Imperial possession. There was to be no reopening with any Spanish Power of the long-vexed question as to British territorial rights in the country. The only point that still remained to be discussed was that of the Colony's precise frontiers or boundaries, especially along the Peten border in the

[1] Burdon, iii, 155.

interior, and the southernmost limits of British rule. From that day to this, a hundred years, the British attitude has been consistent: that Belize is a British possession brooks no argument: that the boundaries of this possession might be adjusted or more clearly defined is another matter.

Thus matters might have remained indefinitely, but by this time the United States was again beginning to worry about the designs of Great Britain upon the Central American isthmus. Chatfield's protracted negotiations with various republics had not gone unremarked, and in particular fears were felt for the future of the great canal which it was planned to cut from the Atlantic to the Pacific Oceans, probably somewhere in Nicaragua. It was felt that the Monroe Doctrine should now be embodied, as it were, in a more formal bilateral agreement. After much negotiating and hard bargaining the CLAYTON-BULWER TREATY of 1850 was the result. With regard to the Canal, America was already in a strong position, for she had signed in the previous year a Treaty with Nicaragua granting to the United States authority to construct and fortify a waterway through the former's territory. The question now at issue was broadly whether England would attempt similar agreements with the adjacent republics, threatening the approaches to the Canal, and thus inaugurating an 'armaments race' in Central America; or whether she could be persuaded by a promise that the Canal should be free to all shipping and completely demilitarized as a *quid pro quo* for her abandonment of any further territorial ambitions in Central America. Sanity and economy in the end prevailed. The projected Canal was neutralized, and in return England undertook to keep out of Central America, on condition, of course, that the United States herself showed equal restraint.

The precise wording of Article I of the Treaty was as follows: 'The Governments of the United States and of Great Britain hereby declare that neither the one nor the other will ever obtain or maintain for itself any exclusive control over the said ship-canal; agreeing that neither will ever erect or maintain any fortification commanding the same or *in the vicinity thereof*, or occupy, or fortify, or colonize, or assume or exercise any dominion over Nicaragua, Costa Rica, *the Mosquito Coast, or any part of Central America*; nor will either make use of any protection which either affords or may afford, or any alliance which either has or may have to or with any State or people for the purpose of erecting or maintaining any such fortifications, or of occupying, fortifying, or colonizing Nicaragua, Costa Rica, the Mosquito Coast, or any part of Central America, or of assuming or exercising dominion over the same,' etc., etc.

To 'keep out' of a place is not, however, at all the same thing as to 'clear out' or 'pull out', as both Mr. Clayton for the United States and Mr. Bulwer for England clearly understood from the beginning. The Settlement of British Honduras (as it had already begun to be called) where England had been firmly established for over two centuries was not included within the scope of the 'any part of Central America' mentioned in the Treaty. Guatemala and Spanish Honduras thought or hoped that it might be, but Bulwer put it in black and white that 'Her Majesty does not understand the engagements of that Convention to apply to Her Majesty's Settlement at Honduras (Belize) or to its Dependencies'. Indeed, if England's holdings in Belize were to be regarded as a European intrusion upon the American continent, the presence of the Americans themselves in the United States might fall in the same condemnation, for there was not much difference in point of time! However, Clayton also put it in black and white that the exclusion of British Honduras from the scope of the Treaty was fully understood. 'The language of Article I of the Convention . . . was not intended by either of us to include the British Settlement in Honduras (commonly called British Honduras, as distinct from the State of Honduras), nor the small islands in the neighbourhood of that Settlement, which may be known as its Dependencies. . . . The Senate perfectly understands that *the Treaty did not include British Honduras*.' He adds that the loose term 'Central America' had been allowed to stand because Viscount Palmerston had assented to it as hardly open to misinterpretation in this connection. Certain anti-British elements in the Senate tried to stir up trouble for Mr. Clayton, on the grounds that he had conceded too much to Great Britain, but the Clayton-Bulwer Treaty was ratified in the end, to the general mutual satisfaction of the two Great Powers, and it was taken for granted that the still unstable Central American Republics would accept the *fait accompli* with gratitude and relief. Guatemala and Spanish Honduras, indeed, the countries most concerned, were in no position to contest an Anglo-American agreement, being hotly embroiled at this time in internal revolutions, external wars, and feverish financial anxieties. Doubtless President Carrera of Guatemala noted the Treaty for future reference, but at this time made no public protest.

It was Great Britain herself who reopened the subject by the sudden proclamation of her British Colony of the Bay Islands, as we saw in our chapter on the Mosquito Coast. There can be little doubt that the phraseology of Article I in the Clayton-Bulwer Treaty had been shaped to include Great Britain's political excursions on the Mosquito Coast and on the Bay Islands of Rattan (Roatan), Utila, and the rest, as encroachments upon the integrity of 'any part of Central America' forbidden by the Treaty. Palmerston's sudden resolve in 1852, only two years after the signing of that Treaty, to interpret the 'Dependencies' of British Honduras as including the Bay Islands, and to annex them unilaterally to the British Crown, can only be regarded as a bold attempt to drive a cart and horse through the lines of the Convention. The roar of protest from Spanish America and the United States very quickly convinced him that he had gone too far. Within less than four years the almost still-born Colony collapsed, as we know, and England's long and carefully built-up edifice of commerce, protective influence, and incipient empire vanished for ever from the Mosquito Shore in the signing of the DALLAS-CLARENDON PACT of 1856.

The Bay Island Colony, however, was not a total loss. Indeed, if one were to judge Lord Palmerston by the standards of modern foreign politics, one might almost suspect him of having made his impossible demand upon the Spanish Republics merely in order to use it as a 'bargaining counter', and to give its abandonment the appearance of a 'concession'. At any rate, the United States Plenipotentiary, Mr. Dallas, received instructions from Mr. Marny, Secretary of State, that in his negotiations with Lord Clarendon he should make it clear that, while no extension of British power in Central America proper could be viewed with indifference, the British tenure of British Honduras could be assured of as firm an approval by the United States as ever. Indeed, 'it would not be of very much moment to the United States, *whether the British tenure at the Belize be enlarged or not*'. Upon this gracious hint, negotiations proceeded with the utmost cordiality on both sides. Mr. Dallas being instructed to 'make concessions on this point, as the means of reconciling Great Britain to other acts which she might be disposed to regard as concessions to the United States', agreed to extend the southern boundary of the Belize Settlement from the Sibun River down to the River Sarstoon. In Article II of the Dallas-Clarendon Treaty of 1856 therefore, it stands that 'Her Britannic Majesty's Settlement called the Belize or British Honduras on the shores of the Bay of Honduras, bounded on the north by the Mexican Province of Yucatan, and *on the south by the River Sarstoon*, was not, and is not, embraced in the Clayton-Bulwer Treaty of 1850, and that the limits of the said Belize on the west shall, if possible, be settled and fixed by Treaty between Her Britannic Majesty and the Republic of Guatemala'. Thus, although the Bay Island Colony and the Mosquito Coast were lost to England for ever, she acquired as a *quid pro quo* the recognition by America of new boundaries for the Settlement of British Honduras which *almost doubled* the area of that colony. President Buchanan and Lord Palmerston shook hands upon it across the water. 'The discordant constructions of the Clayton-Bulwer Treaty between the two Governments,' said the former, 'which at different periods of the discussion bore a threatening aspect, have resulted in a final settlement entirely satisfactory to this Government.'

It was not, however, so satisfactory to the Government of Guatemala, which indeed had not been consulted in the negotiations. By this time Guatemala had convinced herself that Belize and its adjoining territory belonged by rights to Guatemala. President Carrera, bitterly disappointed in the United States, and angered by her 'treachery', but realizing that the Almighty Dollar had spoken, and being badly in need of money, offered to *sell* the territory to England at a reasonable price—or 'in return for some compensation', as he put it.

The British Government, however, felt that England had already paid a good price for the settlement, in the surrender of her Bay Island Colony and Mosquito Protectorate. It was therefore pointed out that Guatemala had never had territorial rights in Belize, and could not possibly sell to England that which was already English. By this time, in fact, the British attitude had hardened. It was forgotten that Spanish territorial rights had ever been conceded. But much water had flown under the Belize bridge since such an admission had last been made, that is to say in 1819, and by implication in the abortive Mexican Treaty of 1826. The break-up of the Spanish Empire—and Palmerston—had made all the difference. The Treaty of 1786, now seventy years old, had become obviously outdated and impracticable in the changed circumstances of the nineteenth century. Yet it was the latest official document relating to the British Settlement in Belize *vis-à-vis* Spanish claimants to the country. It was clearly desirable to have something to show in black and white defining our position. It was decided, therefore, to negotiate an agreement with Guatemala, which, without raising the question of British possessory rights, should settle bilaterally the precise frontiers of the settlement. So eventually the important ANGLO-GUATEMALAN TREATY of September 12, 1859, was signed between the Plenipotentiaries, Lennox Wyke for England and Aycinena for Guatemala, in which, according to the original draft, 'The Republic of Guatemala now and for ever *relinquishes in favor of Great Britain her property and sovereign rights* over that part of territory comprised within the natural and recognized boundaries within her dominions, settled at the present time by subjects of Her Britannic Majesty and known by the name of the Settlement of British Honduras.'

This way of putting the case in a nutshell, so phrased by the Guatemalan Government, was not accepted by the British negotiator. Great Britain could not and would not concede that Guatemala ever had any 'property' or 'sovereign rights' in British Honduras, so that whatever the practical effect of the Treaty might be, it was not in law a 'relinquishing' by Guatemala of any territorial rights at all. These, whatever might be thought about the title of Old Spain, Guatemala had never possessed in Belize, nor had her claim to such possession ever been conceded or even discussed by Great Britain. In this opinion the British Government had been perfectly consistent since the break-up of the old Spanish Empire, and the self-liberation of the Central American Republics. The wording of this first draft, therefore, was rejected at once by Wyke, although it was recognized with satisfaction that Guatemala was prepared to abandon all claims to the country. From the first, therefore, it was made clear to Aycinena that the Treaty was one of *boundaries* only. British Honduras was already a British possession, recognized as such by the Monroe Doctrine, the Clayton-Bulwer Treaty, and the Dallas-

Clarendon Pact, as well as established in the eyes of all the world by the use and custom of centuries and by the final Victory of S. George's Cay. The utmost that Great Britain would concede to Guatemala was her right to ask for a clearer definition of frontiers as between the two countries, especially on the west of the Colony, where Nature had admittedly failed to provide an obvious demarcation. On this basis, accordingly, the final draft of the Treaty began 'Whereas the *boundaries* between Her Britannic Majesty's Settlement and Possessions in the Bay of Honduras, and the territories of the Republic of Guatemala have not yet been ascertained and marked out . . . Great Britain and Guatemala being *desirous to define the boundary aforesaid*, have resolved to conclude a Convention for that purpose.' The boundaries on the north, south and east were then agreed as the Rio Hondo, the River Sarstoon, and the Caribbean Sea respectively. The western boundary, upon which further consultation would be necessary, was roughly drawn as extending from Gracias à Dios Falls on the Sarstoon River to Garbutt's Falls on the Belize River and thence due north to the Mexican border—these being the boundaries of the Colony as defined to this day.

The intention and purpose of this Treaty of 1859 (the last of the treaties, and that which governs the situation to-day) was perfectly clear. But alas! it was soon seen to be no less liable to an aftermath of wrangling and misunderstandings than its many predecessors. British statesmanship seemed to have learnt nothing and forgotten nothing of its inveterate propensity to bungle Belize.

On this occasion it was England's generosity or compassion, or maybe a slight twinge of conscience, which got her into difficulties. Although firmly standing by her territorial rights in British Honduras, and therefore owing nothing to Guatemala for the recognition of those rights, England felt moved to offer the poverty-stricken Republic some sort of compensation for her naturally wounded *amour propre* in the surrender (as Guatemala conceived it) of her title to Belize. The question was, how could England give a *douceur* to Guatemala without at the same time admitting that it was her due? Carrera's proposal that England should *purchase* the territory was obviously out of the question, and had already been rejected. A similar suggestion that the settlers should pay *damages* for unauthorized use of the property was still more unacceptable. The term *compensation* was vaguer, but compensation for what? For loss of face? For loss of business? For the recent extension of boundaries to the Sarstoon River? For the expense and loss of time to which Guatemala had been put in connection with the negotiations and demarcation?

Eventually it was agreed by Great Britain to give, and by Guatemala to receive, an 'inducement' or *quid pro quo* without any particular name, as a kind of gratuitous friendly gift. And the gift, by a brilliant inspiration of the British Plenipotentiary, was to take the form, not of money, but of the building of a trade road from Guatemala to the Atlantic, whereby the commerce both of Guatemala and of Belize would be facilitated. 'It became evident,' wrote Wyke to the Earl of Malmesbury, 'that my negotiations must fail unless I could hit upon a plan whereby the Government of Guatemala would find some inducement for agreeing to my terms. It struck me that the compensation they claimed might in some way be afforded if we aided them in the construction of a practicable cart-road to the Port of Izabal on the Atlantic Coast, whereby the old commercial relations with Belize would be renewed, and both contracting parties mutually benefit, without either appearing to receive a benefit from the other.' The point of this proposal was this: that so far Guatemala City, the 5000-feet-high capital perched among the extinct volcanoes of the interior, was virtually isolated from the Caribbean Sea by the absence of any real roadway, navigable river, or railroad. Transport of merchandise could only be effected by mule- or man-pack, and the provision of an all-weather road suitable for wheeled traffic would meet a real need.

We shall have to return to this road later, for the paragraph which dealt with it caused a great deal of trouble. In the meantime, everyone was satisfied, and the Anglo-Guatemalan Treaty signed on April 30, 1859.

The provisions of the Treaty were briefly as follows: The Preamble has already been quoted, defining it as a Treaty of Boundaries. Article I delimited those boundaries as noted above, from the Rio Hondo to the Sarstoon River and so forth. Articles II and III laid down the method by which the boundaries on the west of the colony were to be marked. Article IV and V refer to the preparation of maps, and the employment of surveyors. Article VI neutralizes for transport by either side the frontier rivers. Article VII speaks of the new road which is to be made.

The relevant clause of this last Article must here be given verbatim: 'With the object of practically carrying out the views set forth in the Preamble of the present Convention for improving and perpetuating the friendly relations which at present so happily exist between the two high contracting parties, *they mutually agree conjointly* to use their best efforts by taking adequate means for establishing *the easiest communication* (either by means of a cart road, or employing the rivers, or both united according to the opinion of the surveying engineers) between the fittest place on the Atlantic Coast near the Settlement of Belize and the Capital of Guatemala; whereby the commerce of England on the one hand, and the material prosperity of the Republic on the other, cannot fail to be sensibly increased, at the same time that the limits of the two countries being now clearly defined, all further encroachments by either Party on the territory of the other will be effectually checked and prevented for the future.'

Despite the engineering alternatives mentioned in the above article, it was at once agreed by both parties that a metalled *road* should be constructed. The precise direction of the road was not settled. The nearest way from Guatemala City to the Atlantic was by Port Izabal on the Rio Dulce, which would not touch British Honduras at all. It was at first in fact, envisioned by the British Foreign Office that the road would be entirely on Guatemalan territory, which would have been entirely within the terms of the Treaty—'a place on the Atlantic Coast *near* the Settlement of Belize'. A more useful, but greatly longer, harder, and more costly road would be one from the capital via Coban and Flores through the Peten forests and so via El Cayo to Belize, but this was not demanded.

Far more serious was the ambiguity of the phrase 'mutually agree conjointly'. Guatemala understood this as meaning that they had mutually agreed with England that the latter should build the road entirely at her own expense as a kind of compensation (albeit not so named in the Treaty) for Guatemala's surrender of sovereignty in Belize. Guatemala in short expected England to foot the bill, whatever it might turn out to be. The British Foreign Office, however, took a very different view. The word 'conjointly' they interpreted as applying to the building of the road—they were to *share with Guatemala* the cost of the work, and share it equally. At first there was some doubt as to how the two countries should pay their fair share. On April 15, 1860, the British Government, a year after the signing of the Treaty, were still discussing this point, and were ready to find the cash and the engineers, if Guatemala would supply the materials and labour. Eventually, however, this was simplified into an offer to pay half the total cost of the construction, this total cost having been estimated at £100,000. England's share was expected, therefore, to amount to about £50,000 sterling. Public money was carefully watched in those days, and the Colonial Office was not too happy about even this comparatively small expenditure on an out-of-the-way colony. But Guatemala was furious with Aycinena. He had sold 22,800 square miles of Guatemalan territory for a beggarly £2 per mile!

But worse was to come. Shortly after the signing of the Treaty, the British Government had dispatched an expert surveyor named Mr. Wray to explore the ground and to prepare a plan with detailed estimates as far as possible of the total cost of the proposed road. Mr. Wray arrived in Central America as directed, but did not seem very anxious to expedite the work, nor was he in the least communicative with the local authorities. After a short excursion through the Republic and the Settlement, he suddenly departed, announcing that he would return in a little while to complete his survey. He was never seen in Central America again. But he was able to report one thing to the British Government, namely, that the original estimate of £100,000 was entirely out of the question: the road, if it could be built at all, would cost at least £300,000. Guatemala protested bitterly: she had not been allowed to see Wray's report, he had never seriously gone into the question of a road through the Republic, his estimate (if genuine at all) was for a road through the notoriously difficult swamps of Belize alone, and in any case Guatemala was not in a position (as England very well knew) to go fifty-fifty on an enormous sum like £300,000.

The British Government replied coldly that Guatemala had mistaken the situation. It had been clearly understood, they said, at the time of the signing of the Treaty that Great Britain was prepared to pay a half share of the sum then estimated for the road, namely £100,000. It was unfortunate for Guatemala that the price had gone up, but that was the Republic's business. England would abide by her promise to pay £50,000, but not a penny more.

It began to dawn upon Guatemala that she had been 'outsmarted' by the diplomats of perfidious Albion. There followed a rather painful exchange of special pleading, indignation, and hard bargaining. A new British Minister, Mr. Mathew, was sent to Guatemala early in 1862. On being confronted by the Guatemalan contention that if the road were not built, then Article VII would be unfulfilled, and the whole Treaty become null and void, he made various propitiatory offers. He suggested that the road should be abandoned, and that Guatemala should accept instead a small pier to be built by the British Government at San José on the Pacific. He asked 'would £25,000 tempt you, without any questions as to its use by your Government?' Other compromises were proposed, until at last Guatemala agreed to a supplementary Convention which should settle once and for all the ambiguities of the Treaty of 1859.

This was the abortive ANGLO-GUATEMALAN CONVENTION of 1863, which has never been fully ratified to this day. In this pact Great Britain promised to pay her half share, namely £50,000, of the cost of the road as originally estimated, provided that Guatemala would pay the balance, whatever it might amount to. By this time, Carrera was in dire need of money, and even £50,000 in cash would have been a godsend. But, to his dismay, the Convention contained a further stipulation. Too canny to pay the lump sum into the bellicose President's sieve-like war-chest, England explained that she would commence payment of the money only after work on the road had actually begun, and then only in instalments of £10,000 a time, as the work progressed to the satisfaction of her inspecting surveyor. Moreover, the road was to be completed within four years. Finally, the Convention to be valid must be ratified by both parties within six months of its being agreed by the negotiators.

The Anglo-Guatemalan Convention of 1863 was signed on behalf of Her Majesty's Government by Foreign Minister Mr. Martin and by Mr. Lennox Wyke on August 5. The pen was then held out to the representatives of Guatemala.

The President of the Republic, however, hesitated to authorize his country's signature to the document. Carrera was at this time involved in a ruinous war with his next-door neighbour on the Pacific Coast, the Republic of El Salvador. To think of starting a cross-country road to the Atlantic, or of entering into unforeseeable financial commitments, was fantastic. So Guatemala kept on postponing her signature to the Convention until the six-months time limit had expired, the Indian President passed to the Happy Hunting Grounds (1865), and the Convention automatically became null and void.

In the meantime, of course, Guatemala did not receive a penny piece from England, not a single sod was cut towards the construction of the transcontinental road, and—an important omission which the diplomats of Whitehall appeared to have overlooked—the 'compensatory' clause, Article VII, of the Anglo-Guatemalan Treaty of 1859 remained unfulfilled.

Not until 1867 did Guatemala feel in a position to raise the matter again. But then, when she professed herself at last ready to sign the Convention, Lord Stanley pointed out that the time limit had now expired. 'H.M. Government declines', he said bluntly, 'to sign *anew* the Convention of 1863, and hold themselves now released from the obligation contracted by Article VII of that of 1859.' He added that it was 'his duty to state in the most explicit manner that H.M. Government never conceded the existence of any territorial rights on the part of the Republic of Guatemala. The 1859 Treaty was merely one of boundaries. H.M. Government did not accept the demarcation of the boundary as involving any cession, or on the part of Guatemala as conferring any title. In the Convention there is not a single syllable which might lead to such a conclusion. England had been ready to perform her engagements: Guatemala declined to do so, but after more than two years called upon its co-signatory to fulfil the engagement which had lapsed.'

Guatemala at once retorted that if the Convention of 1863 had lapsed, then the Treaty of 1859 had lapsed too, owing to the non-fulfilment by Great Britain of the Compensatory Clause in Article VII of that Treaty. England's rights in Belize were accordingly still governed, she maintained, by the London Convention of 1786, merely permitting British timber-cutting in the Guatemalan territory of Belize—if indeed even those rights still survived, seeing that Guatemala had never ratified them in her own Republican name.

Great Britain, however, had done with the matter. In 1862, soon after the signing of the Anglo-Guatemalan Treaty of 1859, Belize had been officially gazetted as a British Colony, and in 1871 was accorded the status of a Crown Colony, which she has retained ever since.

Guatemala, however, did not accept her diplomatic reverses without murmuring as loudly and as often as she dared. Her next overt attempt to reopen the matter was in 1880, when she suggested to Foreign Minister Lord Granville that it might be submitted to arbitration. Granville replied briefly that 'Her Majesty's Government cannot admit that there is any ground for arbitration'. The attack was renewed in 1884 by a letter of protest to Great Britain. On this occasion Lord Granville took the trouble to get legal opinion. Three Judges (Henry James, Farrer Herschell, and Parker Deane) stated that in their opinion 'Articles II, III, IV, and V of the Convention of 1859 are not invalidated by the non-fulfilment of Article VII. . . . The former Articles were in no way made conditional upon the carrying out of Article VII'.

Guatemala's only remaining weapon was a refusal to carry out the bilateral demarcation of boundaries promised in the Treaty of 1859. This poor weapon she used, causing some inconvenience to Great Britain, but more to herself. The boundaries were still unagreed at the end of the century. But in practice the frontiers drawn by Great Britain were accepted, and for many years it seemed that the controversy had died down for ever. All the world recognized British Honduras as an authentic British Colony, a little-known but integral part of the Empire coloured red upon the maps.

Unfortunately the First World War of 1914, which awoke so many sleeping dogs, brought the old trouble to life again. In 1916 a 'lamentable incident' occurred when a party of British soldiers trespassed unwittingly over the still unmarked frontier line of El Peten, and were engaged by Guatemalan patrols in a 'violent skirmish'. Various attempts were made to come to an agreement about the boundaries, but were unsuccessful. In 1929 six British subjects were arrested by Guatemalan police for intruding into Pueblo Viejo, but it was discovered that it was the Guatemalans who were trespassing, and the arrested men were quickly released with apologies.

In 1933 Guatemala renewed the argument in earnest by

announcing that she would proceed with the demarcation, if England for her part would fulfil Article VII, and build the long-deferred road. By this time a perfectly good railway, the Ferocariles Internacionales de America Central, had been constructed between Guatemala City and the new deep-water port of Puerto Barrios on the Caribbean Coast not far south of the Rio Dulce, rendering the proposed cart road commercially superfluous. When Great Britain pointed this out, Guatemala said 'Yes, but England had not contributed one penny towards its cost': which was true. After this, the Belize Government brushed aside all technicalities, demarking the frontier of the Colony itself, unilaterally but with fairness, accuracy, and skill. And so the frontiers are marked to this day upon British maps.

In 1936 Guatemala returned yet again to the attack, hoping no doubt to 'cash in' on the general Appeasement Policy which the British Lion was then adopting to her tail-twisters. Guatemala offered to accept the £50,000 tendered by England in 1863, plus 4 per cent. compound interest accruing since that date, in return for which she would consider Article VII fulfilled, and say no more about it. Lord Halifax balked at this, but in the spirit of the times suggested international arbitration. Guatemala replied that she would accept arbitration from the United States. England demurred: the States were too much like interested parties. She suggested instead recourse to the International Court of Justice at The Hague. It was now Guatemala's turn to refuse: Europe knew nothing and cared less about affairs in Spanish America. She contented herself by reminding Great Britain that the Treaty of 1859 had now lapsed, owing to the non-fulfilment of one of its essential clauses by England. The occupation of Guatemala's territory in Belize by British settlers was therefore illegal: in fact it had been illegal for over eighty years, and England owed Guatemala heavy damages for her long trespass. In 1939 the Guatemalan Government published a voluminous White book in English and Spanish, setting forth its claims, protests, and point of view, with a transcript of the relevant documents. The book was widely read through Central and South America and in the United States. The British Government began to feel that some reply was needed, but at that point the Second World War broke out. On September 30, shortly after the declaration of War, Neville Chamberlain found time to write a pacificatory letter to

Guatemala, promising to go fully into the question 'as soon as ever the War situation permits'.

During the War, Guatemala held her hand in consideration of England's difficulties, but in 1946 renewed her diplomatic offensive with great violence. Foreign Minister Mr. Bevin at once suggested arbitration before the newly established International Court of Justice of the United Nations Organization, devised for just such interstate controversies as this. Guatemala (herself a Member of the United Nations) was agreeable to arbitration, but wanted to know what exactly would be the terms of reference. Mr. Bevin replied that UNO would merely be asked to give a legal opinion on a legal point, namely the interpretation of the Anglo-Guatemalan Treaty of 1859, and how far (if at all) its validity had been impaired by the non-fulfilment of Article VII, and by the non-ratification of the Convention of 1863. It would merely, in short, decide on the point of law. Guatemala, to Mr. Bevin's astonishment, rejected this limitation of the terms of reference. She would go to arbitration only on the basis of '*ex aequo et bono*', that is to say, of general fairplay and equity. It was more than a purely legal question, she claimed—it was a matter to be decided on general grounds of natural right or wrong. In short, it was clear that Guatemala had little faith in her purely legal case. She wanted the whole business thrashing out from the beginning, probably from the Papal Donation of 1493, and decided on the subjective basis of sentiment and sympathy. The proposition, however, did not appeal to Mr. Bevin, and no more was heard of it.

In 1948 a political party rose to prominence in Guatemala which was strongly anti-British, and pro-Action. Secret plans were made to seize the British Colony by force. Airborne troops were trained for a raid on Belize aerodrome. It is said that one Guatemalan plane did actually 'invade' the city, its crew distributing candies to the children in the streets, and promising them still more when Guatemala should rule Belize. At the same time it was reported that Guatemalan troops were massing on the Peten border, which had previously been 'closed' to British commerce, and that a raid was being planned down the river upon El Cayo and Belize, as in the old Spanish days. This was too much. Issuing a stern warning, Bevin sent the armoured cruiser H.M.S. *Sheffield* with marines and troops to the Colony. Another warship was known to be on its way. Guatemala indignantly described this move as a deliberately provocative and hostile action. In Guatemala City an ugly mob, obviously 'inspired' from above, surrounded the British Legation and actually tore down the Union Jack from over the *patio*. But no real damage was done, and after a while the excitement died down. For the time being, Guatemala's protests were confined to the issuing of postage stamps boldly printed with a map of Central America showing British Honduras as a Guatemalan possession, and to the display of a certain amount of 'awkwardness' in diplomatic and commercial relations, such as the continued refusal to allow transit of goods from Peten along the Belize River, and the raising of difficulties over passports and *visas*.

That these pin-pricks are both irritating and bad for business cannot be denied. In September 1949 the Legislative Council in Belize showed its anxiety to have the matter settled once and for all by sending the following unanimous Resolution to the British Government: 'Whereas His Majesty's Government in the United Kingdom has, without prejudice, repeatedly offered to submit for adjudication on a legal basis by the International Court of Justice, the territorial claims made by the Republic of Guatemala in regard to the Colony of British Honduras; and whereas the persistence in voicing the originating claim may, in the minds of some, give rise to uncertainty as to the future status of this colony, and thus tend to discourage to some extent investments from the outside; and whereas the people of this Colony have stated their *unalterable determination to remain British*, and to work out their own independence within the framework of the British Commonwealth: be it resolved that this Council respectfully urges upon His Majesty's Government the imperative necessity to take all proper steps to bring about the speedy determination of the claim made by the Government of Guatemala.'

There was a pathetically familiar ring about this appeal to the Home Government. With a few verbal changes it might have been dispatched at any time within the past two hundred years! Well might Mr. Creech Jones, Colonial Secretary, reply that 'The loyalty of the people of British Honduras to the British connection has never been in doubt, and this latest demonstration of their earnest desire to remain under the British Crown will be a salutary reminder to any who may affect to cast doubt upon its reality.'

As to the main point, the reciprocal loyalty of the Home Government to the Colony and its intentions with regard to it, Mr. Creech Jones stated that 'His Majesty's Government remain inflexibly determined that in the absence of a legal decision by the International Court of Justice that His Majesty has no legal claim to sovereignty over British Honduras, they will not countenance any change in the international status of the Colony or of any part of it'. And there the matter rests at the time of writing.

Chapter XV

*

DEVALUATION AND FEDERATION

UNAVOIDABLE publishing delays make it impossible to bring the story of British Honduras quite up to date, but a word may here be added about the economic and political situation in the Colony at the turn of the half century, that is to say at the end of 1950.

Since the foregoing chapters were set up, the Colonial Office Annual Report for 1949 has appeared, showing that the new Governor, Mr. Ronald H. Garvey, when taking up his appointment in Belize on January 28, was faced, like so many of his predecessors at the beginning of their term of office, with a situation of apparently unrelieved gloom. It is to be hoped that he knew too much of the up-and-down history of his new patient to be unduly depressed, and had enough Latin to read the time-honoured prescription under the Colony's emblem—*Sub umbra floreo*; for the shadow of adversity was undeniably dark, and the assurance that the Colony flourished best under such conditions was a much needed encouragement.

There would be little profit in reproducing the detailed figures shown in the Report. The gist of it lies sufficiently plain in the opening words: "The year 1949 proved to be very difficult for British Honduras. The most disastrous drought in living memory, coupled with a decline in the mahogany and chicle industries, led to widespread distress and unemployment. . . . When the pound was devalued against the United States dollar in September, the currency of British Honduras alone in the colonial Empire remained unaltered. While this reacted favourably upon the cost of living, sterling investors reduced or suspended their activities owing to the unfavourable rate of exchange, and the development and economic life of the Colony was brought to a standstill." There, in a nutshell, is the story of the new Governor's first year in office, crushed (or nearly so) between the upper millstone of an unprecedentedly unkind Nature and the lower millstone of a too kind Home Government.

Mr. Garvey did his best in an impossible situation. Early in the year he secured an allocation of £850,000 from the Colonial Development Corporation (C.D.C.), and created a new British Honduras Development Board to decide how this money could be most wisely spent. Eventually the approval of the Secretary of State was secured, after less than the usual delays, to plans for the reclamation of land north of the capital, for the reconstruction of various streets and a much needed housing scheme, for the completion of various trunk roads, and for agricultural developments on the Old River, especially at Baking Pot. Over half a million pounds were earmarked for these purposes. At the same time, the Governor encouraged the investment of private capital by granting sundry exemptions from customs duties on imports, together with income tax concessions. A licence was granted for soundings for oil, and every encouragement given to all likely enterprises—such as the opening of a newly-discovered salt mine on Ambergris Cay. The result was that by the autumn a distinct lightening in the clouds had become visible. Although the production of the staple industries of the Colony remained at an extremely low ebb—the invention of synthetic chewing gum in America brought no good to the chicle industry—some improvement could be recorded in rice, citrus, sugar, and various kinds of timber, while the membership of that popular Savings Society known as the Credit Union began once more to increase—a sure sign of returning confidence. Unemployment figures began to drop, and discontent to wane. Much satisfaction was felt also in the growing attention paid to the needs of the schools through grants for books and stationery, and the repair of buildings.

Not that the Governor was satisfied with this apparent progress on the long view. He realized only too well, if nobody else did, that much of it was only due to the generous help which the Colony was now receiving from the Mother Country. The economic situation, in fact, was too much like that of modern Israel to be healthy: bolstered up for traditional or sentimental reasons by outside aid from countries, once well-off enough and to spare, but now themselves beginning to feel the pinch. It could not go on for ever. The Colony must learn somehow to stand on its own feet, as in the proud days gone by. In the meantime, one was naturally grateful for the increased interest shown by the Home Government in this one-time 'Forgotten Colony', and for the practical form which that interest had taken. In hard figures, Imperial funds contributed during the year well over a million and a quarter dollars to the Colony's exchequer through C.D.C., grants-in-aid, and remission of the 1931 Hurricane Loan . . . a far larger total than ever before. There were other ways—promises, plans, commissions, and even the prospect of a Royal visit [1]—in which the Home Government was evincing its concern. It was almost embarrassing.

It became definitely so, when in September (1949) the astonished Governor learnt that the Colonial Office intended to single out British Honduras for a singular mark of favour, if not favouritism, denied to any other part of the British Commonwealth. It proposed to exempt Belize from the otherwise universal application of the devaluation of the pound sterling as against the hard currency of the American dollar! It will be remembered that at this time Parliament by a stroke of the pen reduced in one night the value of the pound from 4·03 to a mere 2·80 U.S. dollars. Henceforward, a British pound would only buy about three-quarters of what it had once been able to buy from the States, and, conversely, an American dollar would be able to buy in British shops considerably more than it had ever bought before. This was very nice for America, but not so nice for the British. The only consolation was that British prices would remain the same as among British people, and that the British were all in the same boat.

Except, it appeared, British Honduras.

For generations, the currency of the Colony had been reckoned in dollars, quarters, dimes, nickels, bits, cents, etc. after the American fashion, and the value of the Honduranian dollar had been 'tied' to that of the American in relation to British money. For sentimental reasons, if for no other, it was dreadful to think that the Honduranian dollar might be involved in the devaluation of the pound, and thus lose its ancient parity with that of the States. On the other hand, it seemed rather unfair that the

---

[1] Princess Alice was to be made Chancellor of the new West Indian University in February, and hoped to touch at Belize during her subsequent tour of the West Indies.

British people in the Mother Country and elsewhere should have to stand the losses of Devaluation among themselves, while the British people of Honduras should stand apart, as though within the Empire yet not of it.

It must have been mainly on such grounds that the Home Government hesitated long to make a decision. The Chamber of Commerce waited anxiously for a pronouncement. In London, it was not until October 19 (six weeks after Devaluation elsewhere) that a Mr. P. G. Donald, deputed to elicit the facts, received an official statement from the Colonial Office. In the Colony, however, the news arrived a few days earlier, for on October 13 Lord Listowel himself, Minister of State for Colonial Affairs, arrived in Belize, and informed the Legislative Assembly that a final decision had been made: the British Honduranian dollar was *not* to be devalued, it would be specially exempted, and would remain as before, at par with the dollar of Wall Street.

There was no more popular man in Belize that day than Lord Listowel. The Legislative Assembly, or rather, the majority therein, was delighted. So were the merchants, the shopkeepers, and the masses of the people. Without diminishing one jot their title to the name of British, he had conferred upon them the financial benefits of American affiliation. They turned round and beamed upon their Governor; he had certainly brought them luck. But they failed to catch his eye. He had it firmly fixed upon His Majesty's emissary, and did not look half so pleased as they expected.

The immediate effect of the pronouncement, however, was good; the price of foodstuff and other necessities of life were stabilized, they even tended to go down, while shopkeepers felt able to release their goods from store. One of the Colony's problems at least seemed to have been happily solved.

But it was not long before the Governor's forebodings turned out to have been justified, as we have seen from the first paragraph of the Colonial Office Report quoted above. Present profit, it emerged, could only be accepted at the cost of future disaster. In obtaining exemption from Imperial Devaluation, the Colony had cut herself off from the rest of the Empire, financially speaking, without really winning amalgamation with the States. Every pound received as grants-in-aid and so forth from England was now reduced in value—worth no longer four, but only about three, Honduranian dollars. The same applied, of course, to the large sums coming into the Colony from British private enterprise, and employers found themselves having to pay wages at a correspondingly higher rate. The consequence was that sterling investors shied off, businesses and industries closed down (including every single sawmill), and the Colony's exports, being now as expensive as any other hard-currency exports, sought feverishly for an ever dwindling European market, just at a time when the American importers were beginning to contract their overseas purchases. An additional evil was the wild speculation in currency, which dealt the final blow to public confidence. In the late autumn the situation had become what Mr. Garvey publicly described as 'very grave'. Unemployment was increasing daily, production becoming hardly worth while, savings being withdrawn. The cost of living had indeed gone down a little, but what was the use of that if one had no money at all?—for it must be remembered that British Honduras is ill provided with the shock-absorbers so plentiful in a Welfare State. As exports fell, the wherewithal to purchase foodstuffs from America (North, Central, or South) was lacking, and, owing to the unprecedented drought in the earlier months of the year, the scarcity of homegrown food was even more marked than normal. The Colony seemed actually on the verge of starvation as the winter set in, and to be faced (as so often before!) with utter ruin. Angry disappointment with the Home Government, with the local Legislature, with the Governor, with the United States, and indeed with anything and everything which could be blamed, caused much discontent in the Colony, even to the extent of public disturbances. In England, the *Times* carried several strongly worded letters calling attention to the plight of 'this loyal outpost of Empire'. 'Why must the Imperial Government try the patience and loyalty of this Colony to the uttermost', wrote the Bishop of Honduras (Douglas Wilson), on the eve of his election to the See of Trinidad. 'A Forgotten Colony', cried the *New Statesman*. 'A Challenge to our Christianity!' thundered a Member of Parliament. Adversity had brought her at least advertisement. It was evident that something would have to be done.

In Belize, it was only human nature that the most obvious and immediately effective remedy would meet with most applause—let England put her hand in her pocket and give bigger and better grants-in-aid; let her at least release in actual cash the large sum she had already allocated from C.D.C. to the development of the West Indies in general and of British Honduras in particular. Angry reproaches were flung at the Colonial Office for its meanness and procrastination. What had happened to the high hopes aroused by the Evans Report, now two years old? What practical result had followed upon the special visit of C.D.C. officials, paid to Belize with all pomp and circumstance early in the year? Why had not more been disbursed from the £850,000 long ago earmarked for Honduras? When was the Colonial Office going to abandon its infuriating right to frustrate, delay, and veto expenditure which the local Legislature had sanctioned as urgent? And so forth. All these complaints, among others, were loudly voiced in the Legislative Assembly by its 'unofficial', that is to say by its elected representatives, who, it will be remembered, constitute a voting majority over the 'official' section of that Assembly. It must have been a very trying time for Mr. Garvey, especially as by now he had learned (like many Governors before him) to love his people, yet found himself in radical disagreement with the policy they wished him to pursue.

For Mr. Garvey, though grateful to His Majesty's Government and recognizing the necessity of accepting its help, had no desire to see his Colony permanently on the dole. It was a state of life to which, he felt, God had *not* called it; it was also a state of mind to which it was humanly only too easy to grow accustomed. He was determined that his people should receive only such assistance as would enable them ultimately to stand upon their own feet. To his distressed colleagues in the Assembly, this point of view seemed hard and obstructive. It received even less approval from the small but noisy clique of malcontents outside the Assembly, who were shouting on the Battlefield (Belize's Hyde Park Corner) for adoption by the United States. Not only did he realize that this could only be obtained (if at all) at the heavy price of economic servitude, wherein all the best traditions of the Colony would be violated, but he knew quite well that America desired no further stars on her banner, and was eager rather to circumscribe her commitments, as in the case of the Philippines, than to increase them. He was convinced, in short, that the only way in which to re-establish the prosperity of British Honduras on the long view, was to let the local dollar find its own British level—in other words, Devaluation.

Hints and pleas having failed, Mr. Garvey eventually determined to put the matter plainly before the Legislative Council, and, if necessary, to force the issue. On the last day of the year (1949), therefore, a special *ad hoc* meeting of the Council in Belize was summoned, at which he placed the dilemma bluntly before them. The three months of non-Devaluation had proved a failure. Either the Honduras dollar must swallow its pride, and stoop to conquer, or else it could maintain its high theoretical value, and just cease to exist. The Home Government was willing to accept the Colony's choice; which was it to be? In personally moving that the original decision be reversed, and that the Colony's currency now be allowed to fall into line with the pound sterling, the Governor did his best to justify the proposition by argument. Pointing out the evil effects, already visible for those who had eyes to see, of the refusal to devalue, he assured his hearers that Devaluation would revive waning industries and exports, attract more British capital, and generally create confidence, with an inevitably beneficial result on unemployment. The cost of living, he conceded, would go up, but he promised that he would do all in his power to limit the increases by the imposition of price controls and by the grant of public subsidies, after the example of Great Britain.

But the Governor found, as he had expected, that he was up against a blank wall. The elected members of the Assembly perceived at once that his long-sighted policy could hardly be 'sold' to the excited masses on the Battlefield. No member who voted with the Governor for an increase in the cost of living, however sugared, could hope for the votes of a constituency where the majority lived within a stone's throw of excitable mass meetings, their verandas ready to tremble at the thud of marching feet, their political reading-matter confined to the lurid *Bill-Board* or the respectable but rather flimsy *Clarion*. Moreover, a certain whiff of colour-consciousness was by this time wafting over from Jamaica, even to British Honduras, so long free of that sort of thing; there were some who got satisfaction from opposition to a white man for its own sake. There was also, of course, a more respectable prejudice against Devaluation. Habit and tradition die hard, and the Colony had 'always' had her currency tied with that of the States. Moreover, certain influential sections of the community, such as the importers, genuinely feared the effects of Devaluation on their interests.

At the end of a stormy meeting the unofficial members voted unanimously against the Governor's proposition, and, since they form a constitutional majority on the Council, the noes had it.

But the matter could not so easily be ended. Completely convinced that Devaluation was a matter of life and death for the Colony, Mr. Garvey steeled himself to do what many Governors have had to do before, but all have equally hated. Using his 'reserve powers' under the constitution to act as the finally decisive representative of His Majesty the King, he announced that he intended to override the vote of the majority, and to put his proposal into immediate effect. As from the first day of 1950, therefore, the Honduras dollar was devalued in relation to the American dollar in conformity with the rest of the Empire, and became worth only 2·80 to the pound, instead of 4·03. In other words, its value dropped from 100 to about 70 American cents.

The value of the Governor dropped, in the eyes of the masses, even more steeply. He was accused, like some of his notable predecessors, of 'dictatorial methods'. His effigy was hanged on the Battlefield. 'Garvey must go!' became the cry of the agitators. Conversation in Government House could hardly be overheard above the strains of 'God bless America', and various well-known hymns, such as (somewhat inconsequently) 'Abide with me', played by relays of brass bands. At Stann Creek one of the city councillors who had ventured to say a good word for the Governor was shouted down and forced to parade through the streets under an enormous Stars and Stripes. In Belize an official was chased through the town for saying he hoped Princess Alice, then on tour of the West Indies, would manage to include a visit to Belize. One or two ugly incidents necessitated the use of tear gas at last, and the prohibition of public meetings, but on the whole the temper of the crowds, many of them unemployed and with little to do but work up cheap excitement for themselves, was that of the usual Belisian mob, with its lightning changes from fury to gargantuan laughter, from boyish violence to apologetic sheepishness. The agitators from outside found them poor material to work upon, though of course, for some types, agitation is its own reward. Incidentally, it is to the credit of Guatemala that she took no advantage of these disturbances to inflame the atmosphere still further—indeed, as was her custom when the Colony was in trouble, she deliberately held her hand—save for a formal protest or two, just to give her case an airing.

Through all those anxious weeks of January and early February (1950) the Governor showed no sign of weakening—even when Princess Alice intimated that the time seemed unpropitious for her visit to the Colony, and cancelled it. It must have been a bitter disappointment, but he went forward with a host of remedial and constructive measures, which little by little began to set the minds of his people at rest, especially when it was seen that he was no more susceptible to the complaints of powerful financial interests in the Colony than he was to mob oratory. Price controls were put into effect on most of the necessities of life. On January 15 he broadcast an appeal for labour on various big road construction schemes, to be started immediately with £250,000 actual cash which the Colonial Office had that very day released for the purpose—the principal road being one long needed, but very expensive, linking Stann Creek with the capital. Concessions were granted to various private concerns, such as an exploration company for prospecting for oil, a Jamaican scheme for expanding the citrus industry, and a Canadian enterprise for cultivating a 45,000 acre estate on the Belize river. All this did not prevent the Legislative Assembly from sending a petition in early February direct to the King and Privy Council, begging them to reverse the Governor's decision about Devaluation, and to send them a million pounds by return of post. Neither the Governor nor (as far as I can find) the King seem to have been much moved by it, although shortly afterwards a further £84,000 was released for road construction and for improvements to the hospital, and mention was made of a guarantee by the British Government of the purchase of 25,000 tons of sugar per annum on very favourable terms for the Colony. Also a grant was obtained from the C.D.C. of nearly £7000 for the rebuilding of the Baptist school at Crooked Tree far away up Black Creek, and £3000 for nurses' homes. In the late spring the Governor was evidently rising in popular estimation, for he was asked to assist at the consecration of a new Wesleyan church in Belize, which he did.

By the middle of March, the prospect was already brighter. By the end of April the Governor could travel about his Colony ten times more quickly and comfortably than any previous Governor. Two great trunk roads, (1) from Belize to Corozal and over into Mexico, (2) from Belize to El Cayo and over into Guatemala, were now completed, as well as roads connecting Stann Creek with Middlesex, and Punta Gorda with San Antonio. Other important roads were in process of actual construction, *e.g.* from Roaring Creek to Middlesex (as advised by the Evans Commission), from El Cayo to the Pine Ridge, and from Orange Walk inland. The most difficult and expensive of all was the short road, only fourteen miles, called the Hector Creek Road, eliminating the awkward ferry at Boom on the route from Belize to El Cayo. Each of these roads were now employing hundreds of workmen, either in construction or maintenance (the latter an exacting business in the tropics), and the figures for unemployment were showing a marked decrease. There were now, in fact, only 1699 unemployed in the Colony, of which less than 300 claimed unemployment benefit in Belize itself. But road building was not the only work that could be offered. The re-afforestation of the country absorbed many, as well as its subsidiary activities like the construction of fire-lines, the clearing and levelling of sites, and of course the paper work connected with most industries. Private companies were working on such schemes as the processing of sea-foods, edible oil, soap, tannic acid, tomatoes, salt, and other novelties. Work was begun on the $360,000 hotel in Belize, which, when finished, would prove a distinct amenity and inducement to visitors. Five hundred new acres were laid under cacao, and the banana plantations were extended. Plans were in existence for many more enterprises. In short, although Devaluation had been put into force only five months earlier, events were proving that the Governor had been right after all. By the end of May he was being publicly described in Belize as 'the best Governor in the West Indies'. On this occasion the speaker was not shouted down.

It was not surprising, therefore, though highly gratifying to all concerned, when, on June 9 (1950) his name appeared among the Birthday Honours as Sir Ronald H. Garvey, K.C.M.G.

The following month a new Bishop, Gerald Henry Brooks, lately Archdeacon of Nassau, was consecrated in Belize Cathedral by the Archbishop of the West Indies (Dr. A. Knight), the Bishop of Nassau, the Bishop of Trinidad, and the ex-Archbishop of the West Indies, Dr. Arthur Dunn, to whom this book is dedicated.

By the summer of the year, it seemed clear that the worst was over. Once again the marvellous recuperative powers of the Colony had won the day, or at any rate turned the tide. As a warning against over-confidence, a serious fire swept through the wooden houses of Albert Street, rendering over a hundred people homeless, but it failed to check the onward march. At the end of 1950 Sir Ronald Garvey was able to present at the new session of the Legislative Council a very different report from that of his first year of office.

The 'true' revenue for 1950 had amounted to $2,600,000 which was $150,000 more than any previous record for the Colony! For the first time in its history, Income Tax had exceeded half a million dollars, which was 15 per cent. above any previous record. Such was the heartening beginning of the Governor's Report. Owing to the devaluation of the Colony's dollar, the comparison with previous figures might be a little misleading, yet they showed that the patient, whose life was once despaired of, had turned the corner of convalescence. Tribute was next paid to the Home Government. Whatever might have been said in the past, no one could now complain that the Colony had been forgotten, or grants-in-aid begrudged. The sums allotted to British Honduras in 1950 by the Colonial Development Corporation had 'dwarfed all previous annual receipts'—they were well over $3,000,000. This meant that since the notorious hurricane of 1931 which first gave the Colony its place in the sun of Imperial recognition, the total grants from the United Kingdom exceeded $12,000,000, an average of about $600,000 a year. And more had been promised for 1951, when British Honduras would enjoy a share of the additional $20,000,000 allotted by C.D.C to the West Indies. Many promising plans had been made by C.D.C. in conjunction with the Legislative Council for further development of the Colony and its resources. The Honduras Enterprises Company Ltd. had now been taken into full partnership by the Corporation. Substantial progress had been made in the revival of banana production in Stann Creek, and it was expected that the output for the ensuing year would reach at least 40,000 bunches. The new hotel would be finished by Christmas. At Barton Creek satisfactory progress had been made with the production of ramie. And there were many similar schemes afoot. In fact 'C.D.C. had more projects approved for British Honduras than for any other colony in the Empire, with the exception of Nigeria'.

This new spate of activity was not wholly financed by public funds. The Governor was at pains to record his 'deep appreciation of all who have shown sufficient confidence in the future of the Colony to invest money in its development'. In particular he mentioned the Citrus Company of Stann Creek, the Salt Creek Estate Company, the Spanish Lookout Banana Company, and a number of agricultural development enterprises in which steady progress was being made, encouraged by the new colonial Agricultural Loan Board. During the year many schemes for rural improvement had been carried into effect. $20,000 had been spent on building a new police station at Orange Walk. The Belize Electricity Board was now in working order, financed by a loan of $75,000 which had been fully subscribed locally. 'It was very heartening', observed the Governor, 'to see that local business men were prepared to find the funds required for investment in local development: a very healthy sign'. The Forestry Department had continued the good work of planting mahogany and pine; there were now 493 acres of the former and 862 acres of pine plantation, the growth in either case being 'exceptionally good'. The sawmills had started up again, and a new Sawmillers' Association formed. Trade had improved both with Great Britain and with Canada and the United States. As a result of all this, unemployment figures had been materially reduced, and the whole atmosphere of the Colony changed for the better. As the Belize *Clarion* remarked in an editorial on the last day of the year, 'We firmly believe we are on the road to that development which all of us so ardently desire. Let us then go forward with a firm resolve to do our best for British Honduras in the New Year and all the years to come'.

On this hopeful note, struck on the last day of the first half of the century, our brief history of the Colony may well conclude. It has been a chequered story of light and shade, ruin and recovery, constant battle with the forces of nature, the malignity of enemies, the indifference of friends, the climate and its pests, the impersonal hostility of political and economic situations over which the Colony had no control, the difficulties inherent in its unique geographical situation. At times the final goal of triumph seemed within its grasp, only to recede again. But British Honduras has never yet surrendered to her enemies, nor deserted her friends.

And what of the future? One of these days, if she gets down to work, and manages to retain her traditional qualities of courage, loyalty, and good humour, British Honduras will find her place in the sun. But she will not find it by her unaided efforts, nor in the 'splendid isolation' which a number of her citizens seem loath to relinquish. Time presses now, and will not wait for the slow, haphazard, halting progress which was good enough, perhaps, for the days gone by. It will be a long time before the ground of this neglected Colony is sufficiently fertilized to bear fruit of itself. For speedy and planned development of her latent wealth, still more money, men, machinery, and materials are required, and required quickly. Plans and promises are worse than useless, unless followed up by action; hopes that cannot or will not be realized are best never raised; and there is no more bitter hatred than that of love and trust turned sour. It may even become a matter of life and death for the Colony that she should receive this material assistance promptly and adequately, if not from England, then from other friends. Already voices have been raised, as we have seen, in favour of inclusion within the financial orbit of the United States. It would be a high price to pay for American dollars, if the proud citizens of Honduras were to surrender their British rights of racial equality for such a pottage as is served up in the States for people of 'coloured' stock. Other voices have been raised in favour of submission to Guatemala on the grounds of the Republic's 'natural contiguity', and the future which undoubtedly lies ahead of that great country. From the racial point of view, that would be even worse than union with America, for the Guatemaltecan finds a non-Spanish European almost as distasteful as a Negro, especially if he be a Protestant; and after all that has happened, the attitude of Guatemala to a Belize petitioning for adoption would be that of an exultant victor to a beaten foe. There are a good many Indians and Ladinos in the Colony, but she is a long way yet from a readiness to accept the Spanish-American way of life. Nor, for that matter, is Guatemala financially ready to shoulder additional responsibilities.

Looked at impersonally and sentiment apart, the future of the Colony does seem to lie within the British Commonwealth. Neither Belize nor Great Britain can afford a divorce. The latter needs, and may need still more, both the great wide spaces of this still mostly unoccupied 'possession' of hers, larger by itself than all the British West Indian islands put together, and also the foodstuffs which it is in the power of the Colony to provide—to say nothing of its strategic importance. Belize, for her part, cannot do without Great Britain or the British West Indies, with which her economy has been linked so long, and of which she is a blood relation.

The precise nature of this relationship of the Colony to the Commonwealth, however, will have to be looked into. Colonies, like children, grow up, and there is nothing unfilial in asking for a latchkey. British Honduras, like other parts of the Empire, is afflicted with 'growing pains', disturbing to the maternal though exhilarating to the adolescent breast. Both racially and commercially she is becoming more conscious of herself as a separate personality, with rights and opportunities of her own. An unsympathetic observer might say she wants to have her cake and eat it too, for while she is ready to accept the privileges, she is not always very cheerful about the obligations of attachment to the Old Country. Racially, while acknowledging that she has little to complain of as regards the conduct or ability of the white men who, on the highest level, manage her affairs, she feels that her citizens are still some distance short of that equality of opportunity which can only be gained by education and the experience of responsibility. There may be no discrimination against colour, as such, but discrimination against ignorance and inexperience there is bound to be, and it is time (she feels) that these two disqualifications be removed from large numbers of native Hondurans by better education, by the granting to them of more positions of responsibility, and by letting them make their own mistakes. Such ambition is right and proper, although it may take temporarily unpleasant forms. There are parts of the West Indies where the colour prejudice works bitterly in reverse—where it is enough for a man to be white, for him to be damned, whatever his record or capabilities. This is not so in British Honduras. Nevertheless, there is a feeling that so far, the white man has had all the luck, and now the local coloured boy should have a chance to make good.

The matter is not quite so simple as that either, for in Belize there are natives and natives, poles apart: on the one hand those of predominantly African stock, on the other those in whom European blood is so generously transfused that they can easily be mistaken for English. Many of the latter are well-to-do, physically handsome, cultured, and in the best sense of the term, refined. Intermarriage between their womenfolk and locally resident Europeans is not exceptional. They compose, in fact, a distinct social class. However, that is a problem not confined to British Honduras!

Politically, Honduras is a little restless, like the other British West Indies, under the tutelage of the Imperial Government, and the over-cautious manner (as she regards it) in which democratic rights are conceded. There is a certain amount of wild talk about independence, self-government, Dominion status, republicanism on the Irish pattern and so forth—not taken seriously by responsible elements in the Colony, yet symptomatic of an underlying desire for greater freedom of self-expression. The constitution of a Crown Colony, once the proud goal of the settlement's ambition, is now sometimes felt as an archaic survival which might well be modified. The 'official' membership of the local Parliament, although in a numerical minority as against the elected members, is criticized much in the same spirit as the House of Lords by leftists in England; while the Governor's 'reserved right' to veto or initiate legislation is described, as we have seen, as 'dictatorial'. The claim of the British Government, as the Colony's creditor, to scrutinize local expenditure is on a different footing, but that too is often resented. Finally, although the colonial suffrage is adult and without distinction of sex, there is still a financial qualification which provides the Battlefield demagogues with many bullets to fire at the constitutional *status quo*.

This question of the suffrage is, perhaps, the most difficult of all, especially as the qualifications demanded for the vote are by no means standardized throughout the West Indies. On the one hand we have the doctrinaire theory of complete 'democracy' in the Western sense—one man (or woman), one vote; the only qualifications being those of age, residence, and mental normality: universal suffrage, in short. On the other hand, such a standard presupposes, in the countries where it has been worked satisfactorily (more or less), a certain background of organic political evolution and general culture. It assumes at least, that the vast majority of adult voters can read and write, and are thus able to form a considered judgement of the proposals put forward on the various electoral platforms. Large numbers, probably the majority of the people in Honduras cannot read easily, nor is there much for them to read if they could. There are at least three languages widely used, but not one of them understood universally, whether English, Spanish, or Indian. Outside the larger towns, the constituencies are sparsely populated by people often completely out of touch with each other or with centres of information. Frankly, the time seems hardly ripe for adult suffrage. Yet it is obvious how such a statement could be made use of by a political agitator to stir up trouble on the Battlefield in Belize.

This question of the suffrage is bound to become a major issue in the near future, especially in connection with the proposed Federation of the British West Indies, to which we will now turn.

Federation of the B.W.I. has been 'in the air' for a great many years—ever since the successful federation of the colonies of British North America in 1867, in fact. There are still seven distinct governments—British Honduras, Jamaica, the Leeward Islands, the Windward Islands, Barbados, Trinidad, and British Guiana with their dependencies—but there were originally many more. In 1871 the Islands of Antigua, S. Kitts, Nevis, Montserrat, the Virgins, and Dominica experimented in a kind of loose federation, but without permanent success. In 1885 Barbados was granted a separate government so that the rest of the Leewards and Windwards could combine, but that too failed. In 1899 Tobago was united with Trinidad, and has so remained —the only real success in the direction of Federation up to date. In 1921 Lord Halifax, after studying the question on the spot, reported adversely on the feasibility or advantages of Federation, as did many other powerful influences in the Caribbean. A further attempt was made by a Royal Commission sent out in 1932 to consider closer union between Trinidad, the Leewards, and the Windwards, but this also came to a negative conclusion. So did an unofficial conference of West Indians held in Dominica the same year—the principal difficulty being that of the franchise.

But from this time onwards the weight of progressive West Indian opinion began to make itself felt, until in 1938 a Labour Congress of the B.W.I. demanded Federation, a totally elective Legislature, and a standardized franchise throughout the West Indies, cutting the Gordian knot of the age-old problem by asking for nothing short of universal adult suffrage, with no stipulations save those of residence. By this time the economic advantages of Federation had won recognition nearly everywhere, and the Second World War put the final seal upon it. The scattered British islands and territories of the Caribbean just could not go on any longer as isolated units, each with its separate standards of welfare, civil service, medical, postal, and excise regulations. These units were now admitted to be peculiarly unsuited to economic self-sufficiency; they had been trained from time immemorial to produce specialized crops for export to the Mother Country—timber, sugar, fruits, etc.—and to sacrifice a balanced internal economy to that end. It was neither fair play nor business that in the wild fluctuations of markets in the modern world, each unit should be expected to bear on its own shoulders the brunt of a collapse, say, of the world demand for mahogany, or for cane sugar. Some device for commercial mutual insurance was indicated, a kind of business merger. But this, it was gradually realized, would be impracticable without some sort of political closer association, or Caribbean Federation.

The stage was thus set for the Montego Bay (Jamaica) Conference of 1947, personally attended by H.M. Colonial Secretary, Mr. Creech Jones, where the whole question was discussed by representatives from all the B.W.I. In the end, general approval was given to the idea of forming a B.W.I. Federation, possibly along the lines so successfully followed in the Commonwealth of Australia. Finally a committee was set up, the 'British Caribbean Standing Closer Association Committee', under the chairmanship of Sir Hubert Rance, which published its Report in 1950. The representatives of British Honduras on this committee were the Hon. W. H. Courtenay and Mr. F. R. Dragten. They approved of the proposals in general, and it became their business upon the publication of the Report in that crowded and momentous year, to explain them to the Colony, and to defend them against the criticisms of somewhat suspicious audiences in Belize, Stann Creek, Corozal, El Cayo, and wherever in the Colony a politically-minded crowd could be gathered together.

What everyone, or nearly everyone, wanted in British Honduras, as elsewhere in the B.W.I., was 'real political independence'— at any rate as a long-term policy — but within the protective embrace of the old Empire to which they had adhered so loyally and long. There were many Hondurans who at first sight saw in the proposed Federation, not progress towards the goal of independence, but merely a change of masters. They bitterly resented 'merging their identity' in a general West Indian amalgamation, where their comparatively small population would find British Honduras overshadowed by such more fortunate rivals as Jamaica, or Barbados. And often as they had found fault with their own particular local Government, they far preferred it to some inaccessible and impersonal Federal Government far away across the seas. As to that, what had Trinidad done to deserve the honour of being chosen as the capital of the proposed Federation? Why not Belize? Or even Kingston? There were some who rejected the proposed Federation as a betrayal of the past and an impediment to the future of the Colony; all they wanted was independence, nothing more and nothing less.

Mr. Courtenay made it a whole time business to convert his countrymen to the proposals. Genuine political independence without financial stability was a mirage. The Colony had still a long way to go before it could stand on its own feet in that respect. If it were replied that America would supply the dollars, he could assure them that the acceptance of aid from that source would entangle the Colony in a far more galling subserviency than they had ever experienced under Great Britain or would be likely to experience within a British Federation. 'True liberty must be earned by hard physical and mental effort, and be based upon the solid foundation of financial stability, which in turn rest on economic productivity, or in other words on national income', as the Report put it. At present there was no such stability anywhere in the West Indies, least of all (perhaps) in Honduras. High prices due to world shortages and the War might give an impression of increasing prosperity, but the impression was illusory and the markets insecure. The days of small independent state units were gone; nothing but the co-operation and mutual insurance of inter-state Federation could save the Colony from disaster. In a situation where the B.W.I. were admittedly not to be reckoned among the richly endowed areas of the modern world, it was a case of 'United we stand: divided we fall'. The Colony would be well advised to join in with the rest, all of whom (with the exception of Guiana) were of one mind on the subject. The new Federal Government would not supersede nor be 'over' the local territorial Government, but in partnership with it. The frontiers of authority would be clearly defined. In general, the Federal Government would concern itself especially with external relations, such as trade agreements, inter-communication, defence, and international affairs (the latter, of course, being subject to the final decision of Great Britain), while the local Government would remain in supreme control of public order (police, etc.), education, agriculture, and internal development.

Much concern was expressed in Belize over the large additional expenditure of public money which, by all analogies, would be incurred by such a centralized Government, but it was explained that it would be financed normally by the income from customs and postal revenue, out of which it was hoped to return at least 75 per cent. to the Colonial exchequers. One of the most urgent queries which had to be answered was, would the Colony under Federation lose the grants-in-aid and other financial assistance to which they had grown accustomed? The answer was that grants-in-aid from H.M. Government would not cease, indeed they might well be increased, but that they would be paid henceforward into a central Federal pool, out of which the Federal Government would be able, more promptly and with better local knowledge, to allocate sums to the various units. There were some who would like to have seen the scheme launched on an immediate block subsidy of at least £1,000,000 to the Colony, but on the whole the proposed plan met with resigned approval.

As to the political constitution of the Federal Government, and the electoral system upon which it would be based, there was much apprehension both from left and right. It was explained that an attempt had been made to meet the claims of both. On the one hand, all elections would be decided by direct universal adult suffrage. Qualification for the franchise would depend solely upon British citizenship, age, and residence. There would be no discrimination against sex, race, financial ability, or even educational competence. In this way alone, it was declared, could the present inequality of franchise be levelled up among the various units of the Federation, or be justified before the tribunal of current political opinion throughout the coloured world. On the other hand, any fears of ill-considered or hasty action were to be allayed by the creation of a Second Chamber to be called the Senate, which would have certain delaying powers over legislation. This Senate would consist of two representatives for each unit of the Federation (only one for Montserrat), twenty-three members in all, to be appointed in his discretion by the Governor-General. The qualifications for membership of the Senate would still be as above, except that a residence of at least five years as an adult citizen of the B.W.I. would be required. The Senate would have no control at all of money bills, and its delaying powers over other legislation would be limited to twelve months. Its august counterparts in the United States and Great Britain should commend it to all shades of moderate opinion.

As to the First, or 'originative' Chamber of the proposed Federal Parliament, it would be called the House of Assembly, comprising fifty members elected on the same adult franchise with a fixed proportion of representatives for each unit according to its population. For example, Jamaica would have sixteen members; Montserrat only one. British Honduras, on its present population, would have two. Furthermore, to eliminate the least suspicion that weight might have to be given to the financial standing of any individual candidate, it was laid down that all members, whether of the House of Assembly or of the Senate, should be paid an adequate income out of Federal funds—actually, £600 per annum together with expenses.

Turning now to the Executive Authority, there would be a Federal Governor-General appointed by His Majesty the King.

He would preside over a Council of State of fourteen members. Of these fourteen, six would be nominated by the Governor-General, and eight elected by the House of Assembly. There would thus be a statutory majority of elected over 'official' members. In certain cases the Governor would retain, as was already the case in most Crown Colonies, certain 'reserve powers' in the initiation or veto-ing of legislation, or of action contrary to the advice of the Council of State. The limits and circumscribing conditions of the use of this prerogative, however, were carefully defined in the 'Consolidated Recommendations' of the Standing Closer Committee's Report.

Such was the 'blue-print' of British West Indian Federation. It was certainly not Dominion status, nor did it enlarge the local independence of the Colony, but politically and economically it marked a definite advance. It seemed certain that if the new powers were not abused, they would develop still more in a democratic direction in the not too distant future. The plan was evidently not devised to further the interests of the Imperial Government, but only those of the colonies themselves. It was a healthy sign that Federation was recommended not as an end in itself, but as a means to an end—the economic recovery and stabilization of the West Indies as a whole. It would create a climate in which the efforts of the individual and of the individual colony would no longer resemble those of a man in the stern of a boat propelling it with a single oar, but of a member of the crew in a college eight. All would pull together, and if by any misfortune one of the crew should catch a crab, the momentum of the rest would carry the boat along. Whether in practice it will work out like that, only the future can tell.

ADDITIONAL NOTES

(A) THE MOSQUITO INDIANS

SIR HARRY LUKE, in his recently published *Caribbean Circuit* (Nicholson and Watson 1950) has some further information about Great Britain's protectorate over the Mosquito Indians, which, frankly, is new to me, and which, with his permission, I here append.

It seems that in the time of Charles I, the Earl of Warwick took the heir-apparent of the King of the Mosquitos to England with him, entertaining him there for three years. The protectorate was continued by Charles II and James II, through the Captain-General of Jamaica, and thereafter continuously until, as we have seen, it was ended in deference to American wishes. Thus in 1720, the *Journals of the Assembly of Jamaica* record a military agreement with Jeremy, King of the Mosquitos, for assistance in subduing a rebellion of Maroons.

In the early nineteenth century, the young Mosquito princes were still being sent to Jamaica for their education. In the *Diary* of Lady Nugent, whose husband was Lieutenant Governor of the island from 1801 to 1806, we read of the arrival of one of these princes in Jamaica in 1804. 'I must now describe his little savage Majesty. He is about six or eight years old, a plain puny-looking child, but seems to have a very high and determined spirit. . . . The young King was dressed in a scarlet uniform and wore a crown upon his head, of which he seemed very proud. The crown was of silver gilt, ornamented with mock stones, and was sent from England some years ago for his father. Both the little King and his uncle, who had escorted him here, seemed to hold it in high estimation. When it was placed on the table, and my own children wished to handle it, the uncle got up and placed it in a little box, brought with him for the purpose, shaking his head and saying *na, na*, all the time. . . . At dinner the little King had a small table for himself, and was helped by his uncle who seemed to attend to him quite as a servant. . . . He became quite savage in a short time. He cried, and roared, and yelled horribly, and began to pull off all his clothes in the most violent manner, and was nearly naked before we could have him carried out of the room. He was then put under the care of some of the negro women for the night, but shrieked and roared for several hours before he went to sleep.'

A little later she records, 'Obliged to send the little Mosquito King *forcibly* to school; but not before, in his rage and reluctance, he had broken the poor orderly sergeant's watch to pieces, and scratched his face sadly'.

It is more than probable that the prince who, as George Frederick, was crowned King of the Mosquitos on January 18, 1816, at Belize, was this very child, although Lady Nugent does not actually mention his name.

The last reference to him, in the *Honduras Almanack* for 1830, seems to show that his early promise was fulfilled. It reads:

> 1824 *March. King George Frederick, of the Mosquito Nation, strangled by his wife, and his body thrown into the sea.*

He was succeeded the following year by King Robert Charles, who was also crowned at Belize, in 1825. He, in turn, was succeeded by King George Augustus Frederick, who was crowned at Belize in 1845. Sir Harry Luke was fortunate enough to find a copy of the Coronation Service, probably the only one in existence, and never hitherto published, which he reproduces *in extenso* in Chapter V of his *Caribbean Circuit*. It is 'beautifully printed in red on handsome cartridge paper with the rubrics set out in old face italics as in our Prayer Book . . . technically a remarkable production for the Printing Office of a struggling little Colony of a century ago'.

(B) ADMIRAL BENBOW

The name of the famous Admiral Benbow has often been mentioned, usually without details or references, in connection with British Honduras. The most recent Colonial Office Reports state explicitly, however, that he was one of the seven hundred white settlers who occupied Belize and S. George's Cay after the Godolphin Treaty of 1670.

I have been unable to find any confirmation of this. The first time, as far as I can discover, that Benbow visited the West Indies was in 1697–98, when, as Commander-in-Chief of the King's ships in the Caribbean he sailed to Cartagena, and was able to prevent the Spanish fleet assembled in that port from its projected attack upon Paterson's Scotch colony on the shores of the Mosquito Gulf. He saved the colony's life for a year or two by this action, but the Home Government for some reason were displeased with him for interfering, and ordered him 'not to assist the Scotch Colony in Darien'. His special mission in the West Indies was to hunt down the pirates, in which, however, he had little success. After returning home, he was sent to the West Indies again in 1701, making his headquarters in Jamaica. It was on this occasion that he lost his leg by a chain-shot in action with the French fleet off Santa Marta—an action which brought no glory to British arms. He died of his wounds at Port Royal on November 4, 1702. It is possible that his search for pirates during this period may have brought him into contact with the settlement in Belize.

CHRONOLOGICAL TABLE

*

1492.	Columbus discovers the New World.
1493.	Papal Donation of Terra Incognita to Spain.
1502.	Columbus on last voyage reaches 'Honduras'.
1506.	Pinzon discovers coast of British Honduras.
1524.	Cortés skirts interior of British Honduras.
1527.	First recorded British seamen in West Indies.
1530.	William Hawkins in Caribbean.
1567.	John Hawkins and Drake in West Indies.
1583.	Our first colony in New World, Newfoundland.
1587.	Queen Elizabeth's Declaration of Policy.
1617.	Raleigh's expedition to El Dorado (with Wallace).
1629.	Warwick's settlement on Providence Island.
1634.	British settlements on Coxcomb Coast.
1635.	Spanish assault on Providence Island.
1638.	Shipwrecked sailors on Belize River.
1640.	Captain Wallace founds Belize Settlement.
1641.	Spanish destroy Providence Island Colony.
1642.	Spanish drive British out of Rattan Island.
1642.	Buccaneer Jackson lands in Jamaica.
1655.	Cromwell annexes Jamaica.
1666.	Buccaneer Mansfield recaptures Providence Island.
1667.	Pepys bemoans buccaneer exploits.
1667.	SANDWICH TREATY prohibits buccaneering.
1668.	Esquemelin joins buccaneers.
1669.	Harry Morgan takes Porto Bello.
1670.	GODOLPHIN TREATY.
1670.	Morgan sacks Panama. Morgan and Modyford arrested.
1672.	Lynch claims British logwood rights.
1672.	Modyford supports British rights in Campeachy, etc.
1672.	Godolphin advises 'underhand' cutting.
1674.	Dampier in Campeachy.
1675.	Sir Harry Morgan back in Jamaica.
1675.	Vaughan proposes annexation of settlements by Jamaica.
1677.	Buccaneer Sharpe on S. George's Cay.
1680.	Spanish attack Campeachy settlements.
1682.	Lynch forbids logwood-cutting.
1697.	Buccaneers' last exploit: sack of Cartagena.
1702–13.	War of Spanish Succession.
1704.	Whitehall proposes Colony in Campeachy.
1705.	First mention of BELIZE by name.
1713.	TREATY OF UTRECHT.
1717.	Pirates Blackbeard, Hands, Low, etc.
1718.	Spanish raid as far as Spanish Lookout.
1728.	Spanish claim rights of Papal Donation.
1730.	Spanish raids on Belize River.

1732.	British Government claim damages.
1737.	Spanish raid on Belize city.
1739–49.	War of Jenkins' Ear.
1742.	S.P.G. Mission to Mosquitos.
1745.	Spanish raids on New River.
1749.	TREATY OF AIX LA CHAPELLE.
1754.	Spanish invasion of Belize by land and sea.
1755.	Spanish sack and destroy Belize city.
1756.	British reoccupy and fortify it.
1756–63.	Seven Years' War: Belize a casus belli.
1763.	TREATY OF PARIS.
1764.	Spanish infractions of Treaty.
1765.	Admiral Burnaby defends the settlement.
1767.	More Spanish raids.
1773.	Negro slave revolt.
1776.	American War of Independence.
1776.	Citizens appoint Rev. R. Shaw to cure of Belize.
1777.	American vessels threaten Belize.
1778.	Nelson in command of Port Royal.
1779.	Spanish sack S. George's Cay. Nelson too late.
1780.	British reprisals under Nelson, etc.
1783.	PEACE OF VERSAILLES.
1786.	Despard, first Superintendent of Belize.
1786.	CONVENTION OF LONDON.
1786.	Evacuation of Mosquito Shore settlements.
1790.	Superintendent Despard dismissed.
1790.	Superintendent Hunter fortifies Belize.
1796.	Napoleonic War begins. Superintendent Barrow.
1798.	Victory of S. George's Cay.
1802.	TREATY OF AMIENS.
1803.	Renewal of War with Napoleon.
1803.	Mosquitos fight for England.
1805.	Battle of Trafalgar.
1812.	War with United States.
1812.	Belize Parish Church.
1814.	TREATY OF MADRID.
1815.	Battle of Waterloo.
1819.	MacGregor's Mosquito Shore swindle.
1822.	Pirates around the coast.
1823.	MONROE DOCTRINE. Central American Independence.
1824.	Mosquito King crowned in Belize.
1826.	ANGLO-MEXICAN TREATY.
1831.	Racial Equality Act in Belize.
1834.	Abolition of Slavery Act.
1838.	Emancipation of all slaves.
1839.	Lord Palmerston occupies Rattan, etc.
1843.	British Resident in Mosquitia.
1845.	Mosquito King crowned in Belize Cathedral.
1848.	S. Juan renamed Greytown. British Mosquito Protectorate.
1850.	CLAYTON-BULWER TREATY.
1852.	British 'Colony of Bay Islands' proclaimed.
1855.	The Walker Affair in Nicaragua.
1856.	DALLAS-CLARENDON TREATY.

1857.	*Indian War of Colours begins.*
1859.	ANGLO-GUATEMALAN TREATY.
1862.	*Belize made a British Colony.*
1863.	*Abortive Anglo-Guatemalan Convention.*
1866.	*British reverses in Indian War.*
1871.	*British Honduras a Crown Colony.*
1872.	*Disestablishment of Church.*
	End of Indian Wars.
1880.	*British Honduras Diocese formed.*
1884.	*Colony made independent of Jamaica.*
1905.	*Mosquitia annexed by Nicaragua.*
	Last serious epidemic of yellow fever.
1908.	*Stann Creek Railway opened.*
1912.	*Belize Town Board inaugurated.*
1914–18.	*First World War.*
	Honduras troops serve in Mesopotamia.
1916.	*Clash between British and Guatemalan troops.*
1917–43.	*Anglican Bishop A. E. Dunn.*
1918.	*Great fire destroys Colonial records.*
1924.	*British Honduras pavilion at Wembley Exhibition.*
1925–32.	*Sir John A. Burdon, Governor.*
1925.	*Maya ruins at Lubaantun first explored.*
1926.	*Baron Bliss Bequest.*
1929.	*Burdon Canal opened.*
1931.	*Great hurricane and tidal wave in Colony.*
1933.	*Guatemala repudiates Treaty of* 1859.
1936–38.	*Constitution amended.*
1939–45.	*Second World War.*
1946.	*Guatemala demands possession of Belize.*
1947.	*Montego Bay Conference on Federation.*
1948.	*Guatemala threatens violence.*
1949.	*A year of disasters.*
1950.	*Devaluation of Honduras dollar.*

BIBLIOGRAPHY

*

Central America, by L. E. Elliott. 1924.
The Buccaneers in the West Indies in the XVIIth Century, by C. H. Haring. 1910.
Pirates and Buccaneers of the Atlantic Coast, by E. R. Snow. 1944.
Beyond the Mexique Bay, by A. Huxley. 1936.
Buccaneers of America, by J. Esquemeling. 1678.
A Voyage round the Terrestrial Globe, by W. Dampier. 1690.
A History of the British Empire, by H. W. Clark. 1935.
Mystery Cities, etc., by T. Gann. 1925f.
Beginnings of British Honduras 1506–1765, by E. O. Winzerling. 1946.
Archives of British Honduras (3 vols.), 1670–1884, by Sir John Burdon. 1931f.
Brief Sketch of British Honduras, Past, Present and Future, by Sir John Burdon. 1927. (Enlarged and Revised Edition by A. H. Anderson. 1948.)
Britain and her Treaties on Belize, by J. L. Mendoza. 1947.
Historia de la America Central, by J. A. Villacorta. 1926.
Narrative of a Residence on the Mosquito Shore, 1839–1841, by Thomas Young. 1842.
Colonial Civil Servant, by Sir Alan Burns. 1949.
Belice: Historia de los establecimientos Britanicos del Rio Valis, by Jose A. C. Quijano. 1944.
British Honduras: an historical and descriptive account of the Colony from its settlement, by A. R. Gibbs. 1883.
History of Piracy, by P. Gosse. 1934.
Black Caribbean, by R. W. Thompson. 1946.
A New Survey of the West Indies, by Thomas Gage. 1648.
A Bishop among Bananas, by Bishop H. Bury (1911).
Caribbean Circuit, by Sir Harry Luke (1950).
Short History of British West Indies, by H. V. Wiseman (1950).
The British West Indies, by W. L. Burn (1951).

Colonial Annual Reports (Colonial Office).
Report on British Honduras (Colonial Office), 1934: *Financial and Economic Position*.
Report of the British Guiana and British Honduras Settlement Commission (Colonial Office), 1948.
British Honduras: Survey by British Society for International Understanding, 1948.
Honduras News (S.P.G.), 1921–49.
The Clarion (newspaper) (Belize).
Development and Welfare in the West Indies (Rance Report), 1950.

INDEX

✱

Aix la Chapelle Treaty (1749), 72 f.
Alice, Princess, 212, 217, 218.
Allenby, Lord, 147.
Alligators, 163.
Amatique, Gulf of, 20, 40.
Ambergris Cay, 29, 171, 211.
American Episcopal Church, 118.
Amiens, Treaty of (1802), 100, 128, 188.
Anglo-Guatemalan Convention (abortive) (1863), 203.
Anglo-Guatemalan Treaty of Commerce (1849), 193.
Anglo-Guatemalan Treaty (1859), 131, 198.
Anglo-Mexican Treaty (1826), 129, 191.
Animals, wild, 183.
Archives of British Honduras, 11, 83, 86, 121, 129, 132, 144, 156.
Arlington, Lord, 54.
Armada, 21.
Armstrong, Rev. J., 121.
Arthur, Colonel, 122, 125.
Ashton, Philip, 65.
Axe, Captain, 29.
Aycinena, 198 f.
Azores, 18, 66.

Bacalar, 66, 79, 80, 84, 85, 132, 133, 192.
Baking Pot, 211.
Banana, 135, 141, 142, 148.
Banister, 49.
Barbados, 27, 225.
Barrow, Thomas (Superintendent), 96 f.
"Battlefield", 186, 215, f.
Bay Islands, 71, 85, 92.
Bay Islands Colony, 116, 117, 130, 196, 197.
Baymen of Belize, 60, 65, 71 f., 81, 136.
Belize (name), 31, 63.
Belize Cathedral, 106, 113, 121, 123, 126, 135, 146, 158.
Belize River, *see* Old River.
Belize, S. Mary's Church, 123, 156, 158.
Belize Town Board, 146.
Bell, Philip, 29.
Benbow, Admiral, 62, 232.
Benner, George, 46.
Benque Viejo, 131, 147.
Bevin, Mr. Ernest, 207.
Bicycle Race, 156, 184.
Bill-Board, Newspaper, 216.
Black Creek, 183.
Black River, 41, 72, 87, 103, 107.
Blackbeard, 64.
Bliss, Baron, 153 f., 166.
Bluefield, Captain (Blauveldt), 27, 28, 40.
Bluefields, 41, 62, 114, 117, 118.
Bocas de Toro, 60, 62, 142.
Bonacca, 41, 60, 65, 71, 110, 113, 117.
Bonnet, Stede, 64.
Boom, 170.
Boundaries, 193, 199, 200, 204, 205.
Bragman Town, 88.
"Brethren of the Coast", 26, 48.
Britton, William, Governor, 69.
Brooks, Bishop of Honduras, 220.
Brown, George, 112.
Buccaneers, 21 f., 40 f.
Buonaparte, 96, 100.

Burdon Canal, 134, 155, 166, 170.
Burdon, Sir John, 11, 55, 58, 72, 76, 83, 142, 153, 184.
Burnaby, Admiral and Code, 26, 80 f., 97.
Burns, Sir Alan, 155, 162, 166, 184, 186.
Bury, Bishop of Honduras, 142.

Cabot, 19.
Camock, Captain, 29.
Campbell, Governor of Jamaica, 90.
Campeachy, 30, 34, 37, 42, 43, 51 f., 61, 72, 79.
Canal, 62, 71, 103, 106, 115, 117, 119, 130, 194.
Canul, Chieftain, 133 f.
Caribbean Sea, 33 67, 127.
Caribbean Standing Closer Committee, 226.
Caribs, 109 f., 127, 180.
Carlisle, Lord, 54.
Carnegie Library, 165.
Carrera, President of Guatemala, 133, 193, 196.
Cartagena, 49, 69, 71, 232.
Casas, Bartolomeo de las, 24.
Casinas, Isla de, 48, 81.
Castillo, 18, 41.
Cattock, Cape (=Catoche), 51 f.
Caulfield, Major, 72.
Cedar, 141, 163.
Chamberlain, Neville, 206.
Champetone, 52.
Charles I, King, 37, 51, 221.
Charles II, King, 35, 45, 46, 231.
Chatfield, Mr., 193 f.
Chetumal, 166.
Chichen Itza, 18.
Chicle, 135, 143, 149.
Chinchenha Indians, 132.
Chinese, 127.
Chippendale, 78.
Church of England, 128 f.
Cimarrones, 41, 66.
Cinema, 156, 161.
Clarion, Newspaper, 216, 221.
Clayton-Bulwer Treaty (1850), 115, 116, 130, 149 f., 194.
Climate, 182.
Coban, 201.
Cobb, Superintendent, 105.
Cockscomb Range, 18, 20, 28, 29, 171.
Cocoa, 176.
Coconut, 141.
Codd, General, 123.
Cohune Nut, 144.
Colonial Development Corporation (C.D.C.), 164 f., 175, 178, 187, 211, 218, 220.
Colonial Office Annual Reports, 137, 147, 150, 159, 160, 161, 162, 174, 181, 210.
Colony, 71, 120 f., 129, 131, 205; Crown Colony, 13, 132, 224.
Colour Question, 125, 180, 185, 222, 223, 224.
Columbus, Christopher, 17, 18.
Commis Bight, 29, 142.
Commissions (Government), 145, 161, 162, 174, 226.
Constitution, 71, 81, 90 f., 131, 132, 166, 184, 224, 229.
Convention of London, *see* London Convention.
Convicts, 91.

237

Cook, James, 80, 81.
Corozal, 127, 133, 143, 170.
Cortes, Hernando, 18.
Costa Rica, 73, 87, 113.
Council of State, 230.
Courtenay, Hon. W. H., 227.
Coxon, 48, 49, 57, 61.
Cozumel, 18, 51.
Credit Union, 211.
Creech Jones, 208, 226.
Creole, 179.
Crimean War, 116.
Cristobal de Olid, 18.
Cromwell, Oliver, 30, 42.
Crooked Tree, 183, 218.
Crown Colony, *see* Colony.
Cunliffe-Lister Report (1934), 182.
Currency, 212.

Dallas-Clarendon Treaty (1856), 117, 130, 196.
Dampier, W., 38, 48, 56, 57, 61, 62.
Daniel, Captain, 25.
De Castillo, Bernal Diaz, 18.
De Pointis, 49.
Delgado, Jose, 48.
Denominational statistics, 184.
Depression (1929), 157.
Despard, Colonel, 86 f.
Devaluation, 154, 210 f.
Disestablishment, 124.
Disraeli, 116.
Donald, Mr. P. G., 213.
Dragten, Mr. F. R., 227.
Drake, Francis, 19, 20.
Dredge, Hon. Alan, 147.
Dunn, E. A., Bishop of Honduras and Archbishop of W.I., 9, 124, 148, 220.

Education, 155, 166, 172, 181, 182, 185, 211, 223, 225.
Edward VII, King, 136.
El Cayo, 140 f.
Eldorado, 32, 33.
Elfrith, Daniel, 28.
Elizabeth, Queen, 20, 30, 33, 36, 51, 67.
Emancipation of Slaves, 126.
E.M.L. Launch, 149.
Esquemelin, 7, 22, 32, 45.
Establishment of Church, 122, 123, 124.
Evans Report (1948), 174 f.
Everson, Jacob, 70.

Fancourt (Superintendent), 113.
Federation of West Indies, 225 f.
Ferdinand and Isabella, 18.
Figueroa, 66.
Fingas, John, 63.
Fire, 146, 161, 220.
Fishing, 154, 177.
Flores, 18, 201.
Fonduras = Honduras, 17.
Forestry, 152, 176, 181, 221.
Fort George, 141.
Fox, Charles James, 89.
Freetown, 165.

Gage, Thomas, 42.
Gann, Dr. T., 153.
Garbutt's Falls, 131, 199.
Garvey, Sir R. N., Governor, 210 f.
George I, King, 58.
George IV, King, 106.
George V, King, 147.
Gerrard, Rev. W., 71, 122, 123.
Gibraltar, 89, 91, 92.
Godolphin, Lord, 55, 63.
Godolphin Treaty (1670), 45, 50 f., 61, 67.
Goffe, Christopher, 49.

Golfo Dulce, 17, 60.
Governorship of the Colony, 131.
Gracias à Dios, 17, 41, 62, 111.
Gracias à Dios Rapids, 131, 199.
Gracie Rock, 170.
Graff, Laurence, 49, 56.
Granada, 44, 117.
Granville, Lord (1790), 94.
Granville, Lord (1880), 205.
Grapefruit, 144, 151, 171.
"Green Gold", 143, 175, 176 f.
Greytown, 60, 114, 116, 117, 118.
Guanaja, 17, 112.
Guatemala, 13, 66, 74, 129, 130, 131, 166, 188 f., 218.
Gueux de la Mer, 22.
Guzman, Juan Perez, 44.

Hague, Court of Arbitration, 206.
Hagues, Victor, 110.
Halifax, Lord, 206, 225.
Hall, Colonel, 104.
Hands, Israel, 64.
Harris, 57.
Haulover, 67, 75, 88, 91, 98, 121, 140.
Hawkins, John, 19, 20.
Hawkins, William, 19, 20.
Hay-Bunau-Vasilla Treaty (1903), 119.
Hayti, 125.
Hector Creek, 219.
Hezekiah, Captain, 84.
Hidalgo of Mexico, 128.
Hill, Edward, 86.
Hispaniola, 35.
Hodgson, Robert, 70, 73, 144.
Holme, Bishop of Honduras, 124.
Hondo River, 58, 60, 66, 79, 89, 90, 131, 133, 192.
Honduras = Fonduras, 17, 51.
Honduras, Diocese of, 124.
Honduras Republic, 60, 73, 112, 113, 116, 118, 131, 195.
Hopkins, Roman Catholic Bishop, 149.
Hospitals, 144, 166, 182.
Hotel, 178, 184, 219, 221.
House of Assembly, 229.
Hume, George, 122.
Hunter, Peter, Governor, 95.
Hurricane, 12, 91, 157, 158, 183.
Hutson, Sir Eyre, Governor, 148.

Income Tax, 144, 187, 220.
Indian Mutiny (Sepoy), 127.
Indian Mutiny (Yucatan), 133.
Indians of Yucatan, 132 f.
Italians, 127.
Iturbide, 190, 191.
Izabal, Port, 200, 201.

Jackson, William, 40 f.
Jamaica, 27, 38 f., 71, 75, 102, 130, 171, 229, 231.
Jamaica, Diocese of, 123.
James I, King, 33.
James II, King, 231.
Jenkins' Ear, War of, 69, 72.
Jews, 127.
Jones, Paul, 84, 85.
Joyce, Captain T. A., 153.
Judd, Captain, 84.

Labouring Creek, 74.
Laffite, 129.
Laguno de Terminos, 37, 58.
Letters of Marque, 21, 43.
Levasseur, 35.
Limonal, 170.
Lindbergh, 153, 157.
Listowel, Lord, 213.
Little Falls, 140.

Lobsters, 151, 163.
Logwood, 37 f., 47, 50 f., 77, 78, 135, 139.
London Convention (1786), 91 f., 105, 188 f., 191.
Lovell, 20.
Low, Edward, 64, 65.
Low, George A., 104, 105.
Lowther, Captain, 64.
Lubaantun, 18, 153, 172.
Lucifer, Captain, 42.
Luke, Sir Harry, 231, 232.
Luttrell, Captain, 87.
Lynch, Thomas, 45, 52, 53, 60.

Macdonald, Superintendent, 112.
MacGregor, 103 f.
Machetes, 38.
Maderiaga, 19, 62.
Madrid, Treaty (1617), 91; (1667), 44, 48; (1814), 188.
Mahogany, 58, 78, 90, 92, 135, 139, 140, 149.
Manattee, 127.
Mansfield, Captain, 44.
Maracaibo, 45.
Martinique, 88.
Mary Christina, 156.
Mathew, Mr., 203.
Maya Indians, 18, 126, 133, 152, 153, 171, 172.
Mayflower, 27.
Medical, 182.
Mendoza, J. L., 13.
Merida, 85.
Mesopotamia, 147, 148, 152.
Metcalfe, Sir C., 72.
Mexico, 113, 129, 190, 191.
Middlesex, 142.
Milton, Captain F., 163.
Mineral, 175.
Mitchell-Hedges, 153.
Modyford, James, 44.
Modyford, Sir Thomas, 44 f.
Mona Island, 19.
Monkey Point, 41, 43.
Monroe Doctrine, 116, 129, 190, 194, 198.
Montego Bay Conference, 226.
Montserrat, 225, 229.
Morgan, Sir Harry, 35, 43 f.
Mosquito Indians (Mesquito, Mesekito), 27, 28, 37, 41 f., 51, 60 f., 69 f., 86, 87, 92, 101 f., 231, 232.
Mosquito Kings, 37, 41; Edward, 69; George, 102; John, 102, 103; George Frederick, 103, 105, 232; Robert Charles Frederick, 106, 107, 112, 232; George Augustus Frederick, 113, 114, 116; Robert Henry Clarence, 118.
Mosquito Language, 107, 108, 231.
Mosquito Shore (Mosquitia), 27, 34, 40, 41, 48, 58, 70 f., 82, 84, 87, 91 f., 101 f., 120, 130, 194 f.
Moss, Captain, 96 f., 101.
Motto, 161, 210.
Mullins River, 29.
Munich, 56.
Murray, Archdeacon, 156.

Nassau, 134.
Nelson, Lord, 85 f., 95.
Neville, Admiral, 49.
Nevis, 35, 225.
New River, 66, 72, 79, 89, 133.
Newfoundland, 19, 21.
Newport, Rev. N., 114, 123, 131.
Newton, Professor, 12.
Nicaragua, 41, 44, 73, 92, 111, 113, 115, 117.
Nombre de Dios, 20.
North, Lord, 90.
Nugent, Lady, 231.

Old River (Belize River), 29, 37, 66, 169, 174.
Omoa, 87.
O'Neill, Arturo, 97.

Orange Walk, 127, 133, 134, 143.
Orinoco, 109.
Ormsby, Bishop of Honduras, 124.
Osmar, Captain, 97, 98.
Oxenham, John, 20.

Palmerston, Lord, 111 f., 195.
Panama, 35, 44, 45.
Panama Canal, 119, 147, 149, 167.
Papal Donation, 18, 19, 20, 30, 66, 67, 207.
Paris, Treaty of (1763), 76.
Parker, Admiral, 49.
Paslow, Thomas, 97.
Paterson, William, 62.
Pauncefort-Hay Treaty (1901), 119.
Pavey, Admiral, 83.
Pearl Lagoon, 114, 118.
Pepys, 44.
Peten, 18, 66, 74, 89, 90, 130, 143, 165, 192, 193, 205.
Pimiento, Francisco Diaz, 28.
Pine Ridge, 118, 173, 174, 182.
Pinzon, Vicente Yanez, 17.
Pirates, 45, 46, 53, 64, 129, 232.
Pitt, Billy, 71, 74, 75.
Pitt, William (Junior), 96.
Pitt, William (Senior), 76.
Placentia, 29, 171.
Plantains, 143.
Population, 135, 147, 177, 179.
"Pork and Dough Boys", 38.
Port Real, 51, 85.
Port Royal, 41, 43, 44, 45, 49, 101.
Porter, Thomas, 70.
Porto Bello, 45, 48, 69.
Post, Christian Frederick, 87.
Postage Stamps, 208.
Potts, Thomas, 86, 97.
Poyasia, 103, 104.
Presbyterian Church, 123, 124.
Price, Rev. Nathan, 72.
Privateers, 21.
Prohibition, 152.
Providence Company, 13, 27, 36, 44.
Providence Island, 26, 28, 36, 40, 41, 42, 44, 60.
Providence, New, 28.
Pueblo Viejo, 205.
Puerto Barrios, 171, 206.
Puerto Cortez, 63.
Punta Escoces, 62.
Punta Gorda, 141, 164, 172.
Pye, General, 122, 123.

Queen Cay, 29.
Quetzal, 170.
Quintaroo, 85, 86.

Railway (Central America), 206.
Railway (Stann Creek), 142, 144, 149.
Raleigh, Sir Walter, 32 f.
Rance, Sir Hubert, 226.
Rattan (Ruatan, Roatan), 40, 41, 49, 60, 71, 72, 73, 86, 87, 88, 100, 101, 103, 111, 113, 117.
Regatta, 156, 184.
Rio Dulce, 201.
Rio Grande, 172.
Ringnose, Basil, 57.
Roads, 134, 155, 173, 174, 179, 200 f., 218, 219.
Roatan, Ruatan, see Rattan.
Roberts, Captain Bartholomew, 25.
Robinson Crusoe, 63, 65.
Rodney, Admiral, 76, 83, 84, 85, 88.
Roman River, 111.

S. George's Cay, 48, 81, 82, 83, 85, 87, 88, 90, 91, 92, 96, 158, 168, 171.
S. George's Cay, Victory of, 97 f., 102, 106, 188, 199.
S. Kitts, 35, 225.
S. Vincent, 109, 127.

Salcedo, 68.
Samboler, Chieftain, 110.
Sambos, 41, 66, 88, 108.
San Antonio, 164, 172.
San Jose de Guatemala, 203.
San Juan del Norte (Greytown), 41, 87, 112 f.
San Juan River, 43, 62, 111.
San Paulo, 51.
Sandwich Treaty (1667), 44, 48.
Santa Cruz, 132.
Santa Katarina, Island, 27.
Santiago (Jamaica), 27, 41.
Sapodilla Cay, 64, 129.
Sarstoon River, 118, 131, 197.
Sawkins, 57.
Schools, see Education.
Scotch Point, 62.
Scotch, Scottish, 31.
Senate, 229.
Seven Years War, 76.
Seymour, Sir Frederick, 131.
Sharpe, Bartholomew, 48, 57.
Shaw, Rev. Robert, 87.
Sheraton, 78.
Sibun River, 90, 92, 130, 131, 155, 192, 197.
Sierra de Caria, 17.
Slaves, 26, 41, 67, 72, 73, 74, 83, 84, 90, 97, 98, 99, 117, 125, 130.
Snow, Edward Rowe, 47.
Society for Propagation of the Gospel (S.P.G.), 70, 87, 121, 124, 133.
Solis, Juan Diaz, 17.
Spanish Creek, 133.
Spanish Honduras, see Honduras Republic.
Spanish Lookout, 29, 66.
Sponges, 149, 163.
Spragg, Captain, 49.
Squier, 30.
Stanford, Rev. William, 26, 87, 96, 121.
Stanley Field, 171.
Stanley, Lord, 204.
Stann Creek, 28, 104, 110, 117, 127, 142, 148, 152, 155, 171.
Suffrage, 185, 224 f.
Sugar, 143, 149, 176.
Superintendent, 83, 95, 130, 131.
Sweet-Escott, Governor, 146.
Syrians, 127.

Teach, Edward, 64.
Telephone, 141.
Tobacco, 175.
Tobacco Cay, 28, 74.
Toledo, 17, 110, 127, 131, 172, 173.
Tonks, Bishop, 165.
Tortoise-shell, 149, 163.
Tortuga, 22, 27, 35.

Toussaint l'Ouverture, 125.
Tozer, Bishop of Honduras, 124.
Trafalgar, 100, 128.
Treasure, buried, 46, 64.
Treasure Island, 46, 64.
Trelawney, Governor of Jamaica, 69, 70, 73.
Trinidad, 227.
Trist Island, 38, 53, 56, 58.
Truxillo, 18, 20, 37, 41, 43, 60, 103, 112, 114.
Turneffe Island, 32, 36, 56, 64, 135, 149.

Ubico, President of Guatemala, 165.
Uncle Tom's Cabin, 117.
Union Jack, 102.
United Fruit Company, 142, 143, 148.
United Nations Organization (U.N.O.), 207.
United States of America, 114 f., 140, 206, 215, 222.
Utrecht, Treaty of (1713), 57, 58, 63, 67, 91, 109.

Van Horn, 49.
Vaughan, Lord, 53, 54.
Vera Cruz, 18, 49, 56.
Vernon, Admiral, 69, 71.
Versailles, Treaty of (1783), 88, 89, 91.
Victoria, Queen, 115, 131, 136.
Villalba y Toledo, 40.
Villeneuve, Admiral, 100.
Volunteers, 142, 147.

Walker, Patrick, 113.
Walker, William (Adventurer), 117 f.
Wallace, Captain, 31 f.
Walpole, 69.
War of Colours, 134.
Warwick, Earl of, 27, 28, 40, 231.
Water Cay, 29.
Waterloo, 103, 128.
Watson, Commander, 114.
Wembley Exhibition, 152.
Wilson, Bishop of Honduras, 214.
Winzerling, E. O., 13, 29, 32, 37.
Wireless, 155.
Wodehouse, Superintendent, 116.
Wray, Mr., 202.
Wyke, Lennox, 198 f.

Xumucha, 153.
Xunantunich, 153.

Yallahs (Yellows), 53.
Yarborough, 121.
Ycaiche Indians, 133.
Young Gal, 133.
Young, Thomas, 107 f.
Yucatan, 18, 32, 51 f., 72, 79, 83, 95, 113, 128, 132, 133, 192.

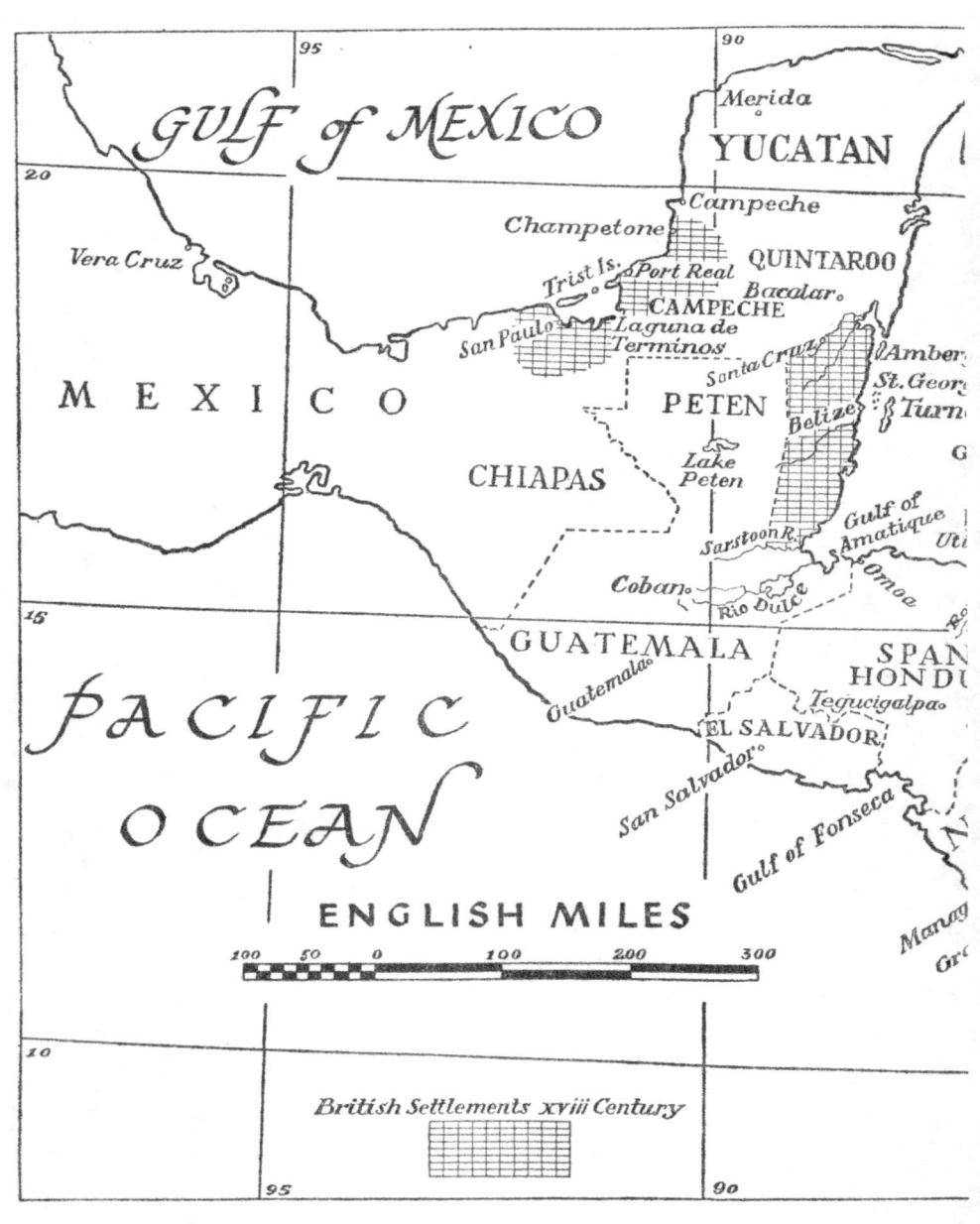

For Product Safety Concerns and Information please contact our EU representative GPSR@taylorandfrancis.com
Taylor & Francis Verlag GmbH, Kaufingerstraße 24, 80331 München, Germany

www.ingramcontent.com/pod-product-compliance
Lightning Source LLC
Chambersburg PA
CBHW070602300426
44113CB00010B/1365